The Mexican
Cinema of Darkness

ALSO BY DOYLE GREENE

Mexploitation Cinema: A Critical History of Mexican Vampire, Wrestler, Ape-Man and Similar Films, 1957–1977 (McFarland, 2005)

The Mexican Cinema of Darkness

A Critical Study of Six Landmark Horror and Exploitation Films, 1969–1988

DOYLE GREENE

McFarland & Company, Inc., Publishers
Jefferson, North Carolina, and London

LIBRARY OF CONGRESS CATALOGUING-IN-PUBLICATION DATA

Greene, Doyle, 1962–
The Mexican cinema of darkness : a critical study of six landmark horror and exploitation films, 1969–1988 / Doyle Greene.
p. cm.
Includes bibliographical references and index.

ISBN-13: 978-0-7864-2999-8
softcover : 50# alkaline paper ∞

1. Horror films — History and criticism. 2. Exploitation films — Mexico — History and criticism. I. Title.
PN1995.9.H6G74 2007   791.43'61640972 — dc22   2007012664

British Library cataloguing data are available

©2007 Doyle Greene. All rights reserved

No part of this book may be reproduced or transmitted in any form or by any means, electronic or mechanical, including photocopying or recording, or by any information storage and retrieval system, without permission in writing from the publisher.

On the cover: Promotional artwork for the 1978 film *Alucarda, la hija de las tinieblas*

Manufactured in the United States of America

McFarland & Company, Inc., Publishers
Box 611, Jefferson, North Carolina 28640
www.mcfarlandpub.com

For Richard Leppert:
in gratitude for the many years
of invaluable insight

Acknowledgments

My thanks first to the following people: Rob Craig, for his always welcome correspondence, comments, and his generous gift of the *El Topo* lobby cards; David Wilt, for his knowledge of Mexican cinema and graciously supplying the illustrated material for the chapters on Juan López Moctezuma.

An immense debt of gratitude is owed to my former instructors and colleagues in the following academic departments: the Liberal Studies Program, and the Department of Cultural Studies and Comparative Literature at the University of Minnesota; the Film Studies Program, the Department of Cinema and Comparative Literature, and the Department of Rhetoric at the University of Iowa. Without the learning experiences in these programs and the possibility to pursue trash cinema in a critical context, this project would not have been possible. A special thanks to Keya Ganguly for her advice and comments on this project, and to Tom Conley for his seminal influence.

Finally, my heartfelt thanks for their continuous support to: John "Ray" Link and Sophia Green, Mr. and Mrs. Link, Matt Potts, Donn Wingate, and Steve "Nacho" Fier. A special thanks to Rodney and Jeni Lynch, and especially to Jim Hoyer.

Table of Contents

Acknowledgments — vii
Preface — 1
Introduction — 3

1. The Counterculture Cinema of Cruelty: *El Topo* (*The Mole*, 1969) — 7
2. Madness and Modernity: *La mansión de la locura* (*The Mansion of Madness*, 1971) — 46
3. The New Dark Ages: *Alucarda, la hija de las tinieblas* (*Alucarda, Daughter of Darkness*, 1975) — 68
4. The Filming of the Disaster: *Guyana, el crimen del siglo* (*Guyana, Crime of the Century*, 1979) — 92
5. Lines of Flight, or Death from Above: *Ataque de los pájaros* (*Attack of the Birds*, 1986) — 116
6. National Oedipus: *Santa sangre* (*Holy Blood*, 1988) — 134

Conclusion — 172
Filmography — 175
Chapter Notes — 179
Bibliography — 195
Index — 199

Preface

The Mexican Cinema of Darkness came about through my interest and research on Mexican horror and *lucha libre* films that eventually resulted in *Mexploitation Cinema* (2005). This project is a continuation of that work, in that my principal argument remains Mexican "trash cinema" is more than a collection of camp oddities, but films which addressed social and cultural issues greatly affecting Mexican society: above all, the question of modernity. However, *Mexican Cinema of Darkness* explores a far different set of films and directors: Alejandro Jodorowsky (*El Topo* and *Santa sangre*), Juan López Moctezuma (*Mansion of Madness* and *Alucarda*) and René Cardona, Jr. (*Guyana, Crime of the Century* and *Birds of Prey*).

While about Mexican cinema, this project was ultimately approached from a perspective of *global* cinema and politics as well as *national* cinema and politics. These films were made with international audiences in mind, particularly the film markets in the United States and Europe. In part, this owed to the restraints the Mexican film industry and government placed on content at the time; however, this was also due to the formal ambitions of the films themselves. Jodorowsky and López Moctezuma (perhaps less so Cardona) were consciously informed by international avant-garde cinema and the arts: Expressionism, Surrealism, Postmodernism, and experimental theater ranging from Antonin Artaud's "Theater of Cruelty" to various strains of Theater of the Absurd. Filmmakers such as Luis Buñuel, Federico Fellini, and Pier Paolo Pasolini can be seen as key influences along with "Eurotrash" exploitation filmmakers such as Mario Bava, Jess Franco, and Jean Rollin — not to mention American counterparts such as Roger Corman or Russ Meyer. (This is *not* to imply Bava, Rollin, or Meyer were necessarily "inferior," or even less "avant-garde" in their own way, in comparison to Buñuel, Fellini, or Pasolini). This improbable nexus of the avant-garde and exploitation — what I have termed "avant-exploitation" — became a defining formal characteristic of these films.

The second issue became historical context. These films reflected awareness that the political upheaval occurring in Mexico — horribly manifest in the Tlatelolco Square massacre in Mexico City on October 2, 1968 — was part of an international wave of political unrest and change: Third World politics in the post-colonial era, the rise and fall of the 1960s counterculture, the political frustration of the 1970s, and the rise of neo-conservatism in the 1980s. My readings consider this context along with the texts themselves. For this reason, this project is interdisciplinary in nature; it draws from film studies, cultural studies, art history, literary theory, world history, philosophy, political science, and especially critical theory ranging from Max Horkheimer and Theodor W. Adorno, Michel Foucault, Herbert Marcuse, and Giles Deleuze and Félix Guattari. Moreover, the interpretations ultimately stem from my own position as a reader engaging these films from a different historical, national, and perhaps even political perspective than the authors of these films.

Admittedly, these readings are not concerned with proving *intentionality*; ascertaining what a filmmaker intended to say is probably best served by simply consulting a DVD commentary track. In other words, I do not claim that my interpretation of *El Topo* as an epic allegory of the counterculture is the definitive analysis of an eminently dense and complex film: yet alone the only valid one. Nor do I claim that *Birds of Prey* was René Cardona Jr.'s conscious effort to make the low-budget film version of Deleuze and Guattari's *A Thousand Plateaus*—but that a comparative reading can indeed be pursued. My interest in these films, and what I believe is their ultimate importance, are as cultural documents that unabashedly chronicle the chaos, desperation, and uncertainties of the modern world after 1968.

Introduction

Nineteen sixty-eight was a year of worldwide political upheaval. In the United States of America, assassinations and riots seemingly became the preferred methods of political practice. Vietnam became synonymous with the status of international relations. In France, the May 1968 movement of student demonstrations and worker strikes paralyzed and nearly toppled the government of Charles de Gaulle. Keeping the Stalinist program alive, the Soviet Union invaded Czechoslovakia in August, crushing a popular uprising.

On October 2, 1968, Mexico experienced its own national tragedy. Between 5,000 and 10,000 students in Mexico City staged a demonstration in Tlatelolco Square (the Plaza of Three Cultures). At 6:00 pm, orders were given to open fire on the protestors: a massacre by police, army, and paramilitary forces resulted. Students were bayoneted and shot, some in execution fashion; government forces also raided nearby apartments searching for fleeing students and murdered numerous residents of the neighborhood. Desperate to maintain its public image in world politics, largely due to the 1968 Olympics set to begin in Mexico City on October 12, the Mexican government claimed less than a dozen people were killed; the "official" figure was eventually adjusted to 32. However, independent news reports and subsequent historical accounts place the number of dead at 325, *ten times* the official admission of fatalities.

Without hyperbole, what became known simply as "Tlatelolco" shattered the Mexican national psyche, and brutally exposed the myths of Mexican democracy and modernity. Héctor Aguilar Camín and Lorenzo Meyer suggested.

> The crisis of 1968 was not a structural crisis that would place at risk the very survival of the nation; it was above all, *a political, moral, and psychological crisis*, a crisis of values and principles, which shook up the triumphant echoes of the governing elite; *it was a bloody announcement that times had changed, without changing the means to confront them.*[1]

In the wake of Tlatelolco, the horror-wrestling films which dominated Mexican cinema in the 1960s succumbed to generic exhaustion during the 1970s, their melodramatic binaries and political visions of a just, modern Mexico rendered obsolete, even scarred, by the events of 1968.[2] A new wave of Mexican directors began making films that were "a bloody announcement that times had changed" not only for Mexican society, but Mexican cinema as well: Alejandro Jodorowsky, a self-consciously avant-garde provocateur; Juan López Moctezuma, an innovator in formalistic, experimental horror; René Cardona, Jr., a purveyor of lurid exploitation.

These directors responded with films unimaginable before Tlatelolco, and this project will focus on six confrontational, and often controversial, landmarks in Mexican horror, cult-film, or the nebulous world of trash cinema after 1968. Their films were not simply difficult avant-garde exercises or cheap exploitation-horror fare, but a startling and challenging combination of both. Their unprecedented levels of sex and violence — often not distinguishable from each other — provided shocking studies of authoritarianism, genocide, revolution, war, religion, politics, family, patriarchy, sexuality, morality, and madness (both individual and collective). Unlike traditional mexploitation cinema's frequent and idealistic affirmation of a modern and modernizing Mexico, these films darkly reflected the aftermath of 1968 and fiercely questioned how "civilized" humanity actually was in an ostensibly civilized modern world.

Although it is debated if the nomadic Alejandro Jodorowsky should be considered a Mexican director, this project begins and concludes by critically discussing two strange and provocative films Jodorowsky made during sojourns in Mexico. First will be his legendary "Surrealist Western" *El Topo* (*The Mole*, 1969), which arguably invented the "midnight movie" cult-film ritual years before *The Rocky Horror Picture Show*, and became an international counterculture phenomenon, despite the criticisms *El Topo* was little more than a postmodern exploitation film. Also to be considered will be Jodorowsky's equally surreal merger of Fellini, Hitchcock, and Italian *giallo* horror films, *Santa sangre* (*Holy Blood*, 1988): a national allegory of the U.S.-Mexico relationship cast in terms of the Oedipal psychodrama.

Following in Jodorowsky's wake was his colleague Juan López Moctezuma, who revolutionized Mexican horror cinema in the 1970s by combining low-budget exploitation and avant-garde formalism — in some respects, much more successfully than his mentor Jodorowsky. Two astonishing López Moctezuma films, *La mansión de la locura* (*The Mansion of Madness*, 1971; alternate U.S. title: *Dr. Tarr's Torture Dungeon*) and *Alucarda, la hija de la tinieblas* (*Alucarda, Daughter of Darkness*, 1975) will be given close critical attention as films that not only radically challenged the established conventions of contemporary Mexican horror films — masked wrestlers versus evil monsters — but their ideological tenets as well: the faith in modern progress. Set in confined, 19th century spaces (the asylum in *Mansion of Madness*, the convent in *Alucarda*), López Moctezuma not only provided provocative critiques of madness, religion, and sexuality, but constructed microcosms of a modern world which prove to be as irrational, unenlightened, and vicious as the dark ages it supposedly transcended.

A veteran of the Mexican film industry and mexploitation era, René Cardona, Jr. is best remembered for notorious trash cinema milestones in the 1970s and 1980s. His films, which often managed a rare combination of tedium and revulsion, have been vilified as the lowest form of cinema, exemplified by the infamous exploitation docudrama *Guyana, el crimen del siglo* (*Guyana, Crime of the Century*, 1979; alternate U.S. title: *Guyana, Cult of the Damned*) and his boldfaced copy of Alfred Hitchcock's *The Birds*, *Ataque de los pájaros* (*Attack of the Birds*, 1988; U.S. titles: *Beaks: The Movie, Birds of Prey*). Like Jodorowsky and López Moctezuma, Cardona's films are also intensely disturbing essays on a modern world perpetually on the brink of disaster, combining frequently offensive exploitation film content with a highly unorthodox approach to film form — the extent of which was intended to be open to debate.

If Tlatelolco represented a political, moral, and psychological crisis for the Mexican national psyche, this crisis of the modern world as a whole after 1968 was graphically expressed in the work of Jodorowsky, López Moctezuma, and the younger Cardona. These films denied the distinctions between art and trash, between morality and transgression, between modernity and barbarism. Their films not only served as a bloody announcement that times had changed, but Mexican cinema had indeed changed its means to confront the times; they represent brutal studies of a modern world in disarray.

1

The Counterculture Cinema of Cruelty: *El Topo* (*The Mole*, 1969)

> *I believe that the only end of all human activity—whether it be politics, art, science, etc.— is to find enlightenment, to reach the state of enlightenment.... I think that the journey of Alexander the Great is a psychedelic trip.... I think that Alexander the Great was journeying into the depth of his being. I think that Odysseus was another great traveler. I want to travel the route of* The Odyssey, *I want to travel the route of Alexander the Great. I want to travel into the deepest areas of my being in order to reach enlightenment.*[1]
> —Alejandro Jodorowsky, 1970

The Art of Provocation

The Renaissance man of cult-cinema, Alejandro Jodorowsky has worked in a variety of artistic mediums and countries throughout his life, ranging from experimental theater to comic books. However, Jodorowsky is arguably most famous—or infamous—for his films, the most important of which were made at various times in Mexico: *Fando y Lis* (*Fando and Lis*, 1967), *El Topo* (*The Mole*, 1969), *La montaña sagrada* (*The Holy Mountain*, 1972), and *Santa sangre* (*Holy Blood*, 1988). With an artistic resume replete with numerous and intriguing projects and collaborations, both realized and aborted, Jodorowsky and his career seem as mythical as his film characters and their journeys, and this perception is strengthened by his tendency to recount his life with an emphasis on evocative power over factual consistency.[2]

Nevertheless, a brief history of Jodorowsky's life and career can be constructed. Born in Chile *ca.* 1929 to Russian-Jewish immigrants, Jodorowsky spent his childhood in the tough, northern coastal city of Iquique; Jodorowsky later claimed one of his strongest childhood memories was a funeral he and playmates conducted for the severed penis of a sailor castrated by a local prostitute.[3] In his teens, Jodorowsky attended the University of Santiago, focusing on such disciplines as philosophy, psychology, and theology: areas of study that greatly influenced his later artistic work. Indeed, Jodorowsky left college for a career in the performing arts, although Jodorowsky suggested it was the arts that chose him: "I am called the new Rimbaud when I am 15."[4] He recounted working as a puppeteer, a circus clown, dancer, a stage actor, and director of his own theatrical troupe before leaving Chile permanently in 1953. Spending the next six years in Paris, Jodorowsky studied mime and worked as a production assistant for Marcel Marceau; he also directed theatrical and concert-hall productions, including a highly-successful show starring Maurice Chevalier. During this period he also made his first film, an experimental short adapted from Thomas Mann's *The Transposed Heads* done entirely in mime which Jodorowsky proudly noted drew the attention of Jean Cocteau, who subsequently wrote an introduction for the film.[5]

Relocating to Mexico City in 1959, Jodorowsky established himself as a force in avant-garde theater. He directed over 100 plays — including works by Samuel Beckett, Eugène Ionesco, and Joseph Strindberg — before returning to Paris in 1962, where he organized the Panic Movement with artist Roland Topper and controversial playwright Fernando Arrabal, whose own brand of the Theater of the Absurd, typified by such plays as *Les Deux Bourreaux* (*The Two Executioners*, 1958) and *L'Architecte et l'empereur d'Assyrie* (*The Architect and the Emperor of Assyria*, 1967), owed less to the bizarre vaudeville of Beckett and Ionesco and more to the episodic brutality of the Marquis de Sade. The initial Panic Movement performance, *Sacramental Melodrama*, was a four-hour piece of experimental theater staged in Paris in 1965: among the highlights were Jodorowsky slitting the throats of two geese; his respective dance numbers with a honey-covered nude woman and a cow's head; and throwing live turtles at the audience from a giant plastic vagina.[6]

The Panic Movement was a deliberate effort to put Antonin Artaud's theories of the "Theater of Cruelty" into practice; Jodorowsky referred to Artaud's *The Theater and Its Double* as his "bible."[7] The Theater of Cruelty demolished the conventions of Western theater — characterization, dialogue, realism, narrative, and good taste — in favor of an intense spectacle that bombarded and assaulted the viewers' senses with disorientating, provocative, often violent and sexual imagery. As Artaud wrote:

> The theater cannot become itself again–that is, can not constitute the means of true illusion — until it provides the spectator with the truthful perception of dreams, in his taste for crime, his erotic obsessions, his savagery, his utopian sense of life and things, even his cannibalism, pour out on a level that is not counterfeit and illusory but internal.[8]

However, Artaud's conception of a Theater of Cruelty was not merely intended to simply batter, bewilder, and offend the viewers with images of sex and violence. It was a deliberate attempt to stir and awaken all that was hidden and forbidden in the spectator's unconscious — a cathartic, even ceremonial spectacle intended to drastically and permanently transform the viewer's psyche. Works such as *Sacra-*

mental Melodrama also generated the criticisms which inevitably shadowed Jodorowsky throughout his career, especially as his notoriety grew with *El Topo*. Critics frequently assailed Jodorowsky's combination of avant-garde stylistics, scandalous subject matter, and heavy-handed symbolism for being simultaneously obscure, obtuse, and obvious. As Hoberman and Rosenbaum observed:

> Despite his theoretical debt owed to Artaud, Jodorowsky's taste for outrage and scandal — characteristically pursued in simplistic terms of paraphraseable content and lurid detail, rather than in those of stylistic or formal expressiveness — virtually reversed Artaud's radical scenario for reforming the spectator. As an artist, Jodorowsky more closely resembles Salvador Dalí: the most literal-minded, self-parodic, and commercial of the surrealists.[9]

Indeed, Dalí was another of Jodorowsky's (many) chief influences, and while Jodorowsky based his artistic mission on Artaud, he learned a valuable practical lesson from Dalí: the power of disturbing and shocking imagery not to confront bourgeois society, but create controversy and publicity — especially if aided by some adroit self-promotion. Jodorowsky admitted shock value was, at least in part, a calculated strategy to snare the attention of the audience, as he described his theatrical work in Mexico: "On the stage I put two naked women. Then I perform Nietzsche, Kant — with two naked women ... I can do anything!"[10]

By 1967, Jodorowsky returned to Mexico City and achieved further success in avant-garde theater, as well as becoming an author and even a newspaper cartoonist (*Fábulas Pánicas*—"Panic Fables"): "I had a weekly comic-strip for a right-wing newspaper in Mexico, *The Herald*. But when they realized what I was saying, it was too late to do anything about it because a million people were reading it every week. It's more successful than *Mandrake the Magician*."[11] An active participant in the growing counterculture movement in Mexico in the late 1960s, he contributed essays to the leading Mexican counterculture publication, *Zona Rosa* (*Pink Zone*), and served as a producer for *1, 2, 3, 4, 5 a Go-Go!* (1968) — a live, weekly television show incorporating rock music, theater, and performance art.[12] This immersion in the counterculture further shaped Jodorowsky's artistic and political sensibilities. As Eric Zolov noted:

> [T]ravels by the hippies ... occurred in a context of a profound historical shift towards postmodern consciousness. This involves rejection of the "codifications of modernism ... based on a teleological view of progress and modernization." The hippies reflected a radical critique of everyday life that drew on new aesthetic strategies and techniques ... a process that involved the techniques of reappropriation and cultural fusion.[13]

It was in this cultural context, the "shift towards postmodern consciousness [and] cultural fusion," that the nomad-hippie-artist-philosopher *par excellance*, Alejandro Jodorowsky, began his filmmaking career. His debut feature film, *Fando y Lis* (1967), was a loose adaptation of an Arrabal play first staged and directed by

The Mexican Cinema of Darkness

Jodorowsky in the days of the Parisian Panic Movement. *Fando y Lis* chronicled the aimless journey of Fando and his paralyzed lover Lis in search of the mythological city of Tar, a place they never locate because it never existed in the first place — a sort of variation on *Waiting for Godot*, replacing Beckett's absurdist comedy with the patented and provocative scenes of sex and violence characteristic of both Jodorowsky and Arrabal's work. The controversy was immediate: premiering at the Acapulco Film Festival less than a month after Tlatelolco, *Fando y Lis* caused a near-riot, and the film was subsequently banned by the Mexican government.[14]

"The Cecil B. De Mille of the Underground"

With the controversy of *Fando y Lis* solidifying his artistic notoriety in Mexico, Jodorowsky secured a sizable financial backing (reportedly in the vicinity of $400,000 dollars) to make his next film: "When I made *Fando and Lis* the film industry in Mexico was closed to me. But the scandal it created opened doors for me. So when we were accepted into the film industry, we decided to make a film that was even stronger than *Fando and Lis*."[15] The result was *El Topo*, which produced a firestorm of debate and outrage as it became a worldwide counterculture phenomenon and briefly situated Jodorowsky at the epicenter of international avant-garde cinema in the early 1970s.

Fearing a repeat of the disastrous reception of *Fando y Lis* in Mexico, Jodorowsky premiered *El Topo* in America in December, 1970, a strategy which proved to be highly successful beyond all expectations.[16] Under the sponsorship of Ben Barenholtz, owner of the Elgin Theater in New York City, the film quickly developed a devout cult-film following through nightly midnight screenings. Among *El Topo*'s more ardent fans was John Lennon, who consequently urged his manager, Allen Klein, to form a business partnership with Jodorowsky.[17] In the summer of 1971, Klein assumed control of *El Topo*'s international distribution and promotion in hopes of establishing Jodorowsky alongside the likes of Ingmar Bergman, Luis Buñuel, Federico Fellini, or Jean-Luc Godard. Jodorowsky, with typical panache, professed his goal was nothing short of becoming "the Cecil B. De Mille of the Underground."[18]

Revolving around the title character, a bearded, bushy-haired, gun-slinging cowboy clad in black leather who wanders through barren deserts and squalid frontier towns, *El Topo* is a surreal, epic journey — using the term "surreal" in the sense of Artaud or Cocteau, and "epic" very much in the Homeric sense. *El Topo*'s narrative is constructed around a series of strange and often shocking events related by their allegorical and symbolic significance rather than any narrative coherency. Amid the desolate landscapes, unreal situations, provocative sexuality, and brutal violence, *El Topo* did not merely incorporate numerous religious, philosophical, literary, and cinematic references; it crushed them together into an inseparable and indistinguishable whole to create a mythological saga appropriate to the 1960s counterculture and its postmodern consciousness: an amalgam — or pastiche — of the Bible, Buddhism, Nietzsche, and the Tarot filtered through *The Odyssey,* Surrealism, Spaghetti Westerns, European avant-garde cinema, and Underground aesthetics (Happenings, psychedelia, and especially underground comics).[19] These myriad influences were arranged in a constellation under the sign of Artaud, and if the Theater of Cruelty was intended for nothing less than a rite of cathartic obliteration and reconfiguration of the spectator's psyche, Jodorowsky expressed similar lofty ambitions for *El Topo*:

> If you want a picture to change the world, you must first change the actors in the picture. And before doing that, you must change yourself ... I must change myself, I must kill myself, and I must be born. I must kill the actors and they must be born. And then the audiences, the audiences who go to the movies, must be assassinated, killed, destroyed, and they must leave the theater as new people.[20]

El Topo became one of the more famous films to emerge from Mexico after 1968. However, the film's success was not necessarily for being an artistic triumph, or for Jodorowsky's vision of the film as "revolutionary" beyond political sloganeering or agitprop. Indeed, Jodorowsky's revolutionary goals for *El Topo* were nothing short of what Artaud's theorized as the end result of the Theater of Cruelty: a complete destruction and reconstruction of the viewer's consciousness.

Nonetheless, *El Topo*'s notoriety owed to achieving considerable counterculture clout in the early–1970s. Critical assessments of *El Topo*, and Jodorowsky, were soon typically polarized.

Young people proclaimed Jodorowsky one of the 20th century's greatest artistic visionaries; veteran movie critics branded *El Topo* a pompous yet vacuous film created by a pretentious megalomaniac and unconditionally embraced by a gullible counterculture. This latter view was quite acerbically expressed by *New York Times* film critic Vincent Canby in a scathing May 1971 review titled with the self-answering rhetorical question, "Is *El Topo* a Con?"[21] Another negative critique was provided by *The New Yorker* film critic Pauline Kael. As suggested by her title, "*El Topo*— Head Comics," Kael viewed *El Topo* as the cinematic equivalent to the underground comics from the era. Some viewed the comics as popular, psychedelic essays against bourgeois society told through sordid acts of transgression; Abe Peck suggested cartoonist S. Clay Wilson's work "went beyond *Candide* and into a grotesque realm of member-chopping violence."[22] Opponents of the comics, including feminist voices in the counterculture itself, condemned them as trashy, trippy exercises in unrestrained misogyny and sadism.[23] Kael contended:

> [Jodorowsky's] an exploitation filmmaker, but he glosses everything with a useful piety. It's the violence plus the unctuous prophetic tone that makes *El*

Topo a heavy trip.... Jodorowsky has come up with something new: *exploitation filmmaking joined to the sentimentality of the counterculture.*[24]

Given Jodorowsky's tendencies to simplify Artaud into episodic, surrealist sex and violence, it could be said that the counterculture intelligentsia achieving enlightenment watching *El Topo* in its ritual midnight screenings at the Elgin Theater in the NYC Chelsea district ultimately bore little difference to the raincoat crowd jerking off to the nudie-roughie productions of Russ Meyer and David F. Friedman shown at grindhouse theaters on 42nd Street.

However, Kael's primary objection to *El Topo* stemmed from what she viewed as Jodorowsky's complete bastardization of Surrealism itself. Comparing Jodorowsky to Luis Buñuel, Kael argued:

> [Buñuel's] surrealist techniques cracked open conventional pieties; Jodorowsky uses those techniques to support a sanctimonious view: Man-God tempted by evil, power-hungry women abandons religious ways and then, through the love of a good woman, becomes spiritual man, only to learn that the world is not ready for his spirituality.[25]

Kael is correct that a key problem with *El Topo* is its highly moralistic subtext, often framed in reactionary gender and sexual politics (issues to be addressed throughout this chapter). However, there is a fundamental difference between the surrealism of Buñuel and Jodorowsky, despite the strong similarities in their imagery. Buñuel's surrealism depicted a world of absurd and meaningless events where bourgeois conceptions of morality, specifically religion and sexuality, were useless in an attempt to provide any semblance of order in the world — or in the film itself. As Buñuel succinctly explained his collaboration with Dalí, *Un Chien andalou* (1929): "NOTHING, in this film, SYMBOLIZES ANYTHING!"[26] Jodorowsky's surrealism was the complete antithesis of Buñuel. *El Topo* presented an allegorical and apocalyptic struggle in which Absolute Truth could be revealed, even if the cynical interpretation might be that this "Truth" was the inevitable result of compressing enough allusions, archetypes, concepts, and symbols into the film until it somehow became profound. In this regard, Hoberman and Rosenbaum unflatteringly compared Jodorowsky to Jean Cocteau, another "aesthetic opportunist" and "professional symbol-monger."[27] Donald M. Lowe provided a similar unfavorable assessment of Cocteau's film *Le Sang d'un poète* (*Blood of a Poet*, 1930) as a failed "allegory of the poet's pilgrimage, told in personal and literary symbols ... [Cocteau] considered film 'a powerful projection of thought.' Thus, the images of *Le Sang d'un poète* were *burdened with excessive representational references.*"[28] Lowe's assessment of Cocteau could easily be applied to *El Topo*, where Jodorowsky took symbol-mongering to its highest order: "I use *concrete symbols in every scene.*"[29]

The Wild West

For *El Topo*, Jodorowsky combined his idiosyncratic brand of surrealism with the most American of all genres, the Western, to house his version of the Theater of Cruelty. To this extent, *El Topo* owed more to Sam Peckinpah's seminal *The Wild Bunch* (1969) and another Italian filmmaker than to Fellini: Sergio Leone's "Spaghetti Westerns," and specifically his trilogy *Fistful of Dollars* (1964), *For a Few Dollars More* (1965), and *The Good, the Bad, and the Ugly* (1966) starring Clint Eastwood as the "Man with No Name." Leone and Peckinpah used the Western to construct "anti–Westerns" that simultaneously embraced the conventions of the Western and yet exaggerated, parodied, and subverted both the genre and its ideological tenets.[30] Moreover, a key aspect of Peckinpah and Leone's work was the depiction of violence, which was no longer inscribed with moral justification as a means to an end, but simply a perennial component of the situation. As Lee Clark Mitchell suggested of Peckinpah and Leone, "Not only did violence no longer offer moral resolution, it also served only marginally as closure to Western plots now loosely defined ... *violent action itself is stasis.*"[31] The same can be said for *El Topo*, where Jodorowsky took the Western and reduced it to its essential clichés while infusing them with surreal spectacle and his patented onslaught of symbols and allegories: an eternal cycle of the gunslinger alternately roaming the frontier and engaging in shootouts, with any closure being full-scale massacre.

Yet despite all of Jodorowsky's avant-garde window-dressing, *El Topo* is very much within certain traditions of the Western genre. *El Topo* begins with the classic establishing shot of the Western: a figure riding a horse in the expansive landscape. However, one is immediately struck by the incongruities between the image and the Western proper, not the least of which being that the figure inexplicably and humorously totes an umbrella in a desert — a Western depicted by Buñuel or René Magritte. Indeed, the landscape plays as pivotal role in the establishing shot as the presence of the rider himself. Within the vast and stark desert, the rider's relation to his surroundings and space itself is one of isolation verses grandeur — the difference between Westerns such as John Ford's *Stagecoach* (1939) and Anthony Mann's *The Man from Laramie* (1955), as described by André Bazin: "In most Westerns, even the best ones like Ford's, the landscape is an expressionist framework where human trajectories come and make their mark ... for Anthony Mann the landscape is always stripped of its picturesque effect."[32] In *El Topo*, the desolate deserts are not simply landscapes "stripped of picturesque effect," but voids in the throes of continuous creation and destruction.[33] Yet the Western in the hands of Jodorowsky is also very much a film where "human trajectories come and make their mark": a Western where Ford and Jefferson are subsumed by Artaud and Nietzsche (or, rather, Jodorowsky's interpretations of Artaud and Nietzsche), and the "human trajectory" is nothing less than the epic struggle to overcome the barriers of civilization and consciousness itself.

As the rider nears the camera, the viewer is introduced to El Topo (played by Jodorowsky), a hippie cowboy dressed in black leather — a look owing more to Jim Morrison than John Wayne.[34] Immediately there is a parodic take of the Western, where the traditional black clothing normally coding the villain is now the garb of the hero: the anti-hero. El Topo also reflects the counterculture's infatuation with the figure of "outlaw" as a revolutionary figure beyond the constraints of bourgeois society: the dashing Clyde Barrow (Warren Beatty) in *Bonnie and Clyde* (1967) or the philosopher-biker "Captain America" (Peter Fonda) in *Easy Rider* (1969).[35] In reference to Mexican culture, El Topo represents a counterculture update of the traditional Mexican Western hero, the *charro*, and especially the "*charro*-as-*macho*" exemplified by actor Pedro Infante as well as the myth of Pancho Villa fighting for revolution and popular justice; as Anne Rubenstein noted, this political image was replaced in post–World War II Mexican culture by the "countermacho," a figure of modernity and moral restraint (represented by Santo and other *luchardores* in the mexploitation era).[36] In *El Topo*, the negative connotations of the *charro*-as-*macho* — the reckless, uncouth, hot-tempered, drunken, womanizing cowboy — are replaced with existential, charismatic cool and "cockiness": the vogue of revolutionary *machismo*. As William L. O'Neill succinctly observed, "Ché Guevara had more political sex appeal than Gandhi."[37] In relation to *El Topo*'s highly problematic representation of sex and gender politics, this revolutionary *machismo* often expressed itself as pervasive and quite overt male chauvinism. As O'Neill noted:

> New Leftists did not automatically shed their masculine personalities by becoming revolutionaries. Sometimes they were even worse than the average man. The prestige of many third-world liberators led many to exaggerate traditional masculine traits. This spurious *machismo* was most readily expressed against movement women.[38]

Father and Son

In the first of many symbolic events thought the film, El Topo sternly instructs the young boy riding with him, naked except for his cowboy hat, to bury his "favorite toy," a teddy bear, and a photo of his mother in the desert sand (the boy is played by Jodorowsky's son, Brontis). The interment of his teddy bear not only represents the renunciation of frivolous childhood innocence, but any bourgeois morality and sentimentality which are not only irrelevant, but a hindrance in *El Topo*'s brutal and desolate Western frontier. Burying his mother's photograph signifies the demolition of the female component of the "holy family" ("mommy-daddy-me") and the Oedipal order (which undergoes a far more complex critique in *Santa sangre*).[39] All traces of the mother — and the woman — are immediately expunged, and the reappearance of women over the course of *El Topo* — Mara (Mara

Lorenzio), the Woman in Black (Paula Romo), and the Small Woman (Jacqueline Luis) — has profound ramifications.

In the next episode of El Topo's journey, father and son come across a decimated town strewn with corpses. The dirt roads are muddied with blood, and the unnerving sounds of cawing condors and buzzing flies are over-amplified on the soundtrack to the point of producing actual physical discomfort for the viewer. It is the first of several references to Tlatelolco which occur throughout *El Topo*, the horror of the massacre still ingrained in Mexican public memory. Among the more disturbing scenes are a child impaled on a pole, eviscerated donkeys, bridegrooms hung from the rafters inside a church, and one hundred dead women in bridal gowns lying raped and murdered–a metaphor of Mexico's loss of political "virginity" after Tlatelolco.[40] As El Topo and his son wander the horrific scene, a badly wounded man crawls through the blood and mud, imploring El Topo to kill him. Indifferently, El Topo hands his pistol to his son, symbolically bequeathing the symbol of phallic power: the gun-as-phallus. El Topo's son tentatively grasps it in both hands and promptly shoots the man. The murder becomes the entry into manhood, the ability to briefly wield the phallic power inscribed in the gun through the definitive act of omnipotence: taking another person's life.

However, this gun-phallus relationship is hardly Jodorowsky's contribution to the Western genre, as it is very much inscribed in the genre itself, and is particularly evident in the aforementioned Anthony Mann–James Stewart Western cycle of the early 1950s (films that can also be read as "anti–Westerns"— to the extent they implode the genre, versus Leone and Peckinpah who explode the genre). In the first, *Winchester '73* (1950), the gun becomes a highly coveted phallic fetish-object. Men longingly stare at the rifle on display before the target competition to decide its ownership; young boys wonder if they too will possess such a magnificent object when they "grow up." The law also does not permit men to wear their pistols in the streets — in effect, castrating them — which men describe as making them feel "naked." The finale of *Winchester '73* consists of a prolonged gunfight between Stewart and his estranged brother for the ownership of the rifle, the struggle to possess the phallus of the absent father and its symbolic authority of the Law. Conversely, in the final Mann-Stewart Western, *The Man from Laramie* (1955), the gun-phallus relationship is established by symbolic castration: another trope that occurs throughout *El Topo*. In the pivotal scene of the film, Will Lockheart (Stewart) is held by two men while the psychotic Dave Waggoman removes a pistol from Lockheart's hand and then shoots him in the palm; Lockheart staggers away, his back to the camera as he cradles his wounded appendage in front of his crotch. It is through this act of symbolic castration that Lockheart, who has been seeking revenge on the men responsible for the death of his brother, slowly begins his acclimation into the frontier community. As Freud observed, "Civilization ... obtains mastery over the individual's dangerous desire for aggression by weakening and *dis-*

arming it."[41] However, in the early stages of *El Topo*, the title character is the sole arbitrator of phallic power in a primitive, surreal, and distinctly phallocentric world.

Frontier Justice

The next section of *El Topo* similarly revolves around political violence and El Topo's phallic mastery. Basking in the afterglow of the massacre in which they participated, three bandits celebrate in sexually-infused comedy routines set to circus music. One sniffs a collection of high heels shoes, simulates fellatio on one of them, and then lines them against a stone wall, shooting them for target practice.[42] Another adroitly slices a banana with a sword and daintily eats a piece (another act of symbolic castration, as well as fellatio). The third draws a stick figure of a nude woman in the dirt with beans and beings to "dry hump" the parched desert sand. However, when the scene suddenly cuts to El Topo and his son riding towards the bandits, the music abruptly stops altogether, signifying what is about to occur as "deadly serious." Confronting each other, they square off in a surreal version of the classic shootout where El Topo exacts justice through the most generic of all Western conventions: the gunfight, although one more reminiscent of Buñuel than Ford. One of the bandits inflates a balloon and sets it on the ground. As it slowly deflates, Jodorowsky constructs and parodies the classic Western gunfight montage: close-ups of steely eyes and stoic expressions; twitching hands next to holstered guns; dramatic long shots surveying the scene; and, of course, the squeaking, shrinking balloon that, when fully deflated, will signal the commencement of the shootout. After a flurry of loud gunshots and jump-cuts that fragment the action to the point of incomprehensibility, two bandits slowly tumble off their horses dead, and El Topo shoots the gun from the third bandit's hand—a parody of the classic Western cliché, as well as symbolic castration (*The Man from Laramie*). With almost sadistic ruthlessness, El Topo steadily pursues the bandit, accompanied by a surreal parody of the Greek Chorus: a herd of goats scurrying about the scene. Not only does their loud, incessant bleating suggest they are mocking the bandit for being "baaaad!," but they suspiciously sound like human voices that were dubbed onto the soundtrack imitating goats, creating a hilarious but quite disorientating effect. After strategically shooting the bandit several times to prolong his torment, El Topo finally corners him in a small pond and shoots him in the heart. As the bandit dies, El Topo demands, "Who?—How many?—Where?"—seeking the names of those responsible for the massacre. It becomes another reference to Tlatelolco; no responsibility was ever assigned to specific government individuals in the wake of the massacre, and El Topo becomes the figure of people's justice demanding answers—and retribution–for the events at Tlatelolco.

With his final breath, the bandit mutters, "the Colonel," and the location of a Franciscan monastery. A long zoom-out of the dead bandit floating in the pond after his baptism of gunfire cuts to a montage of dead bodies strewn about a courtyard; a bandit firing a machine gun; a row of bodies crumpling to the ground after being gunned down in firing squad fashion; and, in a surreal touch, piles of corpses surrounding an antique gramophone. Again, the images bear directly on Tlatelolco, implying many more massacres will occur at the hands of "the Colonels" unless they are stopped. More surreal, savage, sexual, and often sacrilegious images follow. Some certainly recall Buñuel: a bandit reading the Bible pauses to tear out a page to blow his nose while monks are seen tied to the wall behind him; a drunken bandit indifferently fires his pistol at a row of people lined up against a wall, randomly executing a few as he staggers past. Other scenes prefigure the sexually humiliating orchestrations of torture in Pier Paolo's Pasolini's final film — and perhaps the ultimate "avant-exploitation" film — the highly controversial and frequently misunderstood *Salò o La 120 giornate di Sodoma* (*Salò, or, the Days of Sodom*, 1975), Pasolini's adaptation of Sade's writings set in an isolated villa in the final days of Fascist Italy. In one scene, the bandits force the hostage monks to romantically waltz with them in the decimated ruins of the monastery. In another, the bandits ride the naked monks like racehorses, whipping their buttocks with cactus branches — with the monks, in effect, mooning the camera. In a third scene, one bandit lovingly applies make-up and a white veil to a shamed monk, rendering him into a parody of the Virgin Mary. However, in *Salò* the brutal orchestration of sexual torture becomes a critique of modernity's relentless drive towards the systematic organization of domination on all facets of humanity: above all, sex and the body itself—with no orifice left unconquered.[43] In *El Topo*, one is instead struck by the overall homophobia implicit in the scene. The degradation of the devout monks is made particularly odious by their feminization and emasculation at the hands of other men, the bandits. Given the "spurious *machismo*" and phallocentricism which permeated the counterculture as a whole, a pattern is established in *El Topo* where heroic, heterosexual masculinity is frequently pitted against villains codified in terms of femininity, homosexuality, sexual repression, and perversions: above all, conniving lesbians.

As noted, the series of massacres is being led by a Mexican army colonel, played by Mexican cinema legend David Silva, who subsequently starred in López Moctezuma's *La mansión de locura* and *Alucarda*.[44] In a protracted sequence, the bald, heavyset Colonel lounges in his darkened throne room — a commandeered monastery temple — while his servant, a young woman later christened "Mara" by El Topo, assists him in applying make-up and a toupee: again, implying an element of femininity on the Colonel's part to compliment his authoritarian personality. He also dons ornate, antiquated military apparel; his anachronistic and ostentatious appearance certainly references the trappings of European and Latin American dictators. Now properly attired to meet the outside world, the Colonel steps out of his monastery bunker and strikes an arrogant pose worthy of Mussolini himself, his arms akimbo and nose in the air. As he stands motionless for several seconds, a large swarm of grunting pigs stampede from the bunker. The Colonel and his mercenaries are literally denoted as "pigs" — the common, derogatory appellation used by the counterculture to describe the police, military, and other representatives of the Establishment.

After spending several minutes humiliating Mara and his motley foot soldiers, the Colonel grants the men his permission to gang rape Mara. However, the impending assault is interrupted by the timely arrival of El Topo, who bursts onto the scene like Superman (or *Übermensch*) as much as the archetypal Western hero. In a low-angle long shot that exaggerates El Topo's powerful entrance, he kicks open a door in a ruined wall, sending it flying off its hinges as his fires his six-gun. The bandits immediately surrender and El Topo's son removes their guns from their holsters — another act of symbolic castration. When one bandit tries to produce a hidden pistol from behind his back, El Topo nonchalantly shoots him in the gut. Staggering away, the outlaw pathetically attempts to gather a few strewn items from the ransacked monastery before dying. Crosscut with his final moments are approving reaction shots of Mara, El Topo's son, and the monks, who especially demonstrate a particularly strong sense of satisfaction and pleasure watching one of their former tormentors pitifully dying — mirroring the counterculture film audience's own vicarious pleasure in watching one of the "pigs" getting his due.

A brief title card appears, interrupting the sequence: "Genesis," the first book of the Bible. In *El Topo*, the first act of Genesis is the creation of the Universe by establishing El Topo's omnipotent phallic and political power. The guns of those responsible for the massacres are redistributed to El Topo's son and the monks (Mara is *not* bequeathed a gun-phallus). El Topo returns the Colonel's ornate pistol, and dramatically begins to circle him to initiate a duel.[45] Demonstrating complete cowardice, the Colonel flees, even after El Topo stands motionless with his arms outstretched to give the Colonel the first shot: a parody of the Crucifixion cast in political terms, with El Topo, the revolutionary Christ, versus the Colonel, the fascist Pontius Pilate (a scene reenacted later in the film with El Topo's "crucifixion" by the Women in Black and Mara). Various "castrations" of the Colonel follow. First, and not surprisingly, El Topo shoots the gun from the Colonel's hand. Then, in a scene more akin to a Warner Brothers cartoon than a Western, El Topo shoots the toupee: it flies off the Colonel's head, accompanied by a loud ricochet. Not only humorously humiliating him by revealing his (effeminate) vanity, the act also recalls the story of Samson, whose (masculine) power was rooted in his hair (a Biblical reference used frequently by Jodorowsky in his films, including a pivotal scene later in *El Topo*). Literally stripping the Colonel of his power, El Topo removes the Colonel's gaudy uniform, shredding the entire ensemble with a single swipe as if he were tearing a sheer evening gown off a woman — a connotation owing to *El Topo*'s emphasis on phallocentric power and frequent valorization of masculine power (good) over feminine deceit (evil). Aided by monks and bandits alike, now collectively caught up in the aura of El Topo's revolutionary *machismo*, the Colonel is held at bay. He desperately asks El Topo who he is, and quite portentously El Topo answers: "I am God." And, as "God," he carries out the final punishment and castrates the Colonel, severing his penis with a hunting knife. The naked Colonel slowly staggers away before finding his lost pistol, and, in a final symbolic act of phallic power after the loss of his penis, places the gun-phallus in his mouth (also suggesting fellatio) and commits suicide.

Thus, "in the beginning" of *El Topo* the title character is, quite literally, established as the punishing God, the creator of the universe as the sole authority of who may possess phallic power. In turn, the universe is created by the castration and destruction of a political archetype in the form of the Imperialist, the Fascist, and a Mexican Army officer: the last being a particularly politically-charged image given the Mexican military's recent actions at Tlatelolco. Ultimately, the castration also becomes a moment of violent catharsis for both the characters in the film and the film audience, reflecting the affinity between *El Topo* and the underground comics. As Peck noted, the popularity of the underground comics, at least in part, owed to their graphic depiction of "cathartic violence ... [and] hinted at what it would be like 'to win.'"[46]

The Politics of Adam and Eve

After El Topo (God) creates the universe by castrating the Colonel, the other key moment in the book of Genesis begins with the construction of the film's couple: El Topo and Mara as the post-revolutionary Adam and Eve. Mara is clearly enamored of El Topo's revolutionary *machismo*, and she fawningly follows him back to his horse while El Topo's son attempts to come between them, physically forcing himself between the two as they are about to embrace. Faced with choosing his son or the strange, alluring woman for his new partner, he shoves his son aside and abandons him to the care of the monks. As El Topo rides off with Mara, the father-son relationship is replaced by another component of the holy family, the man-woman couple — which is not to say the relationship between El Topo and Mara is no less dominated by the primacy of the phallus.

The scene shifts from the monastery, the site of the massacre and the revolution, to El Topo and Mara cavorting in an environment antithetical to the stark deserts and corpse-littered towns: a waterfall in a lush forest, representing the Garden of Eden. While El Topo plays his wooden flute (referencing him to the Greek god Pan), Mara drinks the water in the pond and complains how "bitter" it tastes.[47] Placing a large tree branch (and phallic symbol) into the pond, El Topo recounts a

Biblical story of Moses stirring stagnant waters in the desert to make them palatable during the Exodus. Mara marvels at El Topo's phallic miracle, delighted he made the water "sweet." El Topo responds, "I'll call you Mara because you are like bitter water." Water also signifies Mara's sexuality, a sexuality that is "bitter" rather than "sweet" except when properly "stirred" by El Topo.[48]

The couple soon returns to the arid desert, the new Adam and Eve beginning their own Exodus as well. Mara soon grows irritable and complains they will not be able to survive, and El Topo responds by performing more Freudian-religious miracles. While Mara stands with her legs spread, he unearths eggs out of the desert sand (a symbol of Mara's womb); he shoots a rock with his pistol, producing a gusher of water to quench her thirst (a metaphor for El Topo's ejaculation satisfying the woman's sexual longing). However, when Mara tries to recreate El Topo's miracles with the eggs and the rock, she fails miserably in being either fertile or orgasmic; while El Topo sits tranquilly in the desert sand, she is reduced to pacing in a circle, muttering, "Nothing... Nothing... Nothing..."[49] Finally, whether to "insert" some of his phallic power into Mara or simply shut her up, El Topo calmly undoes his pants and then viciously rapes her. A close-up of Mara screaming quickly zooms out to reveal her floating naked in a lake, a symbolic shot suggesting both a sexual baptism and that the rape makes Mara incredibly "wet." The montage continues, with Mara now able to produce her own eggs from the desert sand (her barren womb now fertile, courtesy of El Topo), and concludes with an almost unintentionally comic Freudian shot: Mara approaches a blatantly phallus-shaped rock, strikes it with a whip, and bathes her face with a geyser of water, signifying not only male but female sexual climax. Jodorowsky suggested, and completely without irony: "The character is frigid until El Topo rapes her. And she has an orgasm. That's why I show a stone phallus in that scene ... which spouts water. She has an orgasm. *She accepts the male sex.*"[50]

Yet the virtually pornographic shot, the surrealist equivalent of a porn film "facial," becomes the point the power dynamic in the couple relationship changes. The rape, the ultimate expression of male power over women, is also the moment Mara begins to assume her mastery of El Topo: the moment his omnipotent phallus becomes "whipped" (or "pussy-whipped") by Mara. With all the ruthlessness of a hippie Lady Macbeth, she now dictates a plan of action for El Topo:

MARA: Do you love me?
EL TOPO: Yes.
MARA: Well, I don't! *For me to love you, you have to be the best.* Four Master Sharpshooters live in this desert. You have to find them and kill them [emphasis added].[51]

El Topo agrees to kill the Four Masters, drawing a spiral in the desert and explaining, "The desert is circular; to find them we must travel in a spiral." The spiral is a figure used in Jungian psychology to describe the path of self-discovery (individuation); it is also the path of *El Topo*'s narrative strategy: the film is not a linear story, but an ever-expanding, cyclical epic made up of distinct events independent of each other yet metaphorically and metaphysically related as a whole.[52]

Moreover, at this point in *El Topo*, Mara becomes an increasingly diabolical figure. Having achieved a degree of control over El Topo's phallic power, she becomes the archetypal *femme fatale* who simultaneously seduces and destroys men. Moreover, she demands the elimination of those representing a phallic mastery that she herself can not attain (read: penis envy), and uses her awakened sexuality (her "stirred water" after the rape) to manipulate El Topo into fulfilling her wicked designs and thirst for power: her unquenchable fixation on the (presumably sweet) water that gushes from phallic rocks. In this respect, the name "Mara" can be read as a pun on the word *maya*, which translates from Sanskrit as "illusion," and is a Buddhist concept for the (false) reality one sees and experiences through their self-deceptions and self-delusions: the obstacle to *nirvana* (spiritual enlightenment). Mara (*maya*) represents El Topo's own entry into a new reality corrupted by delusion and deception, the dangers of temptation and self-interest: "Man-God tempted by evil, power-hungry women."

The Four Masters

In *El Topo*, each of the Four Masters represents a cultural reference or philosophical school of thought embraced by the 1960s counterculture. The duels with the Four Masters are not triumphs where El Topo exacts counterculture retribution against the Establishment (the castration of the Colonel), but a systematic destruction of the very ideals shaping the counterculture. As El Topo eventually completes Mara's scheme of eliminating the Four Masters, he becomes acutely aware he squandered the immense opportunity to achieve enlightenment through their teachings. In destroying the Four Masters he also destroys himself: a self-destruction prompted by El Topo's succumbing to the wiles of the woman. To the extent *El Topo* is not only an epic *for* the counterculture but *about* the counterculture experience, Mara and the sinister Woman in Black (who will be discussed at length shortly) represent the malevolent force of feminism emerging in the counterculture movement — the dangerous Sirens of the counterculture.

A slender man with long hair and a bushy moustache, the First Master represents Eastern religion, a pervasive influence on counterculture idealism. When El Topo discovers the First Master's secluded temple, the music on the soundtrack abruptly shifts from the parodic Spaghetti Western score to Tibetan music, and El Topo is awestruck by the First Master's sometimes strained Zen platitudes when they meet. Aware that El Topo wishes to duel him, he dispassionately states, "I do not try to win, but to gain perfect control." He orders the servant to shoot him, which has no effect: "I hardly bleed. I offer no resistance to the bullets. I let them pass through the empty spaces of my flesh" (the First Master's servant, billed as "the Double Man," is certainly the most surreal character in *El Topo* and literally a "composite character": a legless man who sits on the back of an armless man).[53] Agreeing to a gunfight, he warns El Topo, "Killing does not bother me because I know that death does not exist." A shot of the First Master sitting in repose after his cryptic statement cuts to a shot of El Topo chest-deep in a pond, forming an associative montage between the two: the master and potential student — now adversaries. Already, El Topo suspects the potential folly of his quest: "He is my superior ... even if I won, I would lose." Disgusted with El Topo's lack of confidence, Mara berates him: "I want a winner. You have to win. *Don't be so honest! Don't fight on the same level. Think of something. Trick him.* You can always win. Find a way!" (Emphasis added.) Midway through Mara's harangue, the shot cuts back to El Topo submerging himself in the water, leaving only his hat floating in the pond. While a kind of old-fashioned, burlesque joke where El Topo sinks into the water to avoid his nagging girlfriend, the gesture suggests something more insidious as well: El Topo is submerging himself, even drowning, in "bitter water"— the scheming influence of Mara.

In this respect, *cunning* is introduced in *El Topo*, a concept integral to Max Horkheimer and Theodor W. Adorno's reading of Homer's *Odyssey,* a key influence on *El Topo*: "Cunning is *defiance in rational form*."[54] As Horkheimer and Adorno observed in their analysis of Odysseus' encounter with the Sirens, the far more prudent course is to simply take a different route and avoid the Sirens altogether. While Odysseus insists on sailing near the Sirens, he also doubts he can resist the Sirens' song simply by tenacious willpower. Thus, Odysseus devises an ingenious strategy which allows him to experience their forbidden song without the inevitable result of being shipwrecked and drowned: he is tied to the mast of his ship and takes the precaution of filling the oarsmens' ears with wax. In Horkheimer and Adorno's interpretation, two essential elements of bourgeois society are already established in antiquity. One is the individual who succeeds through crafty manipulation of his situation. Second is the society based on class, and the many who toil for the benefit of the one; Odysseus' moment of individual privilege and triumph over circumstances comes at the expense of the oarsmen, who must row the ship near the Sirens without experiencing the pleasure of their song.[55]

In keeping with *El Topo*'s underlying sex and gender politics, it is Mara, the devious woman, who becomes the architect of cunning. Like Odysseus, she refuses to veer from her course, yet realizes that she will be ruined if she does not find a means to manipulate the situation: El Topo. Indeed, it is Mara who becomes Odysseus while El Topo is regulated to the status of oarsman, the subordinate who implements the cunning schemes of the epic hero and receives none of the rewards. As El Topo engulfs himself in Mara's "bitter water" and her growing power, El Topo is *already* drowned by the Siren's song — Mara's machinations and badgering which prompts him to submerge himself in the pond. Lacking the sophistication of Odysseus, she simply suggests a crude theorem for El Topo to emerge victorious: winning is the end, and all strategies are acceptable means to prevent losing (the antithesis of the First Master's ideal that he does not wish to win and only seeks perfection). In short, El Topo is situated between the Western bourgeois ideology of competition and domination (Mara) — mastery over others — and the Eastern philosophy of harmony and concordance (the First Master)–mastery of the self. It is this philosophical and political struggle that underscores El Topo's transformation during his quest to kill the Four Masters, and his own enlightenment later in the film.

After a lengthy prologue where the two combatants prepare for their epic battle, El Topo and the First Master face each other in the desert (a surreal merger of Ford and Pasolini), accompanied by overpowering Tibetan music on the soundtrack. However, the building, intensive drama of the confrontation ends quite anticlimactically. In a series of truncated jump-cuts, including a close-up of Mara apparently having an orgasm at the moment of the murder, the First Master plummets into a hole dug into the desert sand and El Topo shoots him between the eyes. The victory is the result of cunning manipulation verses noble heroism — or the moment cunning *becomes* heroism. El Topo is immediately ashamed of his deceitful victory over the First Master, and throws his gun into the sand in disgust — a momentary discarding and renunciation of his phallic power played out after he kills each of the Four Masters. In contrast, Mara is elated. She briefly assumes phallic mastery by taking the dead Master's gun; then, manically and melodramatically cackling, she ruthlessly and repeatedly shoots the Master's servant(s). To celebrate their victory — or, more correctly, Mara's victory — they return to the small oasis where Mara immediately and gleefully throws herself into the water ("bitter water") while El Topo sits next to the pond, glaring at his revolver and pondering the implications of the gunfight.

The Second Master is eventually located, and El Topo sets off alone to confront him in his canyon encampment. The Second Master represents another element of counterculture idealism: the fascination with "native societies" and the cultures of nomads and tribes extinguished by modernity, sometimes reduced to the cliché of the "noble savage" (in the United States, the counterculture infatuation with Native American culture).[56] Like the First Master, the Second Master is also referenced to Eastern culture. His attire recalls the pre-modern Asiatic barbarian tribes (Mongols, Huns), and when El Topo approaches the camp, Tibetan music is again heard on the soundtrack. However, El Topo does not initially meet the Second Master but what Jodorowsky called the "Universal Mother." Similarly clad to the Second Master, she is reading the Tarot and foretells El Topo's future as he approaches their camp: "You are falling. You'll fall even deeper. The deeper you fall, the higher you'll get." However, this Universal Mother — Jodorowsky's version

Showdown: El Topo and the First Master (foreground) prepare to duel in *El Topo*.

of the Jungian archetype of the great mother (the maternal goddess, the earth mother)—speaks to El Topo in a *man's* voice (dubbed in postproduction)—a sexist reconfiguration of the great mother archetype, who must speak in a man's voice to attain any legitimate metaphysical authority.[57]

The Universal Mother informs El Topo that the Second Mater agrees to duel him. A hulking yet graceful presence, he roams around their wagon as a lion similarly paces nearby—both nomadic, primitive hunters combining primal agility and power. However, unlike the loud Tibetan music that appropriately underscored the previous encounter with the Masters thus far, this impending duel is accompanied by a highly incongruent, schmaltzy waltz, a strange and sardonic effect reminiscent of Brecht. As the two circle each other, El Topo draws his revolver, which is immediately shot out of his hand, disarming (castrating) him. The Second Master laughs, "Bang! You're dead ... technically. Now I want to talk to the dead man." He provides El Topo with a second set of lessons, this time based on the principles of Sufism rather than Buddhism, although there are certain similarities in the two trains of thought not lost on Jodorowsky (or a counterculture audience): the dangers and limits of the self that can be overcome through heightened spiritual awareness. However, unlike the First Master's dispassionate discussions, the Second Master's preferred pedagogy is feats of strength. He demonstrates how forging copper made his hands powerful enough to now manufacture and manipulate intricate toothpick sculptures — one of which El Topo promptly crushes when he grasps it. To compare their mastery of the pistol, they each shoot at these small sculptures. El Topo's target is obliterated, while the Second Master's shot only breaks a single toothpick in the sculpture: "A clean shot. Delicate. It destroys the necessary." He then takes a more "hands-on" approach to schooling El Topo. With the lion roaring off-camera, the Second Master lectures and physically beats El Topo as he struggles on the ground: "You shoot to find yourself; I shoot to disappear. Perfection is losing yourself. And to lose yourself, you have to love. You don't love. You destroy. You murder. And no one loves you."

Throwing El Topo at the feet of the Universal Mother, the Second Master explains he has found absolute freedom though his complete devotion to her — the freedom from the self through his fidelity to a spiritual entity greater than himself. "I've surrendered myself to her. I've given her everything. She is within me. Her infinite love fills me. Whatever I do and say are dictated and sanctified by her. I detest anything that is mine because it removes me from her Divine Presence." The lesson complete, the Second Master offers El Topo another chance to duel him, but first gives El Topo a small copper plate: a symbol of the superficial strength he has long forsaken. In his second display of cunning, El Topo drops the plate at the Universal Mother's feet and surreptitiously places some small objects in its place: shards of glass from the hand mirror given to Mara by the Woman in Black and subsequently destroyed by El Topo (the further significance of which will be addressed shortly).[58] When the Universal Mother rises to return El Topo's pistol to him, she steps on the glass fragments and recoils in pain; her cries are the sound of a cawing crow (or more pejoratively, complaining like an old crow). Selflessly drawn to aid the Universal Mother, the Second Master begins to remove the glass from her feet in a parody of Aesop's fable of the slave and the lion (suggesting the lion that roams the camp is a symbol of the Universal Mother as much as the Second Master). El Topo seizes the opportunity to sneak behind the distracted Second Master and coldly shoots him in the back of the head, execution-style. While El Topo's victory owes to the insidious influence of Mara, the Second Master's defeat owes to the Master's devotion, or servitude, to a woman as well: the Great Mother archetype. Yet El Topo realizes this cunning victory is hollow as well; as he leaves the camp, he again throws his gun to the ground in shame.

Jodorowsky noted, "The Third Master is a Mexican Master. In every Western ever made, the Mexican is always the outlaw, the bad guy. In my picture, the Mexican is a very wonderful man, because Mexico has a very wonderful culture.... I wanted to use the nobility of ancient Mexico — the finest of Mexico."[59] However, the Third Master is not represented by ancient Mexican cultures (the Aztecs), but by another counterculture icon of the era: the Third World peasant farmer, a political figure central to Maoism and the wave of "peasant revolutions" during the 1960s, manifest most dramatically with Vietnam. In a surreal addition, the Third Master's farm is entirely populated by white rabbits — all of whom promptly die when El Topo arrives. Beyond the counterculture reference (Jefferson Airplane's anthem of the Psychedelic Revolution, "White Rabbit," itself derived from Lewis Carroll's pre-surrealist *Alice in Wonderland*), Jodorowsky explained, "The rabbit is also a solar symbol of reproduction ... they were killed by a disease ... by El Topo. He was the disease, like the plague."[60] Indeed, the "plague" that El Topo carries with him which kills the symbols of fertility is his own "diseased" manhood and sexuality being steadily "infected" by Mara's influence.

The prologue to the gunfight establishes El Topo as being outmatched by the Third Master's abilities as well; he proudly tells El Topo that his gun "only shoots once ... which is all I need." In a virtual replay of the target practice with the Second Master and the toothpick sculptures, the two simultaneously shoot two crows (a symbolic killing of the wounded Universal Mother from the previous encounter). When they inspect the dead birds, the Third Master notes, "This was yours, it was shot in the head; this was mine, it was shot in the heart." He picks up the respective bodies of the birds and holds them in front of El Topo's head and heart: "The head or the heart —" he ponders, then shifts his hands to changes the bird's positions in relation to El Topo's body: "— It makes no difference." The philosophical lesson the Third Master offers is a rejection of the Cartesian duality of mind and body, that the mind exists in a superior relationship to the body, which his merely the mind's housing. To achieve mastery over the self, the mind and body must exist in a unity, although the more romantic interpretation might be that one must "think with the heart" and "feel with the mind."

The brief lesson concluded, and demonstrating some of his own confident *machismo*, the Third Master initiates the duel. The two square off on each side of a shallow pool of dirty water as the corpses of rabbits litter the scene, suggesting that even while Mara is absent, her presence as "bitter water" and her corrupting sexual influence over El Topo is still central in the scene: a muddy pool surrounded by diseased and dead symbols of fertility. El Topo apparently loses the duel; he falls to the ground, shot in the chest before he can aim his gun. However, he quickly rises and loudly chuckles. After waving his gun across the Third Master's face, he points it at his heart and fires (the previous two Masters having been shot in the head by El Topo). The Third Master falls into the pool, the water turning crimson, and El Topo reveals the secret to his victory: he placed the small copper plate bequeathed by the Second Master over his heart — "hardening his heart" — and correctly surmised it would be the target of the Third Master's only shot (the plate, as noted, is a symbol of mistaken strength). *Cunning* is once again the source of victory for El Topo, the epic hero's triumph owing to shrewd calculation of the situation over rigorous discipline and training: the triumph of the mind over the body. For the first time, El Topo even displays a certain satisfaction with the end result of a duel by tossing his small shield into the pool and muttering, "Too much perfection is a mistake."[61] Nevertheless, the scene ultimately ends with an even greater display of regret by El Topo. A shot of the Third Master's body buried under a pile of dead rabbits zooms-out to reveal El Topo washing his hands in the bloody, dirty pool of water. It abruptly jump-cuts to Mara in the desert excitedly ripping open her shirt to reveal her breasts. Far from aroused, El Topo does not cop a feel, but attempts to wipe the blood off his hands and place it on the responsible party: Mara (and her breasts).

The Fourth Master is soon encountered: an aged, withered man with long, matted hair. Rather than a specific aspect of counterculture idealism, the Fourth Master is the hippie transformed into the Jungian archetype of the wise old man: what El Topo "could be," or "should be," versus what El Topo "is" (although *El Topo* ultimately suggests the First Master may be the most "enlightened" of the Four Masters). The Fourth Master informs El Topo, "You want to fight me? How do you plan to do it?.... I traded my revolver for a butterfly net—you'll have to fight me with your fists." As the Fourth Master hilariously poses in the anachronistic posture of bare-knuckle boxers, El Topo attacks him with exaggerated karate movements. He comically and clumsily flails away against the Fourth Master, who simply dodges El Topo's blows and sends him tumbling in the desert sand: the triumph of non-violent resistance over brute force. Incensed, El Topo draws his pistol and fires; the Fourth Master grasps the butterfly net and the sound of a ricochet is heard on the soundtrack. "My net is mightier than your bullets," he smiles, parodying the adage, "The pen is mightier than the sword." He explicitly warns El Topo: "If you fire again, I'll return your own bullet into your heart" (El Topo's heart being the target, or his "Achilles' heel," rather than his head, or mind). Distraught, El Topo sits in the sand, and the Fourth Master offers sage advice: "How could you possibly have won? I don't fight. I have nothing. *Even if you tricked me*, you couldn't have taken anything from me" (emphasis added). El Topo snarls in response, "I could have taken your life." The Fourth Master simply responds that life "means nothing to me," and he nonchalantly takes El Topo's gun and shoots himself in the stomach, and utters his final words to El Topo: "*You lost.*"[62]

It is with this final "victory" that El Topo realizes what he suspected all along: "Even if I won, I would lose." As a surreal coda to his quest for domination, El Topo returns to the scenes of the three previous battles: the Third Master's rabbit burial mound now engulfed in flames; the Second Master and the now-dead Universal Mother entombed in a giant toothpick sculpture which El Topo promptly destroys; the First Master laying in a fetal position in his rectangular hole in the desert, a parody of Christ in the tomb. In one of the more startling images of the film, El Topo performs a perverse parody of the communion by "eating the body of Christ" as an act of cannibalism, manifest in a close-up of El Topo gnawing at a honeycomb removed from the grave. This shot cuts to El Topo throwing himself against the walls of the First Master's temple — now adorned with a crucified lamb — until the entire structure collapses. Standing in the ruins, El Topo releases a pair of doves, and, in his definitive renunciation of violence and his (phallic) power, he smashes his gun to pieces with a piece of rubble from the temple. However, having definitively disarmed himself, the stage is set for his next battle — his confrontation with the Woman in Black.

The Fifth Master: The Woman in Black

At the moment El Topo and Mara locate the First Master, another crucial character is introduced to the film, the mysterious Woman in Black: she is seen sitting on horseback, applying mascara while looking in a hand-held mirror, patiently awaiting a chance to duel the First Master. Her presence constructs a classic romantic triangle with El Topo and Mara, although the object of the romantic battle is ultimately Mara rather than El Topo. Furthermore, she completes the dialectic of man (El Topo) and woman (Mara) which reaches its synthesis in the Woman in Black. In short, she is El Topo-as-Woman, dressed almost identically to him, with selected feminine accouterments (make-up, a white scarf tied around her neck) — the *charro* as *Vogue* fashion model versus *macho* revolutionary. Most importantly, she is a woman with dormant masculine, or phallic, power. While not immediately noticeable, and like the voice of the Universal Mother, Jodorowsky used a *man* to dub the Woman in Black's sparse dialogue in post-production: the image of woman who is invested with inherent power, and therefore must necessarily speak with the man's voice and authority.[63]

In this sense, the Woman in Black embodies an even greater threat to El Topo than Mara, who is content to manipulate El Topo with seductive deceit in the framework of the man-woman couple relationship. The Woman in Black represents the force of the woman no longer content to parasitically influence phallic power, but a force that can, and will, potentially usurp it altogether. In this regard, the Woman in Black is a distinctly political symbol, the force of feminism emerging within the contradictory counterculture politics of revolution and sexism: the underground comics, rock music, trends in underground theater and cinema that amounted to avant-garde burlesque revues and stag movies (Ed Sanders' *Mongolian Cluster Fuck*), and even the organizational structures of the 1960s radical movements themselves.[64] These sexual politics were cogently expressed by Wayne Kramer, guitarist for legendary 1960s rock band MC5: "We were sexist bastards.... We all had the rhetoric of being revolutionary and new and different, but really what it was, was the boys get to go fuck and the girls can't complain about it. And if they did complain, they were being bourgeois bitches — counterrevolutionary."[65] In a 1969 editorial, "Goodbye to All That" (published in *Rat*, the leading New York City underground newspaper), Robin Morgan proclaimed:

> We have met the enemy and he is our friend ... the friends, brothers, and lovers in the counterfeit male-dominated Left.... We are rising with a fury older and potentially greater than any force in history, and this time we will be free or no one will survive. Power to all the people or to none. All the way down this time.[66]

In this context, the Woman in Black can certainly be seen as a reactionary gesture by Jodorowsky in response to the growing resentment and rage of women within the counterculture, with the demand for gender and sexual equality presented in *El Topo* as a dangerous manifestation of penis envy and women overstepping their proscribed roles. The idealistic and lofty principles of the counterculture are represented by El Topo and the Four Masters: all men. Mara, the "power-hungry woman," and the Woman in Black, the sinister woman with inherent phallic power and a revolutionary *machismo* of her own (feminism incarnate), not only become the eventual betrayers of El Topo, but the counterculture era as a whole.

Each epic contest between El Topo and the Four Masters alternates with crucial sequences depicting the shifting power dynamics between El Topo, Mara, and the Woman in Black. The First Master simply refuses to acknowledge the Woman in Black, who also wants to duel him, but he immediately grants El Topo an audience. "The Master will see you immediately," the First Master's servant announces, adding, "How strange! He's never received anyone without making him wait ... your woman should wait here." Both the Woman in Black and Mara are excluded from any direct contact with the First Master, while El Topo is granted instant access, suggesting that in his more enlightened state the First Master understands the women are potential threats, and the great metaphysical conference must be strictly between men. When Mara seizes the First Master's pistol after El Topo's cunning victory and shoots the First Master's servant(s), there is a brief inserted close-up of the Woman in Black smiling in approval at Mara's newly-seized power. After El Topo and Mara depart, the Woman in Black, in an almost punitive gesture demonstrating her own latent phallic power, shoots the First Master's corpse with her own revolver, which otherwise remains holstered until her eventual confrontation with El Topo on the bridge.

After she joins El Topo and Mara in their quest to murder the remaining three Masters, a bond between Mara and the Woman in Black is soon established. In the Biblical context of *El Topo*, if El Topo and Mara are Adam and Eve, the Woman in Black represents the Serpent: the seducer and corruptor of Mara. The two women bathe topless in a pond (water being the site of female sexuality), and the Woman in Black bequeaths Mara her hand mirror: the first of two scenes where the Woman in Black (the Serpent) tempts Mara (Eve) with the forbidden fruit of knowledge. Mara immediately becomes fascinated with her own image in the mirror, constantly holding it up to her face and gazing at her own reflection, enacting Jacques Lacan's "mirror-stage," the moment the subject recognizes oneself and the mirror and also defines oneself as a subject. In Lacan's formulation, the mirror-stage is a type of *misrecognition*, a fragmenting of the subject; it encompasses *narcissism*, in that the subject becomes fixated on the image-ideal of the self, but also entails *alienation*, in that the subject sees oneself as the Other (seeing oneself as someone else) and within a much greater order — the Symbolic Order of other innumerable signs and images.[67] However, Mara's relationship to the mirror is entirely one of narcissism (in contrast to *Santa sangre*, where the mirror-stage only brings about alienation). Beyond the infatuation with her own image ("Vanity, thy name is woman"), the mirror bestowed by the Woman in Black allows Mara to contemplate and articulate her own growing power over El Topo.

This becomes apparent when El Topo and Mara have sex covered in the desert sand — a space antithetical to the "bitter water" of women's sexuality.[68] However, Mara is not so much a partner or even participant in their intercourse. Instead, she impassively lays motionless underneath El Topo while staring into the mirror, contemplating her own "position" in the man-woman couple and a pivotal moment in Mara's own self-recognition that El Topo does not control her, but she controls El Topo in all ways, including sexually. Not surprisingly, El Topo, whether annoyed by her narcissism or sensing the mirror signifies an increasing threat to his own status, finally reacts with phallic violence. As the trio rides through the desert to find the Second Master, he draws his pistol. There is a close-up of the mirror and Mara's reflection within its circular borders, and the mirror explodes as a gunshot reverberates on the soundtrack. With her dominated status momentarily reestablished, she hands the broken pieces of the mirror to her master — El Topo. As noted, it is these broken pieces of the mirror that El Topo uses to disable the Universal Mother and gain his advantage over the Second Master: the symbol of growing female empowerment destroyed by the male is subsequently utilized to defeat the great mother archetype.

These growing power struggles between El Topo and Mara, mediated by the Woman in Black, suggest Hegel's "master-slave" dialectic (a concept also central to *Santa sangre*): Hegel's famous example of a dialectical contradiction and its resolution when a slave realizes they can exist without the rule of the master, but the master can not exist unless there is a salve to obey.[69] As the quest to eliminate the Four Masters is realized, El Topo — the phallic Master of the first third of the film — is steadily weakened by Mara's own increased realization of her power (abetted by the Woman in Black) to the point of El Topo's subordination and even dependency on her, ultimately reversing their roles in a master-slave relationship. Yet this shift in control is depicted as distinctly evil, and the very reason this struggle in *El Topo* cannot be adequately read through Nietzsche's critique of "master-slave morality." As the power dynamic shifts between El Topo and Mara, the rise of Mara as master is equated with her becoming an oppressive monster, and El Topo's relegation to the slave is infused with victimization and eventual pious martyrdom — the very aspects of master-salve morality Nietzsche found so contemptible.[70]

Immediately after El Topo's killing of the Second Master, a title card appears on-screen: "Prophets." However, like the first title card ("Genesis"), the card is used to announce a key symbolic or allegorical moment in the film as much as dividing it into narrative acts. One of the film's more infamous moments occurs: Mara and the Woman and Black duel with whips in the desert. While Hoberman and Rosenbaum suggest the scene could be out of Russ Meyer's *Faster, Pussycat! Kill! Kill!*, the reference point could also be the notorious line from Nietzsche: "Are you going to woman? Do not forget the whip!"[71] While the battle is provoked by Mara's jealously, it becomes apparent Mara is actually the object of the Woman in Black's sexual designs. After the two battle with whips on horseback in a perverse parody of the medieval joust, Mara is knocked to the ground and quickly whipped into submission by the Woman in Black, who then lifts Mara's bloody shirt and begins to lick the wound she inflicted, culminating in a passionate kiss. While certainly catering to male lesbian fantasies, it is also a Sadean moment where domination and sexual pleasure converge through the flow of blood (recalling the perverse wedding between Alucarda and Justine in López Moctezuma's subsequent *Alucarda*). Mara and the Woman and Black are now united as the film's "prophets."

A similar scene occurs after the Third Master's murder and the three principals sit in the desert sand at dusk, physically forming a (romantic) triangle around three small cacti, also arranged in a triangle. Leaving very little to the imagination, the Woman in Black picks up one of the cacti; in a long, fetishistic close-up, she cuts a vertical gash in it with a knife and run hers finger in the slit to widen it and release its juices, and then runs her tongue in the expanded slit in the cactus. Again, the Woman in Black as the Serpent offers "forbidden fruit" of knowledge to Mara: not only the knowledge of each other's potential power (the mirror), but the opportunity to "know" each other's vaginas (or in the context of the cactus and its thorny outer casing, a potential *vagina dentata*). Intrigued yet repelled, Mara rejects the forbidden fruit, and the Woman in Black responds by roughly grabbing Mara and kissing her on the lips. On the verge of succumbing to the Woman in Black's sexual advances, and thus "accepting" the *female* sex (just as El Topo's rape of the "frigid" Mara makes her "accept the male sex"), Mara pushes her away and promptly runs into El Topo's arms. The growing threat of the Woman in Black is not only as a romantic rival for the affections of Mara against El Topo, but the growing threat of woman assuming masculine roles and power: feminism cast in the stereotype of the butch lesbian.

After El Topo kills the Fourth Master and definitively destroys his gun-phallus, the scene shifts to the trio at an expansive suspension bridge traversing an immense canyon. El Topo desperately wanders on the bridge in his crisis of faith (a psychological crisis motivated by his self-castration as well as the spiritual void resulting from killing the Four Masters). A voice-over reads Biblical verses, including the opening line of Psalm 22 and Christ's question while undergoing the Crucifixion: "God, why hast thou forsaken me?" As El Topo stands on the bridge, at one point standing on the railings and contemplating suicide, a "Fifth Master" emerges: the Woman in Black. She determinedly walks towards El Topo and tosses one of her pistols at his feet, challenging him to a duel for his newly-acquired Master status. When El Topo refuses to fight, she simply and callously shoots him, fully demonstrating her previously dormant phallic power and "fury older and potentially greater than any force in history." More allusions to the Crucifixion are overtly made: El Topo is first shot in each palm while his arms are stretched out to each side, and then in each foot; a long close-up of El Topo's bare, bloodied feet insures the audience will not miss the reference. As El Topo staggers towards the two women, the Woman in Black hands Mara the pistol and indifferently mutters, "It's either him or me." In Mara's final act of female treachery, she shoots El Topo in the left side, referencing the fatal wound of Christ on the cross, and completing El Topo's crucifixion in a hail of bullets and at the hands of women. To add insult to injury, the new couple rides away as El Topo pathetically follows them for a short distance before collapsing, the Woman in Black having now committed the ultimate exercise of phallic power: stealing another man's woman.

El Topo's crucifixion also marks the exit of Mara and the Woman in Black from *El Topo*. Initially, Jodorowsky envisioned the women being killed in an explosion after their betrayal of El Topo. Jodorowsky later explained:

> I didn't use that scene. I didn't use it because I thought ... why destroy the women? *I am not a moralist. If I destroyed the women, it would be a form of punishment.* I didn't want to say that, but the audience can think it.... They can imagine the women will eventually destroy each other, if they wish.[72]

However, as the film unfolds through the second part, Jodorowsky indeed infuses *El Topo* with a "moralist" and sexist binary: the man as good and the woman as evil. The vilification of women in *El Topo* is consistent with Laura Mulvey's argument that much of the cinematic treatment of women revolves around a two-fold process of undervaluing the woman through narrative punishment while simultaneously overvaluing the women as a sexual fetish-object.[73] This overvaluing process is epitomized in *El Topo*'s gratuitous nudity and forays into male lesbian fantasies (the bathing and especially the whipping sequences). Moreover, Mara and the Woman in Black are indeed undervalued and "punished" by the film precisely *because* of their victory; they are seductive destroyers who go unpunished for their ruthless corruption and destruction of the spiritual man. Their triumph over El

1. *The Counterculture Cinema of Cruelty*

The Holy Trinity? A none-too-subtle comparison between Christ, El Topo, and Jodorowsky used for *El Topo* lobby card illustration.

Topo does not allow them to escape final punishment, but reinforces the narrative undervaluing and punishment of women that occurs during the film, which has profound political implications. Wilhelm Reich suggested, "*Sexually awakened women, affirmed and recognized as such, would mean the complete collapse of the authoritarian ideology.*" [74] In *El Topo*, "sexually awakened women" are not "affirmed and recognized," but *vilified*: traitors against the man who is solely responsible for "stirring" woman's sexuality — through rape. The awakened sexuality of women that could confront and dismantle authoritarian ideology is depicted as unequivocally evil: a disruption, if not outright commandeering, of the phallocentric order.

Thus Spoke El Topo

The crucifixion of El Topo by Mara and the Woman in Black ends the second part of the triptych and begins the final third of the film: El Topo's spiritual rebirth, his enlightenment via "resurrection." Apparently mortally wounded, El Topo staggers across the bridge and collapses. A group of various handicapped peasants gather around him and cart his body away, a moment taken from the opening sentence of "On Redemption" from Nietzsche's *Thus Spoke Zarathustra*: "When Zarathustra crossed over the great bridge one day, all the beggars and cripples surrounded him."[75] As Jodorowsky confirmed

> I took it from Nietzsche's bridge. I'm very familiar with Nietzsche because I've just directed a play called *Zarathustra* which is adapted from his work. And the symbolism of the bridge is the symbolism of the passage of the man and that beyond him.... It's the moment when El Topo passes from one stage to another. *And I think that's where he reaches the first stage of enlightenment*: when he crosses the bridge.[76]

As El Topo is dragged away by the "beggars and cripples," accompanied by more voice-over Biblical quotes and loud choir music, another title card appears onscreen to inscribe the next section of the film: "Psalms." The title cards inserted midway through scenes or sections of *El Topo* emphasize the symbolic importance of what will follow: "Genesis" the castration of the Colonel and the formation of the couple, El Topo and Mara; "Prophets" the bonding of Mara and the Woman in Black through a ritual of blood, sex, and violence. The "Psalms" title card also corresponds to a distinct narrative as well as thematic shift for the final third, or triptych, of the film: El Topo's resurrection. The title card cuts to a startling close-up of El Topo surrounded by darkness: his long hair sticks straight out, akin to a fright wig, now dyed copper along with his beard. He sits in a catatonic trance in the bowels of a cave — a locale figuring prominently in the Fourth Part of *Thus Spoke Zarathustra* as the site of Zarathustra's own transformation to higher man. Tended to by the Small Woman, so named because of her dwarfism, her attention to El Topo is akin to the maintenance of a religious totem or statue as she gently refines his facial make-up. However, while make-up is frequently connected with vanity, femininity and therefore evil in *El Topo* (the Colonel's rouged cheeks and toupee, the Woman in Black's mascara), the Small Woman is nonetheless irresistibly drawn to El Topo, or his masculine essence, under the ornate appearance. Tentatively, she kisses him on the lips, and in a parody of the classic fairy-tale convention (*Snow White*), El Topo awakens from his slumber, much to the Small Woman's shock and fascination. As she genuflects before him, he responds, "I am not a god; I am a man." Yet in the first third of the film, El Topo was God ("I am God"); while the second part of the film depicted the death of Man-God (his crucifixion on the bridge). With El Topo's proclamation that he is not a god, but a man, the final third of *El Topo* attempts to fulfill Nietzsche's credo of "the death of God and birth of Man" while framing the birth of Man, or rebirth of man, in terms of the Resurrection. Here Jodorowsky attempts a dialectical *tour de force* through an unlikely synthesis of Christianity and its avowed archenemy, Nietzsche — the piety of Christ merged with the "overcoming" of the *Übermensch*—and the remainder of *El Topo* chronicles the efforts of the title character, the Christ-*Übermensch*, to bring peace and enlightenment to a violent and unenlightened world. As will be addressed shortly, this becomes a highly problematic element of the film.

El Topo learns he has been a state of hibernation for many years, and the denizens of the cave are the exiled outcasts of "the Great Town."[77] Trapped in the caverns due to their physical disabilities, which the Small Woman explains are the deforming effects of generations of incest, they have become "freaks," to use the word in a non-pejorative sense — for two reasons. One is that "the freak" is a common figure in Jodorowsky's films, and always attains a position of privilege: a person who is outside the normalcy of society by virtue of physical differences designated as "deformity," and thus a figure who can be victim, critic, and opponent of bourgeois society (not coincidentally, Jodorowsky cited Tod Browning's classic 1932 horror film *Freaks* as a major influence on his own work).[78] Second, "freak" was a common counterculture self-appellation, and the freaks in the cave become metaphors for the freaks of the counterculture.[79] Prophecy foretold of a man who would one day liberate the cave dwellers, and El Topo undergoes his transformation into savior: beginning with a version of the peyote ritual by his eating a giant beetle and madly hallucinating, and culminating with the Small Woman shaving his head and beard (accompanied by the almost unintentionally humorous choral and organ religious music first heard at the bridge). Another allusion to Samson, the voluntary removal of El Topo's locks becomes a symbolic gesture of his renunciation of phallic power, domination, self-interest, the ego itself. As Jodorowsky noted, "He loses everything. He loses his sexual life. He loses his material possessions, his revolver. He loses his personality."[80] In effect, El Topo transforms into a Buddhist monk, which is explicitly manifest in the film's conclusion. This aspect of El Topo's transformation is also quite compatible with Nietzsche, who spoke in favor of Buddhism versus Christianity in *The Antichrist*: "[Buddhism] no longer says 'struggle again *sin*,' but ... 'struggle against *suffering*.' Buddhism is profoundly distinguished from Christianity by the fact that the self-deception of the moral concepts lie far behind it ... it stands *beyond* good and evil."[81] Now enlightened, El Topo announces his plans to fulfill the prophecy and build a tunnel connecting the cave's inhabitants with the Great Town, creating a unity of the two worlds. No longer the avenging God punishing (Establishment) *sins*, El Topo now becomes the selfless man dedicated to ending (counterculture) *suffering*.

However, El Topo and the Small Woman's arrival in the Great Town coincides with a return to the viciously surreal depiction of the West that defined the first third of the film. The Great Town is an appalling, brutal, and depraved place, as if Pasolini had set *Salò* in the American West rather than Fascist Italy. As Hoberman and Rosenbaum suggested, "Clearly this frontier Sodom is meant to suggest the United States of America."[82] The Great Town is decorated with innumerable hand painted signs of the "Eye in the Pyramid," the Masonic symbol on the back of the U.S. dollar (with the symbol's companion on the dollar, the Eagle, figuring prominently in *Santa sangre*). Prostitutes are brought into town in wooden crates; African-American men are branded like livestock in rodeos and sold into (sexual) slavery to ostentatious old women. Mexicans peasants are chased through the streets like cattle and, in another scene referencing the recent events at Tlatelolco, forced to lie in the road to be executed by the town's sadistic sheriff— to the polite applause of the citizens. The Sheriff (José Antonio Alacraz) and the Deputy (Felipe Díaz Garza) are parodies of an American icon, the Western cowboy. Moreover, the Sheriff and Deputy are coded around the equation of authoritarianism and homosexuality, an effect certainly intended by Jodorowsky in describing the characters: "The Sheriff, dressed in green satin, is a totally effeminate queer. His Deputy is a quiet, obese homosexual. He is dressed in sheepskin. His beard is bleached yellow."[83] In the scene at the church, the lawmen are seen sitting in the pews dressed in women's clothing. In a later scene at the jail, which is decorated like a brothel, the Sheriff lines up male prisoners against the jail cell, inspects their asses, and chooses which one will be raped.[84]

In order to earn money and acquire the necessary materials to construct the tunnel, El Topo and the Small Woman become street performers for the amusement of the citizens of the Great Town (sequences which allow Jodorowsky to showcase his considerable skill in mime and the art of clownery). However, the townspeople soon grow bored with street theater, and demand a more titillating form of entertainment: El Topo and the Small Woman are paid to have sex at the local whorehouse for the voyeuristic and derisive pleasure of the Great Town's finest citizens. While this act of prostitution provides money to purchase dynamite and hurry the completion of the tunnel, the Small Woman is humiliated by the fact that her love for El Topo was consummated in such a setting — not because the act degraded her, but that El Topo is now "ashamed" of her. To assuage her concerns, El Topo asks her to marry him. While the relationship between El Topo and the Small Woman is undeniably poignant, it also becomes problematic from a political standpoint. El Topo's enlightenment is essentially the path of the epic hero *"from digression to salvation.... * Like the heroes of all true novels later on, Odysseus *loses himself to find himself.*"[85] As Kael previously suggested, El Topo's digression into a spiritual abyss of destruction and domination is motivated through the machinations of a "power-hungry woman," and his salvation stems from the devotion of "a good woman." Given *El Topo*'s emphasis on equating homosexuality with authoritarianism, and especially the relationship between Mara and the Woman in Black that usurps male domination, El Topo and the Small Woman's love reflects a synthesis of the Jungian *anima* and *aminas,* the unification of masculine and feminine essence that define the metaphysical universe; Jodorowsky suggested when they leave the cave the two "could be brother or sister, father and daughter."[86] Yet, ultimately, they become "husband and wife" (or, in the outmoded phrase, "man and wife"). El Topo and the Small Woman's relationship is not only cast within bourgeois conventions of the romantic heterosexual couple as the natural order, but the clichés that "behind every good man is a good woman" and that a woman's sexuality is affirmed only if the man "still respects her" after the act.

In addition to El Topo and the Small Woman, another stranger arrives in the Great Town: a tall, bearded Franciscan monk (Robert John). He promptly becomes involved in a local church service, but the source of parody is not the Catholic mass but evangelical, fundamentalist Christianity, specifically displays of faith such as snake-handling and faith-healing. The minister, wearing a frock adorned with the Eye in the Pyramid logo, passes a revolver around to the faithful, who play Russian roulette to demonstrate their faith. When the gun is passed to the monk, the minister informs him, "Don't worry ... it's a blank." The monk unloads the gun, takes a real bullet from a parishioner's gun belt, reloads, and pulls the trigger while pressing the barrel to his temple. The click of the gun sends the congregation into a greater fervor, delighted a miracle has indeed occurred — until a young boy gleefully takes possession of the pistol. A loud gunshot is matched by a jump-cut of the boy lying dead, his head bathed in blood, followed by the final title card with its none-too-subtle announcement of the final act — or book — of *El Topo*: "Apocalypse," the impending destruction of the world inadvertently initiated by El Topo.

In the first scene after the "Apocalypse" title card and the immediate aftermath of the boy's death, the minister abandons the church to the monk: "The circus is over — they'll never return" (the circus again prefigures *Santa sangre*, where the *Circo del gringo* performing in Mexico City is an overt metaphor of the United States of America's cultural and political domination of Mexico). A far more righteous man than the minister-huckster, he immediately tears down the Eye in the

Pyramid signs, leaving only a large drawing of a cross, signifying that the church is indeed a holy space again: the one space in the Great Town that is no longer desecrated by the sign of the Eye in the Pyramid. Thus, when El Topo and the Small Woman decide to marry, they arrive at the now-sanctified church under the guidance of the monk. This moment also begins the reconstruction (or resurrection) of the holy family — as awkward as that moment initially becomes. When El Topo and the monk meet, there is an instant recognition that he is the son El Topo abandoned earlier in the film. El Topo's son immediately reacts with violence, with El Topo spared from being killed only by the impassioned pleas of the Small Woman.

El Topo's son agrees to allow El Topo to finish the tunnel before killing him, and adopts the black leather gunfighter attire his father wore in the film prior to his enlightenment, patiently watching El Topo work until he can murder him. An accord is soon struck, and El Topo convinces his son to help them complete the tunnel, which will hasten the process of freeing the exiles in the cave — and El Topo's own execution. Yet when the tunnel is completed, and El Topo accepts his inevitable fate, El Topo's son cannot bring himself to kill his father: "How can I kill my Master?" he asks El Topo. Jodorowsky noted that this scene was taken from a story in *Zen Flesh, Zen Bones*, but "*I changed it completely*. The only thing that remains is: 'I can't kill my master.' Then the master kills himself."[87] Given Jodorowsky's conscious alteration of the source, the status of "the master" becomes highly ambivalent in *El Topo*. Jodorowsky noted, "The Masters need to be killed; they ask to be killed. A true Master always asks for death. Because if no one kills him, he'd live forever. So he needs to leave this world. And for a Master to step down, someone has to push him, so that someone can take his place."[88] The significance of the Fourth Master is that, realizing El Topo cannot kill him, he must kill himself. In contrast, while El Topo is willing to die, he does not choose to relinquish his status when his son, a potential new Master, cannot "push him" by pulling the trigger. Instead, El Topo kills himself in response to the devastation resulting from his effort to unite the Great Town and the freaks, leaving his son to assume his role by default. For all the drive to overcome the Masters, an essential master-slave relationship remains unchanged and even endorsed in *El Topo*: the mastery of the Father over the Son.

With the tunnel complete, the cave-dwellers begin their mass migration, while well-dressed Great Town citizens flood the streets, armed with rifles. As the cave-dwellers enter the town, their arrival is depicted in a montage of shots echoing the harrowing climax of Browning's *Freaks* when the freaks exact their revenge on the vain circus performer who wronged one of their own. However, Jodorowsky's "freaks" do not seek retribution, but acceptance into the community. Instead, they are summarily gunned down in a lengthy montage: the counterculture version of the "Odessa Steps" sequence in Eisenstein's *Potemkin* (1925). Certainly, the slaughter in the streets is the film's most graphic commentary on Tlatelolco; for the Amer-

1. The Counterculture Cinema of Cruelty

Apocalypse: El Topo amid the aftermath of the massacre of the freaks at the conclusion of *El Topo.*

ican counterculture audience, it also had a specific reference point in the killing of four anti-war protestors at Kent State University on May 4, 1970. The montage of the massacre is crosscut with El Topo, clad in his Buddhist attire, rushing toward the scene, and the Small Woman lying near the tunnel in the throes of labor, giving birth to another son fathered by El Topo. The massacre of the freaks and the birth of El Topo's second son becomes a moment of Jungian synchronicity.

As El Topo surveys the aftermath carnage, he is overcome with rage. He is shot numerous times, but refuses to die as he advances on the Great Town citizens (while intended to suggest the First Master, who allows bullets to pass through his body, the effect is more akin to Superman comics). Seizing a rifle, El Topo begins to fire indiscriminately at the townspeople, leaving no one spared. Immediately afterwards, distresses by the horror of the massacre, his own regression into violence and destruction, and the disastrous results of his mission to unite the Great Town and the freaks, El Topo's final act is to destroy himself, now acutely aware the world is unwilling or unable to accept the reborn and vastly improved El Topo:

that enlightenment is possible, but not in the world as it presently exists. Calmly sitting in the middle of the street littered with bodies, El Topo sets himself on fire, and the shot of his self-incineration is specifically based on a famous photograph of the era: a Buddhist monk who burned himself to death in protest of the war in Vietnam. The evolution of El Topo is complete: from the archetype of the Western cowboy (a caricature frequently used in anti–American, anti-war marches in other countries) to a famous image of pacifist protest "burned" into public memory in the 1960s.

Besides its topicality, the self-incineration suggests a mythological reference: the Phoenix reborn in a funeral pyre (and yet another symbol central to *Santa sangre*). Indeed, El Topo is reborn, in that his first-born son becomes the El Topo seen in the beginning of the film — the black-clad gunslinger who assumes the Father-Master position and his role in the world. In a parody of the classic Western ending and the triumph of social order in the frontier, the new holy family as Holy Trinity leaves the decimated Great Town and rides off into the distance: the new El Topo (God), the newborn son (Christ), and the Small Woman (Holy Spirit). Yet *El Topo* does not end; it completes the cycle of historical transformation that will begin when the film is viewed again (its next ritual midnight screening). This new El Topo will one day bring his brother-stepson into the desert to bury the remnants of his childhood; become the castrating God of justice; forsake his stepson-brother by falling prey to another Mara; murder a new set of Masters; be crucified and resurrected; achieve enlightenment only to tragically realize the world will not accept an enlightened man; inadvertently initiate an apocalyptic slaughter; abdicate the role of El Topo to the brother-stepson he once abandoned, and father a *new* son who will one day begin his own transformation into the *next* El Topo under the tutelage of *his* stepfather-brother: a historical cycle ritually acted *ad infinitum* in the surreal battlefields of the West. Rather than any utopian conclusion, *El Topo* suggests a profound pessimism: Christ's second coming as the Nietzschean eternal return may entail El Topo achieving personal enlightenment, but the world will forever remain unenlightened.

Homer, Nietzsche, Jodorowsky: The Dialectic of El Topo

In *El Topo*, the Homeric epic and Nietzschean philosophy — among numerous other sources — become intertwined, and the questions of enlightenment, morality, the epic, and myth ultimately raise issues of how *El Topo* is unable to escape the bourgeois and even authoritarian ideology it intends to oppose. While frequently interpreted as proto-fascism, Horkheimer and Adorno contend, "It was Nietzsche who expressed [Enlightenment's] *antipathy to domination*."[89] They suggest that Nietzsche recognized the potential for enlightenment to expose the myths and deceit of the Church and the State, "So that the priests become priests with a bad conscience ... to make princes and statesmen unmistakably aware that everything they do is sheer falsehood," as well as realizing enlightenment's vast potential to deceive the masses in the hands of the "great manipulators of government."[90]

As noted, the Nietzschean overtones of *El Topo* are highly problematic. Returning to the issue of gender politics, the construction of El Topo and Mara as the counterculture Adam and Eve is best expressed by Nietzsche:

> Has the famous story that stands at the beginning of the Bible really been understood? The story of God's hellish fear of *science*?... Only from woman did man learn to taste the test of knowledge.... Man himself turned out to be his greatest mistake, he had created a rival for himself, science made godlike ... science is the first sin, the seed of all sin, the original sin. *This alone is morality.* [91]

To this extent, Mara achieves a further sense of denigration in the film — Man as spirituality (good) versus woman as science (evil): El Topo, the saintly man, seeking enlightenment versus the corrupting influence of Mara, the woman who introduces him to cunning. Her seductive power over man is not merely manifest in sex, but *science*—a fundamental misreading of Nietzsche by Jodorowsky where the Eve-woman-science equation is interpreted as a condemnation of the moral "evil" of science and knowledge in the form of the woman.[92]

Nietzsche sought to employ enlightenment and the figure of the *Übermensch* to destroy the mythic elements contained in modern enlightenment: its hypocrisy, its self-confidence, its insidious ability to enslave as much as liberate. *El Topo* seeks to destroy the myths of modern enlightenment by abandoning modern enlightenment altogether, replacing it with new myths of spiritual and personal enlightenment entrenched in the "postmodern consciousness" of the counterculture's eclectic fusion of politics, cultures, philosophies, religions, and mythologies. As Jodorowsky remarked, *El Topo* was conceived as a kind of psychedelic version of *The Odyssey*, and the quest for enlightenment in *El Topo* is a journey of self-discovery and redemption from cunning gunslinger to selfless monk. As Horkheimer and Adorno contend, the enlightenment of Homer's Odysseus became the precursor for the enlightenment of modernity and the bourgeois individual: "All bourgeois enlightenment is the requirement of sobriety and common sense — a proficient estimate of the ratio of forces."[93] However, it is precisely this bourgeois enlightenment that El Topo, the counterculture Odysseus, repudiates. In the epic struggle as a quest for individual domination through shrewd cunning, even if El Topo wins, he loses. El Topo's enlightenment is much more comparable to sentiments expressed in Theodore Roszak's *The Making of the Counterculture*. Roszak urged a rejection of "'the myth of objective consciousness' (science, reason) in favor of 'the beauty of the fully illuminated personality [as] our standard of truth ... not simply to muster power against the misdeeds of society, *but to transform the very sense men have of reality.*'"[94] Similarly, Jodorowsky envisioned *El Topo* as a film that would change the world — not through political polemics, but it own brand of Artaud-inspired enlightenment: the crucifixion and resurrection of the viewers' consciousness.[95]

The only moment in the film El Topo — "the Mole" — achieves true enlightenment is in the solitude and darkness of the cave where El Topo is shielded from the "light of reason." The narrator explains during the opening credits montage, "The mole is an animal that digs tunnels underground searching for the sun. Sometimes his journeys lead him to the surface. *When he looks at the sun he is blinded*" (emphasis added). In this regard, *El Topo*'s opening recalls the definition of unreason offered by Michel Foucault in *Madness and Civilization*:

> [We] must not understand it [unreason] as reason diseased, or reason lost and alienated, but quite simply *reason dazzled* ... the madman sees the daylight, the same daylight as the man of reason ... but seeing this same daylight, and nothing but this daylight and nothing in it, he sees it as a void, as night, as nothing.... Descartes closes his eyes and plugs his ears the better to see the true brightness in essential daylight; thus he is secured against the dazzlement of the madman who, opening his eyes, sees only night, and not seeing at all, believes he sees what he imagines.... Unreason is in the same relation to reason as dazzlement is to the brightness of the daylight itself.[96]

Foucault's argument is a rejection of the modern conception of reason and unreason as exclusive binaries of light and darkness (central to Juan López Moctezuma's work as well, specifically *La mansión de la locura*, the focus of the next chapter). Madness is the state of dazzlement, being overwhelmed by the light of reason. *El Topo* takes place in a *dazzled world* — the deserts and frontier towns saturated by the glare of the sunlight as well as the rivers of blood (also, the symbolic importance of the umbrella in the film's opening shot as a shield against the sunlight and dazzlement). This effect was specifically intended by Jodorowsky: "I took a position on color. Everything I looked for — all the costumes, all the location — I looked for a lack of color: black, brown, beige. And the only strong colors you see are the *blue of the sky*, different greens of the plants, and *the red of the blood*."[97] The West, both in the sense of the Western genre and Western civilization, becomes an unreal but unreasonable world not only awash in blood but perpetual daylight. While Dalí famously proclaimed, "The only difference between myself and a madman is that I am not mad," Jodorowsky stated, "Yes, I am absolutely mad like all the civilization on this planet.... *I think all of humanity now is completely crazy*."[98] In *El Topo*, the light of reason can only result in bourgeois enlightenment and/or dazzlement, and the only escape is from the sun altogether and into the dark recesses and solitude of the caves (and eventually death). As alluded to, it is the First Master who is ultimately the most enlightened; when El Topo is brought into his darkened monastery, the First Master explains that he needs no light because he is *blind*—the light of reason now unnecessary in his higher state of enlightenment, and also immune to the effects of dazzlement."[99] Reason *itself* becomes the avowed enemy of enlightenment, best expressed by Jodorowsky's own aphorism, "Logic is stupidity."[100] Yet the abandonment of reason in favor a conflation of politics, mythology, and mysticism ignores how myth and mysticism were vital in constructing the ideologies of Fascism and Nazism. Rather, as Herbert Marcuse wrote, "Reason ... was instrumental in creating the world we live in. It was also instrumental in sustaining injustice, toil, and suffering. *But Reason, and Reason alone, contains its own corrective.*"[101]

A second issue concerns the status of El Topo as the epic hero. *El Topo*'s New York City premiere in December, 1970, coincided with an American counterculture growing increasingly disillusioned, fragmented, and, above all, angry. The Summer of Love in 1967 gave way to "Convention Summer" and the police riots at the 1968 Democratic National Convention, which, in turn, gave way to the Days of Rage on October 8–11, 1969, a three-day exercise in street fighting and vandalism in Chicago. Moreover, in late 1969, Charles Manson (who bears an uncanny resemblance to the pre-shorn El Topo) emerged as the dubious poster-boy of the counterculture with his arrest for the Tate–LaBianca murders, prompting a polarizing debate in the Underground whether to deify or vilify Manson.[102] His trial, which itself became a kind of Theater of the Absurd, was well underway when *El Topo* premiered. As Hoberman and Rosenbaum observed:

> Jodorowsky's film served to comfort its original audience by investing hippie violence with a religious aura. If the film's devotees identified with the "holy killer" in the first and second sections of the movie, by the third he presented himself as their savior, the champion, quite literally, of the freaks.... Jodorowsky played El Topo as perhaps the most potent counterculture hero ever to appear on the screen.[103]

Hoberman and Rosenbaum were acutely aware of the film's more pessimistic moments, specifically their adroit reading of El Topo leading his flock of "freaks" to slaughter rather than victory as a metaphor of the impending demise of the counterculture: the brutal antithesis of the utopian hippie order envisioned in "the counterculture's *Triumph of the Will*, the three-hour *Woodstock*."[104] Nevertheless, their descriptions of El Topo as a "potent counterculture hero," both "savior" and "champion," suggests the possibilities of how El Topo could easily be (well)endowed with both messianic charisma and epic heroism. In part, this can be attributed to El Topo being an all-purpose fusion of classical, religious, philosophical, and contemporary pop culture heroic icons, particularly Jodorowsky's unlikely (and untenable) synthesis of Christianity and Nietzsche as an attempt to cast El Topo as a destroyer of the corrupt morals of the old order (*Übermensch*) and the new messiah (Christ) who can lead his flock to creating a morally superior "new order"—a quest ultimately not only unsuccessful but disastrous.

The Mexican Cinema of Darkness

However, the effect of *El Topo* was precisely the opposite for the film's counterculture legion, as epitomized in Glenn O'Brien's ecstatic review of *El Topo* in the *Village Voice* (March 1971):

> El Topo is a killer, but he is a holy man. Like Zarathustra, he wants to overcome all men. He is a seeker who seeks to overcome all masters. And blood is the sacrament of truth by which El Topo soars/falls towards enlightenment.... Jodorowsky is here to confess, the young audience here for communion.[105]

For Jodorowsky, and despite his own admitted awareness of the sheer power of shock value, the obsession with sex and violence in *El Topo* is not simply gratuitous; they are inseparable forces of transgression and transformation. Jodorowsky stated, "I don't love violence in the way that you see in American pictures. When a child is born, it is violent. When a flower opens up, it is violent. Even when you die, it is violent. Life is very strong."[106] El Topo's violence as a messianic mixture of Christ, Zarathustra, Buddha, and Weatherman righteously offing the pigs is presented far more ambivalently and far less romantically than O'Brien would have it, especially given that much of El Topo's "overcoming masters" is a metaphor for the destruction of the counterculture. At worst, it becomes steeped in the same specious morality Nietzsche repudiates, and reflects the same corrupted interpretations of Nietzsche's "master morality" used as a blueprint for the Third Reich: the perversion of Nietzsche's "*antipathy* to domination" into a *thirst* for domination piously recast as a romanticized, counterculture "holy war [where] blood is the sacrament of truth." To inscribe sanctimonious nobility in El Topo as a "killer-holy man" is as ignoble as the Crusades or the Inquisition's merger of religious mystification and brutal domination, and Kael is quite correct in suggesting *El Topo*'s apparent "fundamental amorality" was not even "honest amorality."[107] As far as "amoral Westerns" go, Leone and Peckinpah ultimately serve as far better examples.

Ultimately, the issue of the implicit authoritarian ideology in *El Topo* lies with the influence of Homer and not with Nietzsche, who actually recognized the "bourgeois Enlightenment element in Homer."[108] Horkheimer and Adorno contend that Homer constructs the formative relationship between epic, myth, and bourgeois ideology:

> There is no work which offers a more eloquent testimony to the mutual implications of enlightenment and myth than that of Homer ... epic and myth, form and content, do not so much emerge from and contrast with, as expound and elucidate, one another.... The adventures of Odysseus are all dangerous temptations removing the self from its logical course. He gives way to allurement as a new experience, trying it out as a novice still impervious to good advice ... or as an actor continually rehearsing his parts.... [Yet] the knowledge which comprises his identity and which enables him to survive, draws its content from experience ... *from digression to salvation; and the know-*

ing survivor is also the man who takes the greatest risks when death threatens, thus becoming strong and unyielding when life continues.[109]

Thus, the appearance of the "rugged individual" who triumphs over adversity through a series of contests testing him physically and mentally to become a stronger and wiser person can be traced back to Odysseus himself, and this is the aspect which resonates with El Topo's journey as much as the overt allusions to Nietzsche's Zarathustra seeking to overcome the bourgeois order. Indeed, the reliance on the epic form and the construction of myth in *El Topo* inadvertently reiterates what Horkheimer and Adorno suggest is the fundamental ideological problem of the epic and myth: "What epic and myth actually have in common [is] *exploitation and domination*."[110] In fairness to Jodorowsky and the many problems of *El Topo*, it is clear that his intention is to repudiate "exploitation and domination." Yet by its very aspirations to become an epic and create a myth, *El Topo* is inherently tied to authoritarian ideology, despite its 1960s revolutionary aspirations. The film's emphasis on the hero's epic journey of suffering and triumph that culminates in the formation of the stronger and smarter individual can easily be construed into the gross misreading of *El Topo* supplied by O'Brien, where El Topo's desire to "overcome all men" and punish the sins of the Establishment, infused with the currency of revolutionary *machismo* and a pastiche of mysticism, is tantamount to using El Topo as an iconic "bridge" between hippie radical and the new Master Race.

For Horkheimer and Adorno, a crucial issue of modernity is the dialectic of enlightenment, as expressed by Richard Leppert: "The ironic regression of enlightenment, reason's alleged goal, into myth, whose deadly consequences at the level of the subject and society were so dramatically enacted in the Aryan myths of the Third Reich."[111] This is certainly not to say that Jodorowsky is a closeted Fascist (so to speak).[112] Rather, as *El Topo* consciously strives to become a modern myth and El Topo the epic hero for the chaos of the late 1960s, the film embodies the very process by which "enlightenment becomes myth." *El Topo*'s repudiation of modern enlightenment does not seek to offer a warning, or provide a study of the regression of reason and its catastrophic impact. With *El Topo*, Jodorowsky constructed the counterculture epic: a postmodern mythology as a comprehensive answer to alleviate the crisis of modernity — or a reactionary myth for a rapidly declining counterculture.

2

Madness and Modernity:
La mansión de la locura
(*The Mansion of Madness*, 1971)

The Mexican tradition for [horror] films is very simplistic and very conformist, in my opinion, despite their surface delirium. I don't really like them very much.... I think my films much more belong in the surrealist tradition than in the Mexican one.[1]
— Juan López Moctezuma, 1977

The Art of Horror

During the turbulent 1960s, Juan López Moctezuma became an influential figure in Mexican popular culture. He created a long-running jazz program for Mexican radio ("Panorama de Jazz"), and also worked extensively in television production; director Guillermo del Toro (*Cronos*, *Blade II*, *Hellboy*) fondly recounted that a favorite television program from his youth was a late-night movie showcase for silent horror films (*The Golem*, *Nosferatu*) produced and hosted by López Moctezuma.[2] However, other than a few minor acting roles, López Moctezuma was unable to break into the highly-restrictive Mexican film industry, and subsequently turned his creative attention to avant-garde theater. Through this work, he became a friend and colleague of Alejandro Jodorowsky, and López Moctezuma assisted in the production of both *Fando y Lis* and *El Topo*. Yet in their discussion of Jodorowsky in *Midnight Movies*, J. Hoberman and Jonathan Rosenbaum make only passing reference to López Moctezuma as "another Mexico City avant-gardist ... and future director of *cheap horror films*."[3] What appears implied in Hoberman and Rosenbaum's comment is the status of "avant-gardist" and "director of cheap horror films" is mutually exclusive. While Jodorowsky, to varying degrees of validity, was accused of masking exploitation films in avant-garde flourishes and delusions of grandeur, López Moctezuma obliterated the boundary between avant-garde and cheap horror films with *La mansión de la locura* (*The*

Mansion of Madness, 1971) and *Alucarda, la hija de las tinieblas* (*Alucarda, Daughter of Darkness*, 1975).[4]

A key aspect of López Moctezuma's work was his appreciation, knowledge, and adaptation of divergent strains of cinema: he freely admitted numerous shots in *La mansión de la locura* were citations from the "directors from the Golden Age of American horror cinema, Buñuel, and, of course, the silent filmmakers."[5] In discussing *La mansión de la locura* and *Alucarda*, comparisons can be made to contemporary European sources: on one hand, the avant-garde films of Buñuel, Fellini, and Pasolini; on the other, Hammer horror films and the Eurotrash exploitation-horror cinema of Mario Bava, Jean Rollin, and Jess Franco. The influence of the drive-in era of Roger Corman and American International Pictures can be seen in tandem with silent German horror and the Universal horror classics. Indeed, *La mansión de la locura* suggests an unlikely and unholy combination of Roger Corman and Luis Buñuel, *Alucarda* a "nunsploitation" film directed by Pasolini. Yet despite his eclecticism, López Moctezuma explicitly distanced himself from the tradition of Mexican horror cinema; as Guillermo del Toro noted, López Moctezuma demonstrated "horror could be done in Mexico in a different way than just masked wrestlers with tongue in the cheek."[6] Yet, ultimately, López Moctezuma's horror films share many of the same ideological concerns of the mexploitation era—above all, the status of modernity.

Poe-tic Horror

Due to the unprecedented success of *El Topo* and his close ties with Jodorowsky, López Moctezuma was afforded the opportunity to direct his own film, utilizing many of the people involved in making *El Topo*. The result was *La mansión de la locura*—henceforth referred to as *Mansion of Madness*—an adaptation of the Edgar Allan Poe short story "The System of Doctor Tarr and Professor Fether." Critically praised throughout Europe at the time of its release, in the United States it was marketed as a "cheap horror film" and released under the more sensationalistic title *Edgar Allan Poe—Dr. Tarr's Torture Dungeon*. In fact, the original U.S. title seems to be a deliberate attempt by its American distributors to pass the film off as one of Roger Corman's many Poe productions which flooded American drive-ins in the 1960s and 1970s. *Mansion of Madness* begins with a psychedelic credit sequence, with scenes of the film shown in negative and saturated with crimson and turquoise hues. Combined with the film's title change, which is much more lurid and directly referential to Poe, the opening of *Mansion of Madness* could easily be mistaken for one of Corman's Poe film—if only initially.

In this regard, the respective adaptation of Poe's literature by Corman and López Moctezuma merits some comparison. *The Masque of the Red Death* (1964) was a fairly faithful and visually striking Corman adaptation of Poe's story. With *The Raven* (1963), Corman retained the title of Poe's poem and the sporadic appearance of a raven in the film (Peter Lorre dressed in a bird costume), but otherwise made a broad comedy and horror film parody. López Moctezuma delved into the very essence of Poe: narratives juxtaposed with lengthy, descriptive passages that are simultaneously disorientating, disturbing, and darkly comical. As Walter Benjamin suggested, "Poe's manner of presentation *cannot be called realism. It shows a purposely distorting imagination at work*, one that removes the text far from what is commonly advocated as the model of social realism."[7] Indeed, Poe's stories achieve a precarious balance where the purely descriptive becomes as essential as the narrative drive, where the adjective become as important as noun and verb, where the poetic and the prose are interwoven.[8]

In "The System of Dr. Tarr and Professor Fether," an unnamed first-person narrator decides to visit a famous insane asylum, *Maison de Santé* ("House of Health"), which happens to be in the vicinity of where he is traveling. He meets the asylum director, Dr. Maillard, and the two have a long, evocative conversation about the asylum and its innovative approach to treating madness, "The Soothing System." As Maillard explains:

> We contradicted *no* fancies which entered the brains of the mad. On the contrary, we not only indulged but encouraged them; and many of our most permanent cures have been thus affected. There is no argument which so touches the feeble mind of the madman as the *reductio ad absurdum*.[9]

The narrator is surprised to learn Dr. Maillard recently and abruptly abandoned the Soothing System in favor of new methods, but further explanation is postponed in favor of a lavish dinner party. These proceedings are the bulk of Poe's short story: strange, vivid accounts by the raucous party guests discussing the inmates of the asylum; at times, these guests begin to mimic the inmates before being sternly interrupted by Maillard. After being pressed by the narrator, Maillard eventually begins his delayed explanation of the new procedures: after an inmate led a successful revolt in the asylum, the Soothing System was replaced by a new system of confinement and punishment — the system of "Tarr and Fether." Poe summarily concludes the story at this point; another inmate revolt breaks out during the party and the guests begin to act like the inmates they were previously describing. The narrator is beaten during the melee and, after regaining consciousness, learns the truth in a brief epilogue: Maillard was the inmate who led the initial takeover of the asylum, and the party guests were the liberated inmates discussing themselves in the third person. Surreal descriptions of asylum life and the mystery narrative are juxtaposed in Poe, the same elements that become central to López Moctezuma's filmic adaptation of Poe's story as *Mansion of Madness*: not a *blending*, but a *collision* of poetics and prose.[10]

The "Outsider"

Mansion of Madness begins with a languidly paced opening sequence as a horse-drawn carriage traverses a fog-shrouded forest, strongly recalling the period Hammer horror films of the era, although the horror eventually manifest in *Mansion of Madness* is not the "bosoms and blood" formula of Hammer but the horror inherent in the black comedy of Buñuel's surrealism or Jean Genet's brand of the Theater of the Absurd. Inside the carriage are three well-dressed bourgeois occupants — traveling journalist Gastón Leblanc (Arthur Hansel); his friend Julién Couvier (Martin LaSalle), owner of an estate adjacent to the asylum; and Julién's young cousin (Mónica Serna). The carriage and clothing, contrasted with the asylum's technological status–its massive foundries and burgeoning electrical capabilities — situate the film in the late 1800s. However, as will be discussed, historical references — past, present, and future to the film's setting — abound in *Mansion of Madness*.

Gastón's narration begins over these images and serves two immediate purposes. One is providing a condensed summary of the back story for the viewer. The entire plot of the film is essentially summarized in the space of the opening few minutes. Gastón is visiting France from North America in order to write a news story on Dr. Maillard's renowned asylum and his innovative methods for treating the insane (an important modification by López Moctezuma; in Poe's story, the main character's detour is a spontaneous decision when his vacation route happens by the asylum). Throughout *Mansion of Madness* much of the plot is actually conveyed by using, or even *parodying*, the classic mexploitation narrative strategy — long monologues or dialogues in which characters provide plot exposition, versus depicting said events onscreen.[11] As David Wilt observed regarding the wrestling-horror classic *Santo y Blue Demon contra Drácula y el Hombre Lobo* (*Santo and Blue Demon vs. Dracula and the Wolf Man*, 1971; dir. Miguel M. Delgado), "Events are described rather than shown."[12] With *lucha libre* films, plot exposition was frequently provided largely to organize and compress the film's narrative around the requisite wrestling matches, which might or might not have any actual bearing on the film's narrative (in the aforementioned *Santo y Blue Demon contra Drácula y el Hombre Lobo,* three divergent wrestling sequences alternate independently to the events in the horror film proper). Yet using the standard mexploitation narrative device of plot exposition intertwined with strange, dramatic, and even astringent action sequences allows López Moctezuma to structure *Mansion of Madness* very much like "The System of Doctor Tarr and Professor Fether" — a general situation is quickly established and abruptly resolved in the conclusion. Little emphasis is placed on developing a teleological, realistic story in favor of an array of comical, confusing, and disconcerting events in the asylum which are not depicted through "social realism" (the depiction of the horrors of the mental hospital in *One Flew*

Over the Cuckoo's Nest), but *surrealism*, combining comedy, horror, and melodrama (with "melodrama" specifically *not* used in its pejorative sense).[13]

Beyond providing a condensed plot premise for the film to unfold within, the opening narration is also crucial in two thematic aspects. One, the opening monologue begins with Gastón's exhalation of the pleasures experienced in nature, and that nature can *only* be appreciated in solitude and seclusion, passages which could have easily been taken from Henry David Thoreau's *Walden*. He is an "outsider" through his very status as a devotee to the joys of the outdoors, a status that is placed in jeopardy as he becomes immersed in the claustrophobic confines of the asylum. Moreover, Gastón is returning to France, the land of his birth, after being raised and educated in North America by his tutor on the family dime following the mysterious fate of his parents: his father died in an asylum after he allegedly killed Gastón's mother. His visit is both investigative and nostalgic, motivated by his "inherent craving to see my homeland" and reconnect with his European heritage, which one presumes was one of bourgeois affluence. Gastón is a character born of the Old World (Europe) and reared in the New World (North America), a figure connected to the Old World's structures of aristocracy and class privilege and yet an embodiment of the New World man who combines contemplation and adventure in his solitary exploits in nature. He represents elements of both the Old World and the New World, rather than the historical break the New World posited itself to be from the Old World as the antithesis of Europe.[14] Gastón is most cognizant of his European heritage, and even melancholy for that tradition. Trapped between the Old and New World, he is an "outsider" tied to both but belonging to neither. As the film progresses and numerous allusions are made to the great disasters of European history and culture within the walls of the asylum, Gastón's relationship to the Old World slowly evolves from one of longing to disgust. In this way, López Moctezuma constructs a cultural debate common in classic mexploitation films: dangerous forces representing Europe or coded as European (the various monsters and mad scientists referencing Greek and Roman antiquity, Spanish colonialism, Nazism).[15] The diabolical Dr. Maillard and his asylum empire signify a (mad) Old World versus the "outsider" Gastón from the (sane) New World. Ultimately, Gastón not only becomes trapped in that order, but realizes he can never escape that order from which he is descended.

When Gastón and the others arrive at the gates of the asylum, they are greeted by two guards dressed as disheveled French soldiers armed with muskets; one is dressed much like Napoleon himself (one of the classic "role models" for the modern madman). The bloodbath of the Napoleonic Wars is the first of several European historical catastrophes inscribed into the film. It becomes quickly apparent that the guards are not stationed to simply prevent escape from the asylum, but to deny any encroachment of the outside world into the asylum. When Juilén confronts them and demands entrance, the guards respond with a definitive gesture:

aiming their rifles at them. A montage alternates between close-ups of the understandably nervous Gaston and Julién, and point-of-view shots from their perspective, the guard's muskets pointed directly at them, the camera, and the film audience. The technique not only disrupts the filmic barrier between the screen image and the audience (the theatrical technique of "breaking the Fourth Wall"), but does so in a rather sardonic way, an overt signal to the film viewer that they also are not welcome into the film world of the asylum. However, the tense standoff is abruptly ended — or, more correctly, undercut — through a moment of strange and even burlesque comedy. Accompanied by a xylophone flourish much more appropriate to a cartoon than a horror film, the guard's commanding officer saunters into the shot; it is the first of several occasions comedy is incongruently inserted into *Mansion of Madness* to destabilize the ominous mood of the horror or the dramatics of the action sequences. Gaudily dressed in Napoleonic military accoutrements, and demonstrating highly fey qualities, the officer prances about to defuse the situation, exercising his authority with campy flamboyance. While succumbing to the same problem of *El Topo*'s depiction of authoritarian figures as flaming homosexuals, one might also suggest the officer is a sort of homage to, or even parody of, Corman stalwart Vincent Price's droll, tongue-in-cheek performances in Corman's Poe adaptations.

This sequence establishes a central theme of *Mansion of Madness*: the specious binary and separation of madness and sanity. In Poe's story, Dr. Maillard explains that the "rigid process of exclusion" at the *Maison de Santé* is not to control the public danger of the insane but to bar "injudicious persons who called to inspect the house."[16] In effect, the asylum exists to exclude the sane from the world of madness as much as to exile the mad from the world of the sane, an assessment of the asylum Michel Foucault made a century later in *Madness and Civilization*:

> [C]onfinement functioned ... not in the direction of the liberation of the mad, nor ... a more philanthropic or greater medical attention to the insane. On the contrary, it linked madness more firmly than ever to confinement, and this by a double tie: one which made *madness the very symbol of the confining power and its absurd and obsessive representative within the world of confinement*; the other which designated the madness as the object *par excellance* of all measures of confinement.[17]

This dual status of the modern asylum is essential to *Mansion of Madness*: a space where madness must be segregated, yet where madness must be allowed to flourish as evidence of what needs to be separated from society. In this context, *Mansion of Madness* is not only a critique of the status of madness in modernity, but of study of modernity as madness: the asylum as a mock-up of the modern world and its historical development rendered through the Theater of the Absurd — or the *reductio ad absurdum*.

It's a Mad, Mad, Mad World

The carriage is allowed into the asylum grounds, but the commander insists a guard accompany them. As he sits beside the driver Henri (Jorge Berkin), riding shotgun (or rather, "riding musket"), it constructs a surreal parody of the Western stagecoach venturing into the frontier, with the carriage ride becoming a descent to a distinctly European world of horror and madness. Even before the carriage reaches the asylum proper, the first of many disconcerting events occurs. A highly-agitated man careens into the path and blocks the way of the carriage. Dressed in a red suit and top hat, branches attached to the hat to resemble antlers, and brandishing a pitchfork made out of tree limbs, he spends several seconds jumping up and down in the road and yelling incoherently. Soon, an elderly monk also emerges from the woods, wielding a lantern and frantically chanting in Latin to banish him back into the forest. As the bewildered occupants in the carriage watch the bizarre battle, a sort of absurdist parody of Milton's *Paradise Lost*, the confrontation between the monk and the man he calls "Lucifer" is depicted primarily through point-of-view shots of the combatants, the two lurching directly toward the camera and, by extension, the film audience. Like the sequence with the guards leveling their rifles at the film viewer, the barrier between the screen and the audience is actively and comically disrupted.

With the unsettling encounters becoming too much of a strain for his fragile cousin, Julién leaves Gastón at the gates of the asylum. Unfortunately, the carriage is ambushed as the party tries to leave the asylum grounds. Julién's cousin is raped; later, she and Henri are seen as inhabitants of the asylum—Henri as a prisoner, Julién's cousin as a key participant in the film's bizarre climatic banquet. While Julién is able to escape his captors, much of his role in the middle portion of the film is to provide comic relief and an absurd running joke—or, more correctly, a hopping joke. During Gastón's tour of the asylum with Maillard, the film periodically cuts back to Julién, bound hand and foot, aimlessly hopping through the woods like a rabbit, accompanied by cartoon-inspired xylophone music—recalling Warner Brothers cartoons or Monty Python's Flying Circus as much as classic horror.

Now venturing into the asylum alone, the intrepid Gastón meets the Priest (David Silva), who wears a horned, animal skin hood and red robes adorned with a spiral: the Jungian symbol for the process of individuation, which foreshadows Gastón's own journey of self-discovery within the asylum as a "downward spiral." Resembling a cross between a Druid cleric and Catholic priest, he is a synthesis of pagan religion and Christianity (which also becomes pivotal in *Alucarda*); the Priest raises his arms and announces, "Welcome to the Owl's Castle"—Silva's only line of dialogue throughout the entire film. Gastón follows the Priest, the camera remaining stationary as a long take depicts Gastón walking into the background of the shot and into the asylum, which cuts to an extreme low-angle shot suggesting German expressionism by way of Ken Russell. Standing in the asylum lobby, Gastón gazes upward in an immense tower, the balconies resembling prison "shooting galleries" (the catwalks armed guards patrol); naked men dart back and forth, and a topless woman stares indifferently down at Gastón. From the moment he enters the asylum, Gastón is enveloped by madness simply by his diminished status in its vast, overwhelming space. Wandering into another section of the asylum resembling a Dickensian slum or the "dark, satanic mills" William Blake termed the cities of England during the Industrial Revolution, Gastón passes a building which appears to have been racked by an explosion, stares at soot covered workers peering out of windows in a brick wall, and is startled when the door of a mammoth blast furnace swings open and a curious laborer stares at him — his head emerging from *inside* the furnace. As well as the Industrial Revolution, the images suggest a *future* crisis point in modernity caught within the late–1800s time-frame of the film: World War Two encased a section of the asylum composed of bombed ruins, ghettos, and ovens fueled by human beings.

Amid the machinery stands a figure in a black suit and cape: Dr. Maillard, portrayed by Claudio Brook.[18] An actor ideally suited for López Moctezuma's nexus of cult-film horror and experimental cinema, Brook was a well-known actor in the Mexican film industry, equally proficient in mexploitation movies and avant-garde films: he portrayed the mad scientist Dr. Karol opposite Santo in *Santo en el museo de cera* (*Santo in the Wax Museum*, 1963, dir. Alfonso Corona Blake; U.S. title: *Samson in the Wax Museum*) as well as starring in the title role of Buñuel's *Simón del desierto* (*Simon of the Desert*, 1966), a baffling film even by Buñuel's standards of surrealism.[19] As alluded to, much of *Mansion of Madness*' plot is supplied courtesy of the verbose and nonsensical expository monologues of Dr. Maillard; they are delivered in a manner quite consciously and often hilariously histrionic, permeated with macabre melodrama and dark comedy. In this sense, Maillard could easily be a character from the Theater of the Absurd as much as a horror film — as if a character from a Genet play were transplanted into a Corman-Poe film. Yet while Malliard's ravings are effective absurdist comedy, his orations are comparable to the definition of madness posited by Foucault:

> Madness ... does not designate so much a specific change in the mind or body, as the existence ... under the oddity of conduct and conversation, of a *delirious discourse*.... *Language is the first and last structure of madness* ... a discourse which liberated passion from all its limits ... it is this delirium, which is of both body and soul, of both language and image, of both grammar and psychology, that all the cycles of madness conclude and begin.[20]

Indeed, it is "delirious discourse" by which Maillard's world-view is expressed: stream of consciousness *non-sequiturs* and imaginary cause-effect relationships in which Maillard can define, explain, coordinate, and manufacture a new world order within the asylum that seamlessly functions according to his whims and divine powers simply because he decrees it to be so — the world according to Dr. Maillard.

Another issue raised by Foucault in *Madness and Civilization* is the necessity of situating the very definitions of "madness" in their specific historical and cultural contexts, with the historical eras prior to modernity — Antiquity, Middle Ages, the Renaissance — having primarily conceived of the delirium and hallucinations of madness as "a sign of another world."[21] Similarly, the madman's existence was "a life more disturbed than disturbing, *an absurd agitation in society, the mobility of reason.*"[22] With the advent of modern Reason, the status of madness was shifted from "another world" to a "non-world." In short, madness evolved from *different* ways of perceiving the world to *erroneous* ways of perceiving the world. Madness became the negation of reason, its antithesis; the metaphor of the "light of reason" versus the dark, shadow world of madness — the modern binary of reason and madness so forcefully depicted in the expressionism of *The Cabinet of Dr. Caligari*. As discussed with *El Topo*, this is a fundamentally incorrect metaphor according to Foucault, who contended unreason is not *blindness* to the light of reason, but *being blinded* by the light of reason — *reason dazzled.*[23] Nonetheless, the status of madness in the modern age underwent a profound shift as well: no longer an object of fascination and sympathy, but disgust and derision. Thus, the mobility of reason was replaced with the confinement of unreason. As Foucault argued:

> A sensibility was born which had drawn a line and laid a cornerstone, and which chose — only to banish. The concrete space classical society reserved for a neutral region, a blank page where the real life of the city was suspended.... Madness was thus torn from that imaginary freedom which still allowed to flourish on the Renaissance horizon ... [where] it had floundered about in broad daylight: in *King Lear*, in *Don Quixote* ... it had been superseded and, in the fortress of confinement, bound to Reason, to the realm of morality and to their monotonous nights.[24]

It is this historicism of madness that becomes essential in *Mansion of Madness*, where the dual-function of the modern asylum to both quarantine and display madness entails a possible rupture point. Within the interiors of confinement, madness can reclaim its former status as "a neutral region, a blank page" — "*another* world" versus a "*non*-world" — provided the remainder of the world is confined *outside* the asylum walls. As the asylum becomes an enclosed and immanent space defining its own ethics, morality, politics, and, above all, *reason* entirely from within, modernity is taken to its own unreasonable conclusions.

In perhaps the most astounding sequence of the film, Dr. Maillard leads Gastón on an afternoon tour of the vast courtyard of the asylum, hard at work while it "flounders in broad daylight." Heightened by Maillard's explanatory "delirious discourses," the two make their way through Maillard's self-described "kingdom," courtesy of a carriage being pulled by inmates — an idea Maillard proudly notes he modified from the practices of English coal mines. With great pride, he points out the wonderful inventions and amazing achievements in the arts and sciences, all created within the asylum through the unbridled imagination offered by the Soothing System, and waxes enthusiastically about their potential for social, cultural, and technological progress. First, the *Deus ex machina*: "A real marvel that can generate three storms in five minutes time. It never works, but it keeps them occupied." As they roll by a young handmaiden cranking a squeaking wheel, Millard points out "'The Golden Mare' ... a compendium of all musical instruments known and unknown." The scene cuts to a long shot of guards in military uniforms on a rooftop patrolling the asylum by marching back and forth in repetitive patterns and compulsively saluting each other, akin to mechanical clock tower figures: one of several commentaries in the film on military precision and efficiency in the era of Vietnam. Maillard and Gastón enter the frame, continuing the tour on foot; the camera slowly zooms back to reveal a sloping wall lined with massive chimneys — each encasing a human being: "The people lodged in the chimneys have such human warmth, and they pour energy in such great quantities we use it in the heating system.... Latins are the most rewarding, because of the hot blood, I suppose." Again, the allusion is to the Holocaust, with Dr. Maillard's empire literally fueled by human bodies. Maillard then proudly displays the technological masterpiece of the asylum: "'Madame Gronaphobia,' better know as 'Eritgroovia.'" As men in loincloths traverse the girders and wires of a rudimentary electrical power plant and its crucifix-like poles, the Priest stands next to the contraption alternately bowing and raising his hands to the sky. Maillard provides a convoluted and priceless explanation of its magnificent powers:

> A fantastic machine which generates luminous matter; if all goes according to plan, it'll become an integral part of man's nervous system. A metallic womb uniting man to the universe.... A religion has just come out of the bowels on an electric golem.... And those people that are now worshiping the crux, and building the pyramids, feed the mother larvae of this religion. The Goddess of the future is now facing you! Will you dare question her: the Electro-Sphinx?!

The asylum becomes a preposterous parody of the utopian aspirations of modernity: the faith in progress, science, and technology; the triumph of industry and urbanity (Gastón "the outsider," who rejoices in the solitude in nature, versus Maillard's celebration of the asylum as a frenetic hub of production); the fascination with the machine, and the ultimate unification of man and machine (Futurism, with Maillard's description of the coming of the "Electro-Sphinx" rivaling the hyperbolic rhetoric in Futurist founder F. T. Marinetti's manifestos). Under Maillard's vision ("vision" used in both the sense of "foresight" and "hallucination"), the asylum represents the degeneration of enlightenment into an absurd synthesis of man, machine, magic, and myth. In this sense, the asylum explodes the contradictory concept of "utopia"; as Matei Calinescu noted: "The utopian drive involves modern man in the adventure of the future ... the only way out of 'the nightmare of history' ... but on the other hand, the future ... is suppressed by the very attainment of perfection."[25] In *Mansion of Madness*, the asylum does not escape but *encapsulates* the "nightmare of history," from antiquity to the Holocaust, and the perfect future is not realized, but ridiculously *unrealizable*. Past (ancient empires), the film's present (Industrial Revolution), the film's context (the counterculture era), historical disasters (Napoleon, World War II) and an untenable future (Maillard's "vision") are all compressed and crystallized into a mechanistic-organic utopia composed of utterly *useless* phantasmal machines and mythological technogods — with Dr. Maillard acting as designing God, crazed ruler (*King Lear*), fervent crusader (*Don Quixote*), labor supervisor (or exploiter), and, to keep the film within the horror genre tradition, mad scientist.

By way of comparison, *Mansion of Madness* and Pasolini's *Salò* construct insular, immanent spaces representing the regression of modernity. In *Salò*, modernity's drive towards rationalized, systematic domination becomes an obscene, often vile theater where reason is pursued to its unreasonable conclusion — Fascism and genocide. In *Mansion of Madness*, unreason, able to flourish within the very confines established for it by modern reason, constructs its own skewed variant of modernity: the modern world rendered through Bosch rather than Sade, which is nonetheless equally hellish as *Salò*. The utopia of Dr. Maillard is absurd and even comical to be sure, but no less nightmarish when, as Herbert Marcuse observed, "It may be justifiable, logically as well as historically, to define Reason in terms which include slavery, the Inquisition, child labor, concentration camps, gas chambers, and nuclear preparedness."[26]

Madness: The Dark Side and the Lighter Side

Proudly completing the display of technological progress attained in his kingdom, Maillard proceeds with Gastón to another section of the asylum. In a long take, Maillard explains that he has recently begun new modifications to the Soothing System based on the work of "Dr. Tarr and Professor Fether." As they pass, they ignore a group of inmates reenacting another historical pivotal moment in European history in the street: a mob of roaming peasants beating each other with clubs; nobles merrily skipping; a soldier obsessively and indifferently marching back and forth. It is the first of *Mansion of Madness*' two key references to the French Revolution, which signaled the end of the "Age of Enlightenment"; and the "end of enlightenment" is precisely the moment when Maillard leads Gastón to the dungeons where the Soothing System is implemented in much more overtly cruel and punitive methods. Away from the sunlit courtyards and pathways of the asylum ("reason dazzled"), the dungeons' dim inner recesses are the realm of modern madness consigned to the darkness and shadows.

Quoting the line from Poe's "Dr. Tarr" almost verbatim—"There is no argument which so touches the feeble mind of the madman as the *reductio ad absurdum*"—Maillard immediately adds the famous aphorism of the dean of 20th century Black Magic, Alistair Crowley: "Do as Thou wilt is the Whole of the Law." Foucault suggested that one aspect of the modern definition of madness is the seeming degeneration into a state of animal impulse, and the madman's inherent danger to society is that he is indifferent — or immune — to the constraints of civilization by viewing himself as "the Whole of the Law": "Madness would be regarded as ... an impulse from the depths *which exceeds the juridical limits of the individual, ignores the moral limits fixed for him, and tends towards an apotheosis of the self*."[27] With the Soothing System, the "impulses from the depths" constituting madness is not discouraged, but exacerbated within the asylum to exhaust it, which is not to say the Soothing System is an inherently more humane method of treating madness, especially as implemented in the dungeons. Maillard presents Gastón the case of "Mr. Chicken," a man who believes he is a chicken and therefore fed grubs and seeds, covered in feathers (literally "tarred and feathered"), and placed in a filthy coop. Another inmate, the religious fanatic "Dante," is chained to a chair with his outstretched arms secured in order to perpetually act out the Crucifixion (an image certainly reminiscent of Buñuel). Disgusted at the display, Gastón mutters, "Abandon all hope ye who enter here"–the words written in blood on the walls of the entrance to Hell in *Dante's Inferno* (again, comparable to *Salò*, which also incorporates *Dante's Inferno* and the "Circles of Hell" in Pasolini's organization of the film into a three-act play of torture—"The Circle of Obsessions," "The Circle of Shit," and "The Circle of Blood"). Indeed, if the battle between the monk and "Lucifer" outside the asylum was a parody of *Paradise Lost*, Gastón's entrance into the depths of the asylum is his own descent into the Inferno (with Dr. Maillard playing Virgil to Gastón's Dante in *Mansion of Madness*' "divine comedy"). Growing annoyed at Gastón's repeated concerns that these improved methods are as barbaric as any other method in the modern asylum, Maillard, in a brilliant absurdist *non sequitur*, petulantly exclaims: "Blame it on the less soothing part of my soothing system!" By his own admission, Maillard concedes the fundamental function of the asylum, be it through soothing or punishment (methods that are ultimately of little difference): correcting behavior deemed socially unacceptable through coercive measures, instilling the constraints of civilization and limits of the individual, and effecting the transition from pleasure principle to reality principle by any means necessary. The binary constructed in modernity is not only "madness versus reason," but also "madness versus civilization."[28]

Aware of Gastón's disdain of the newer practices within the asylum, Maillard escorts him to a chamber for a more pleasing display of madness, courtesy of his daughter Eugénie (Ellen Sherman). She does not appear in Poe's original story, but is referenced from another literary source: Eugénie is a character who under-

"Abandon all hope ye who enter here": Gastón (Arthur Hansel, on left) and "Dr. Maillard" (Claudio Brook) tour the asylum dungeons in *Mansion of Madness* (courtesy of David Wilt).

goes a wicked sexual education in one of Sade's more acerbic essays on sexuality and power, *Philosophie dans le boudoir* (*Philosophy in the Bedroom*). Announcing she will deliver a treatise against "the indecent practice of people who prefer to rest rather than to dance," the Priestess (Susana Kamini) removes Eugénie's red gown, revealing that she is clad in an ornate bikini to complement her ornamental headdress, resembling an Eastern goddess. After the Priest places her in a hypnotic state, Eugénie begins her discourse through an interpretive dance, accompanied by a hippie band on a ledge in the chamber. A bald woman in a black gown and an elaborate white hood recites increasingly garbled poetry (her voice distorted through electronic effects) while musicians play bongos, flute, and sitar: a reference to the contemporary counterculture, with the sequence as a 1960s-style happening in a 19th century asylum. It is also the scene in *Mansion of Madness* most visibly influenced by Alejandro Jodorowsky, and could have easily appeared in *The Holy Mountain*—not only in the visual presentation, wealth of cultural references, and the density of symbolism, but in reference to an implicit issue Jodorowsky addressed much more overtly in *The Holy Mountain*. In both *The Holy Mountain* and *Mansion of Madness*, the counterculture is no longer an opponent and alternative to the nightmare of history, but is increasingly absorbed into, even becoming complicit in, a progressively more unreasonable modern world. Maillard's butler is a bushy haired, obedient, stoic (read: stoned) hippie in Mod fashions; in the climactic banquet sequence, an agitated hippie with a headband and antiquated military jacket functions as the court jester to Maillard's mad king and enthusiastically parrots his every decree. During the courtyard tour of the asylum, Maillard points out that some of the heat siphoned from the people in the chimneys is "processed and crystallized into a miraculous drug that conquers laziness and aggression." The reference is not only to the methods of forced medication of mental hospital patents but to the Psychedelic Revolution. The social impact of Maillard's "miraculous drug" is not the individual and collective enlightenment of Timothy Leary's credo of psychedelic liberation, "Tune in, turn on, drop out," but the State-sanctioned use of mind-altering drugs to promote the docility and passivity of the citizens in Aldous Huxley's *Brave New World*.[29] With the denizens of the asylum tranquilized, they cavort, labor, obey, and even become fuel for the heating system in ignorant bliss.

As Eugénie begins her gyrations, Maillard notes that the dance-discourse is based on those he observed on the island of Java; a woman's voiceover recites the lines, "Inaction rots and gnaws the roots of the tree.... It binds the sailor; the sailor wins the wings." The last line is a reference to Coleridge's "Rime of the Ancient Mariner" and the dead albatross which hangs around the sailor's neck—the symbol of all that limits human happiness and progress (nostalgia, obligation, regret, or, more broadly, the nightmare of history). The Priestess hands Eugénie a large conical seashell, a fairly blatant phallic symbol, which she suggestively fondles as she dances. At one point, Eugénie's movements imply she is having an orgasm, which becomes even more perverse considering Maillard is intently watching his daughter's erotic dance as he provides more obscure, symbolic commentary: "From the height of the baobab tree fall the leaves of the yea and the nay. Eugénie will have ceased to exist and the world will stop, yet the cycle will start anew. The resurrection will take effect and the world itself will inhabit the roots of the baobab." The baobab tree is an indigenous tree to Africa, characterized by its massive trunk and small branches; it is known as the "Tree of Life" and considered sacred by several African cultures. "The leaves of the yea" is referenced from the last lines of the poem "Scent of Irises" by D.H. Lawrence: "Dark fires burn on untroubled, without clash of you upon the dead leaves saying me yea." Maillard's cryptic mention that when Eugénie dies the world will be reborn in the roots of the baobab (the Tree of Life) is matched in the next shot by Eugénie raising the seashell over her head; it appears she will conclude the performance by impaling herself with the phallic symbol at the command and for the pleasure of her father. However, Eugénie instead maneuvers towards Maillard and is about to kill *him* when Gastón intervenes. Incensed, Maillard immediately halts the performance and orders Eugénie taken away, prompting a very sarcastic remark from Gastón about the Soothing System that leaves Maillard, for once, speechless.

Gastón retires to his guest quarters following the troubling tour of the asylum, and the scene opens with an expressionistic overheard shot of Gastón in the room, composed of black backgrounds and shadows punctuated by white decor ranging from lace furniture covers to thick cobwebs. Moreover, having removed his black overcoat and cape, Gastón now wears a white shirt. Gastón's last name is "Leblanc"—"the White"—and inscribes him as the antithesis of "the Black," the darkness and blackness of madness, denoted by his and Maillard's black suits and capes. During the tour of the asylum, Gastón and Maillard are both dressed almost identically, all but indistinguishable figures in the frequent long shots, emphasizing the spiral of madness unfolding around them versus the individuation of the main characters in its midst. After witnessing and realizing the horrors of the asylum, the Soothing System, and Maillard himself, Gastón's wardrobe change from black to white establishes him as the figure of Reason within the Unreason surrounding him. This recalls the moment earlier in the film when Julién's cousin grows ill as a result of the encounter with the guards and witnessing the battle between the monk and "Lucifer." Her reaction prompts Gastón to remark: "I'm worried about her *color*" (emphasis added). The characters in the carriage are all dressed in black as they near the asylum, and the initial surfacing of reason within *Mansion of Madness* occurs when the "color" of Julién's impressionable cousin begins to change as she grows pale-turning white — in response to the bizarre, early events.[30] While one of the more visually striking aspects of *Mansion of Madness* is the use of color, ultimately the most important colors in the film are black and white. However, while they become key signifiers in the film to designate madness (black) and reason (white), they do not strictly and uniformly designate reason versus madness in the traditional light and darkness dichotomy (*The Cabinet of Dr. Caligari*), but rather chronicle the nebulous and shifting status of reason and unreason constructed within the enclosed space of the asylum. The growing conflict between Maillard and Gastón is ultimately much more ambiguous than a simple, binary clash between reason (Gastón) and insanity (Maillard), as it questions the distinction between sanity and madness in modernity — the "grey area" between Reason and Unreason.

After a hallucinatory montage of flashbacks and a topless Eugénie appearing at his window, beckoning him to the garden (presumably brought on by a dose of

2. Madness and Modernity

Black and white: Eugénie (Ellen Sherman) led through the eerie asylum grounds in *Mansion of Madness* (courtesy of David Wilt).

Maillard's "miraculous drug" surreptitiously placed in his beverage), Gastón staggers to the balcony and sees Eugénie being taken into the foggy forests between the asylum and its outer gates by the Priestess, accompanied by a monk and a soldier (respectively, Church and State). Eugénie is now dressed in a *white* gown, signifying her as a figure of reason as well (when first introduced to Gastón early in the film, she is also clad in black). Stumbling through the hallways, Gastón soon encounters Maillard — still in his black coat and cape. The modern binary of madness is now represented by the main characters, the hero Gastón (reason-light-white) and villain Maillard (madness-darkness-black); however, this distinction is also problematized by Gastón's black suspenders and Maillard's white shirt barely visible under his black outerwear, reflecting the inherent ambiguity of what ultimately constitutes reason and madness, despite the highly melodramatic battle developing between the two. Maillard dismisses Gastón's concerns over Eugénie's safety and informs him that his daughter is merely being punished for her impertinent behavior during her dance recital. Now aware of Maillard's disciplinary methods, Gastón presses the issue only to earn the wrath of Maillard. Asking Gastón if he believes in "sorcery," the Priest, who suddenly and rather mysteriously appears in the background, claps his hands; Maillard tells Gastón he now casts "three shadows" against the wall. Of course, Gastón only casts one shadow, although there is an element of truth to Maillard's contention if one grants Freud's structure of the psyche: Gastón casts one visible shadow — his ego — and two invisible shadows — his id and superego. Two guards enter the shot to seize Gastón by each arm, and Millard hilariously proves himself vindicated, using his absurdist logic: "Can you see them now? Three — precisely three! HA HA!"

Gastón is roughly escorted back to his chambers and locked in his room, still accompanied by the melodramatically diabolical and long-winded laughter of Maillard. However, he escapes by scaling down the walls of the asylum via a rope of *white* sheets tied to the balcony — the rope of reason which provides an escape route to the madness unfolding around him. Heeding the hallucination of Eugénie summoning him to the garden, he hurries to the asylum greenhouse, where he witnesses a bizarre ritual in progress: the Priest crushing grapes over Eugénie's naked body (her genitalia strategically concealed by plants and grapes) — a bizarre convergence of Aztec human sacrifice and the rituals of Catholic mass (the wine of communion) occurring within a surreal and enclosed Garden of Eden. In a burst of valiant derring-do, Gastón rescues Eugénie from the Priest and the guards and carries her into the woods: his familiar realm of nature and reason, the "outside world" opposed to the asylum. However, their flight is not underscored by a dramatic (or bombastic) musical overture commonly used in action films, but wonderfully incongruent bassoon-driven jazz: again, music one might associate with cartoons and comedy shorts rather than a horror film. Indeed, while Gastón and Eugénie's attempt to escape the asylum grounds could be a source of tense drama and action, it instead transpires as pure slapstick comedy. They encounter and free the long-suffering Julién, still bound and hopping pointlessly through the woods. Dr. Maillard, leading his guards through the woods to apprehend Gastón and Eugénie, barks hopelessly complicated and contradictory orders, sending the troops literally running in circles in the forest, akin to the Keystone Cops, while blaring bugles and rattling snare drums are heard on the soundtrack (also a commentary on the war in Vietnam still raging when *Mansion of Madness* was produced). The series of fisticuffs with the guards play out as slapstick vignettes recalling early Laurel and Hardy, the Three Stooges, and even the epic battles between Bugs Bunny and Elmer Fudd. In this way, these sequences also effectively parody the swashbuckling excitement period action-adventure films of the era (*The Three Musketeers*).

Amid the hectic, comedic activity, *Mansion of Madness* also pauses to allow for some plot exposition, or much-needed clarification. As Gastón and Eugénie embrace in the woods, she explains that "Dr. Maillard" is actually Raúl Fragonard, a famous criminal who came to the asylum seeking a cure for his madness and sub-

2. Madness and Modernity

Black mass: The Priest (David Silva) performs his version of communion with Eugénie in *Mansion of Madness* (courtesy of David Wilt).

sequently "led a *coup d'etat*." Her father, the real Dr. Maillard, and the others formally in charge of the asylum are now confined in the dungeons. When she came to the asylum to visit her father, she was forced to remain as Fragonard's hostage. This plot revelation negates the surprise ending that concluded Poe's story, and constructs a different narrative impetus: the eventual comeuppance of the villain, Fragonard. (For the purposes of clarity, Brook's character will be referred to as Fragonard for the remainder of this chapter.)

Exit the King

Gastón, Eugénie, and Julién are recaptured in the woods and brought back to the asylum. The scene cuts to the dungeons, where waving arms extend out of the jail cells just out of reach of a malicious guard in the corridor: a shot quoted from Mark Robson's 1946 horror film *Bedlam*, a chilling study of the insane asylum set

The Mexican Cinema of Darkness

in the early modern era.[31] Julién is thrown into the cell teeming with filthy prisoners; among them are his servant Henri and the real Dr. Maillard (Max Kerlow). However, while Julién is thrust into a throwback to a 1940s horror film, Gastón and Eugénie become immersed in a parody of Fellini's *Satyricon* (or, perhaps, if Pasolini had directed the film). In a section of the asylum recreating the Holy Roman Empire (another historical European reference point), Fragonard lounges in a throne and verbosely waxes philosophical. Gastón is massaged by two naked women while a naked man attends to Eugénie's hair; naked women indifferently lounge at Fragonard's feet; a slender, naked man pretends to fish in front of Fragonard; and men and women have sex in the public bathtubs in the room. Moreover, Fragonard, Gastón, and Eugénie are all clad in *white* togas, breaking from the pattern of the previous scenes where reason (white) and madness (black) were contrasted. This is *not* to say unreason has conquered reason; rather, unreason and reason have become indistinguishable. Maillard's dazzled vision of modern utopia — the consolidation of all history, equal parts fantasy and brutality — is now the *status quo*.

The scene abruptly cuts to a close-up of a young man staring at the camera, his hands and face pressed against a plane of glass. The camera tracks upward and towards the right, revealing a nude woman on a white horse (Lady Godiva) and the Priest leading Gastón and Eugénie through the bowels of the asylum's heating system: people locked in glass cages over the furnaces, their body heat being siphoned to provide the fuel for the ovens. The shot cuts to a high-angle pan moving slowly across a massive dinner table and a surreal feast, the sequence that makes up the bulk of Poe's original story. The banquet plays out as if Fellini directed *Salò*, concluding the film in scenes combining carnival and degradation: a fantastic celebration

The great dictator: Fragonard/"Dr. Mallard" (Claudio Brook) in full regalia presides over the concluding banquet in *Mansion of Madness* (courtesy of David Wilt).

taking place in the middle of the human-fueled furnaces — a bizarre dinner party in the midst of the Holocaust. Like the people in glass cages over the furnaces, children are locked in glass booths around the table (presumably better to be seen and not heard); a soldier courteously salutes Lady Godiva; the centerpiece of the table is the "house band" of gaudily dressed nobles plucking plants and blowing into crustacean shells. At the head of the table, Fragonard sits on another throne — a chair draped in a red sheet framed by a rack of cobwebs holding dangling animal bones. He is now dressed in a regal, *white* military costume: modern unreason-as-reason embodied in a figure of authoritarianism and genocide, reminiscent of the Colonel's ostentatious wardrobe in *El Topo* and its similar allusions to the well-known dictators of modern history — Napoleon, Maximilian, Mussolini, Hitler, and the contemporary figure of Fascism in the 1970s, Francisco Franco. Fragonard joins their ranks as the megalomaniacal mad scientist–king who is the "Whole of the Law" within the asylum as the *reductio ad absurdum* of modernity.

A skinned animal is presented to the guests for dinner. The peasants consigned to the galleries rush to partake, only to be pushed away by the soldiers. A man sitting near the throne mounts the carcass, simulating sex with it as he holds the hind legs in the air and everyone giggles in delight. When an inmate dressed in a tacky Pope costume rises to denounce the act as "blasphemy" (the man copulating with the gutted "Lamb of God"), he is brusquely thrown to the ground by the Priest. As the evening's entertainment, inmates in various combinations of peasant and military attire tote a large vegetable basket to the banquet table. Fragonard, in a parody of carnival barkers or even television game-show hosts, grills Gastón: "And now, my dear Monsieur Leblanc, if you're as clever as you think you are, tell me: what lies under the celery?!" As the vegetables are removed, it is the real Dr. Maillard, bound and gagged, who lies under the celery, briefly brought from the depths of the dungeons to be reunited with his daughter before he is returned to captivity.

Fragonard then announces his final decree of judgment on Gastón and Eugénie. Of course, the verdict is death. He stands and proclaims, "The time has come to feed our famished fowls.... All together now: call our fowls!" In more absurdist comedy (again recalling Monty Python much more than a horror film), Fragonard suddenly begins squawking and flapping his arms, leading those at the banquet in mass chicken imitation: the descent of the masses into a collective of "Mr. Chickens," with their animalistic frenzy to be sated by Gastón's public execution. Two inmates roughly seize Gastón and hold him in place as menacing, *film noir*-style jazz erupts on the soundtrack. Three dancers in mime makeup and ghoulish, feathery outfits perform an extended dance number, echoing both the stylistics of modern dance and the Hollywood musical (certainly by now a drive-in audience expecting a Corman-style, low-budget horror film with some obligatory blood, comedy, and "tits and ass" must have been positively reeling). Finally, the fowls are presented with scythes, which they begin waving and poking at Gastón, further prolonging his execution.

Suddenly, a shot rings out, killing the lead chicken-executioner. Like the uprising that ended Poe's story, the real Dr. Maillard, Julién, Henri, and the others have escaped from the dungeons to begin the "counter-revolution" Fragonard took great measures to prevent: ostensibly, the revolution that will mark a return to reason. In a fittingly surreal finale to the film (a moment also recalling Godard), Julién's cousin steps out of the crowd dressed as a peasant, now armed with the pistol, and proclaims: "*Vive la Révolution!*" The allusion is to both the French Revolution as the conclusion to the Age of Enlightenment, as well as the counterculture movement, with the assassination of the mad dictator by the peasant as politically charged as *El Topo*'s castration of the Colonel. However, in *Mansion of Madness* the counterculture is also established as merely part of the madness in the whole of the asylum (versus *El Topo*'s "freaks" who are gunned downed in the sunlight streets of the Great Town). Three consecutive slow-motion shots from different angles depict Fragonard struck in the chest by the bullet before he finally collapses onto his throne, bringing to mind another cinematic reference — Sam Peckinpah (whose influence can be seen in the apocalyptic finale of *Alucarda* as well). In close-up, the fatally wounded Fragonard ponders, "The tree, the baobab tree ... the leaves of the yea and the nay ... the roots...." Suddenly he grimaces, briefly looking at the camera, and exclaims: "Can this be the end of Maillard?!" A parody of Edward G. Robinson's final line from *Little Caesar*—"Can this be the end of Rico?"— his reign ends with an absurd punchline rather than portentous rumination.

Initially, *Mansion of Madness* appears to close with the triumph of reason over madness: Fragonard, the insane villain (the disturbing madman) conquered by the daring and dashing man of reason, Gastón. However, despite the death of Fragonard, *Mansion of Madness* does not end with the triumph of reason, but the final *loss* of reason. The low-angle shot of the dead Fragonard sprawled on his throne cuts to a shot of the carriage presumably leaving the asylum, and Gastón's voice-over epilogue provides a disturbing coda to the film:

> Well, men may call me mad. I at least admit to the existence of two adverous [sic] elements striving to steal my soul. The one, *ruled by reason and related to the memory of events that occurred in my former life*. The other, *that world of shadows and doubt leading to my present condition*, born in the recollection of violent events so recently experienced. Therefore, believe whatever you wish, for anything that I say concerning the first stage you may accept, and trust or dismiss altogether whatever I might say about the last [emphasis added].

Fragonard's death has indeed been "the end of Maillard"— Fragonard's outward visage and alias of reason. However, his death also heralds "the resurrection [that] will take effect and the world will itself reside in the roots of the baobab"— the modern world reborn and entangled in the roots of the Tree of Life.[32]

Gastón has become the resurrection of Fragonard by going mad himself, unable to resolve the struggle between his "former life" in the domain of reason (nature, the outdoors) and his entrance into madness and "that world of shadows and doubt" (the asylum). If Gastón descends into madness, it is also because he is a descendent of madness: his father, the Old World, the nightmare of history, the Tree of Life. He was "always-already" part of the order of madness, long before he officially entered the asylum.[33]

When Gastón finishes his closing narration, the shot of the asylum grounds becomes saturated in the same psychedelic appearance that began the film — the negative image tinted in brilliant crimson and turquoise hues that began the film. The final shot of the film expresses the non-world of madness: the conversion of the shot into its negative image. However, this negative image is also saturated by vivid and incongruent colors. Madness is not only a "non-world" versus reason (its negative); it is "another world," a recognizable but altogether distorted world of vibrant and extraordinary colors — a world of dazzlement. The modern binary of Reason and Unreason is both erased and exploded; Gastón can no longer negotiate the specious binary that ostensibly separates reason and madness. Unreason — "Reason dazzled" — is merely a different manifestation of Reason, and ultimately Reason may simply be a version of Unreason accepted and endorsed in modernity's own *reductio ad absurdum*.

3

The New Dark Ages:
Alucarda, la hija de las tinieblas (*Alucarda, Daughter of Darkness*, 1975)

Her feet go down to death; her steps take hold on hell.
— Proverbs 5: 5

The New Vampire Women

Following *Mansion of Madness*, López Moctezuma's next project was the horror-thriller *Mary Mary Bloody Mary* (1974). A Mexican-American co-production, the film was made in Mexico with a largely Mexican supporting cast and production crew, possibly as a cost-saving measure. The producers, writers, and leading cast were all American; fashion model–actress Cristina Ferrare starred in the title role, and B-Movie icon John Carradine appeared as Mary's deranged father.[1] While essentially a director-for-hire on a B-horror film, López Moctezuma nevertheless included some highly distinctive and disturbing touches. One unconventional aspect is that the title character is the killer throughout the film rather than the pursued victim: a role reversal from most horror movies, specifically the American slasher film vogue of the 1980s, where an attractive woman was usually the object of murder. Moreover, *Mary Mary*'s violence is infused with highly sexualized aspects; Mary murders with a blatantly phallic weapon, a long needle disguised as a hairpin. While slasher films certainly have highly sexualized components as well, *Mary Mary* is much closer to contemporary Italian *giallo* horror films (Mario Bava, Dario Argento). The strange, naturalistic world of *giallo* depicted a Sadean world where eroticism and violence became inherently connected and inseparable; the slasher film often constructed a rigorous binary of Puritanical cause-effect where sexual behavior inevitably resulted in violent punishment.[2] To make *Mary Mary* even more chilling, Mary compulsively drinks the blood of her victims. While the film offers some incidental explanations by Mary's father that the family is afflicted by a genetic malady that requires them to consume blood, Mary is not a vampire in the established conventions of the horror film. While she shares an affinity for vampirism, Mary's sexually-infused bloodlust is not satisfied by ethereal, nocturnal visits and seductive bites on the neck, but the direct and decidedly non-supernatural method of thrusting a phallic needle into the throats of her victims and producing geysers of blood to devour. In *Mary Mary*, murder and the flow of blood are synonymous to sexual intercourse and orgasmic discharge, and, as Georges Bataille noted in discussing the literature of Sade, "Murder becomes the pinnacle of erotic enjoyment."[3]

The reinterpretation of vampirism depicted in *Mary Mary* also figures prominently in his subsequent film, *Alucarda*. In a 1977 interview, López Moctezuma stated that *Alucarda* was not a vampire story, but added:

> The name is certainly a homage to Count Dracula ... the film draws on the vampire tradition, and in a way the protagonist is a female vampire ... but not in the sense of a blood drinker. In fact, she has all of the powers and attributes of the classic vampire except she doesn't drink blood. I've given her all the vampiric powers Bram Stoker mentions that never got shown on screen, as well as the ones you'd expect.[4]

In this respect, *Alucarda* provides a dialectical contrast to *Mary Mary*: Mary drinks blood but is devoid of vampirical powers; Alucarda is endowed with vampirical powers but does not drink blood (the highly-eroticized moment of blood-tasting in *Alucarda* notwithstanding). While Mary and Alucarda are both "vampires," each represents a vastly different representation of the classic horror film depiction of vampirism, specifically the mexploitation horror films of the same period, which by the early 1970s were still largely confined to depicting female vampires as eerie, seductive, undead women with oversize fangs, heavy mascara, flowing nightgowns, and glamorous hairdos roaming the night — the only major change being the occasional topless vampire woman scenes included in versions released outside of Mexico.

The Mind's Eye

López Moctezuma stated, "In *Mansion of Madness* I wanted to show the link between eroticism and madness; in *Mary Mary*, the eroticism heightens the violence and serves as a counterpoint to the fantastic."[5] In *Alucarda*, these themes become indistinguishable: madness, eroticism, violence and the fantastic *all* merge into a disturbing whole. Through disorientating editing, vertigo-inducing camera angles, obliterating the first person (character) versus the third person (camera) perspectives, scenes of sex and violence rivaling anything in contemporary Eurotrash

The anti–Catholic girl: Promotional image for *Alucarda* (courtesy of David Wilt).

horror cinema, and a depiction of Catholicism that might make Buñuel blush, *Alucarda* is the shocking account of strange and disconcerting events in a 19th century Mexican convent where all the characters appear to be suffering from varying degrees of mental instabilities and sexual proclivities.⁶ One could describe *Alucarda* as *Mansion of Madness* set in a nunnery rather than an asylum proper. Foucault suggested, "The asylum is a religious domain without religion."⁷ In *Alucarda,* the convent becomes a psychiatric domain without psychiatry.

In this respect, *Alucarda* is frequently compared to Ken Russell's *The Devils* (1971), another film set in a convent where sexual repressions explode into collective madness (*The Devils* also inadvertently heralded the wave of Eurotrash "nunsploitation" films of the 1970s which focused of the sexual "habits" of cloistered nuns — a genre *Alucarda* is often associated with).⁸ However, the crucial difference between *Alu-*

carda and *The Devils* is Russell's psychoanalytic formula where religious obsession plus sexual repression equals mass hysteria: dogmatic Catholicism and pent-up libido climaxes in an orgy of mass insanity. Certainly, *Alucarda* presents a similar depiction of Catholicism as a repressive religion expressing abhorrence for sex and the body which is conversely expressed through sadistic and masochistic sexual rituals staged as religious ceremony. However, rather than the simplified Reichian psychoanalysis posited by *The Devils*, *Alucarda* liberally incorporates supernatural overtones and implications in its violence and eroticism: occultism, demonic possession, and vampirism. In *Alucarda*, the strange and disturbing events in the convent cannot be explained by sexual repression, mental affliction, demonic possession, or vampirical seduction: *all* are equally and inherently related. The main characters in *Alucarda* exhibit various states or stages of mental distress: Alucarda (Tina Romero), whose manic dementia may be the result of being an agent of supernatural evil; Justine (Susan Kamini), consumed by melancholia after her parents' untimely deaths; Sister Angélica (Tina French) and her frenzied religious-sexual obsessions and visions; Father Lázaro (the one and only David Silva), whose revulsion for sex and the body is pathologically expressed in sadism, masochism, and dictatorial control over the convent. As these characters' individual psychoses coalesce, the fantastic events grow increasingly more surreal and horrific, and, in direct proportion, more violent and erotic. In *Alucarda*, a dangerous collective madness is not simply rooted in organized sexual repression (*The Devils*), nor does the encounter with supernatural evil become a means to explore the troubled psyches of the main characters (*The Exorcist*). The relationship between the characters' worsening psychological states and a world becoming immersed in supernatural horror is not simply ambiguous in *Alucarda*, the two become inseparable. Madness and the supernatural work in an inexorable tandem to produce a crescendo of erotic, fantastic, and apocalyptic violence.

While López Moctezuma's films are certainly comparable to Buñuel and Fellini, the work of Pier Paolo Pasolini offers a crucial reference point. In *Alucarda*, there is the extensive use of a film technique Pasolini termed "free indirect discourse" or the "free indirect subjective," as articulated in his essay "The Cinema of Poetry" (1965).[9] To admittedly simplify Pasolini's theory, the free indirect subjective can roughly be defined by a free interaction between subjective and objective points of view.[10] However, this is not simply juxtaposing the first person (character viewpoint) with the third person (camera viewpoint) without clarification of which point of view is being presented to the viewer. Rather, the subjective perceptions and objective events become entangled in the filmmaking itself. As an example, Pasolini hailed Michelangelo Antonioni's *Il deserto rosso* (*Red Desert*, 1964):

> Antonioni no longer applies ... his own formalistic vision of the world (the problem of the neurosis of alienation), but he looks at the world at one with his neurotic heroine, [realigning] it through the "look" of the woman.... He

> has finally succeeded in representing the world through *his* own eyes *because he has substituted, wholly, the world-view of the sick woman for his own vision, which is delirious with estheticism.*[11]

The alienation and ennui of *Il deserto rosso*'s tragic, overwhelmed heroine (Monica Vitti) is expressed by her relationship to the camera, which manifests her perceptions of the modern world: endless long takes utterly devoid of any action or dramatic tension as she wanders urban landscapes until the sheer monotony indeed become "delirious with estheticism." A similar cinematic process occurs in *Alucarda*, where López Moctezuma's "formalist vision of the world" also adopts "the world-view of the sick woman," with Alucarda's delirium, and the other characters' own neuroses, depicted through a barrage of shocking and surreal images equally "delirious with estheticism."

The free indirect subjective entails that the objective camera necessarily reflects and compliments the character's subjective states, attitudes, even ideologies. In Pasolini's *Porcile* (*Pigpen*, 1969), two parallel stories are told: one in a pre-modern world where a young man wanders a desert, resorting to murder and cannibalism to survive; the other in the modern world as a bourgeois young man lives in affluence and his wealthy industrialist father looks identical to Adolph Hitler (perhaps not his actual appearance, but how he appears to the world). The pre-modern story is depicted by alternations between abrupt jump-cuts and languorous long takes; the modern story depicted through a constant regularity and regulation in its shot structure, exemplified by the constant and monotonous shot–reverse shot configurations in conversations between characters. In *Salò*, the degradation of the modern world as an unyielding organization of brutality is as powerfully expressed by the unremitting symmetrical staging of action as much as the extremely grisly and offensive particulars of the torture (*Salò*'s notorious banquet of human excrement). In *Alucarda*, the repression and control within the convent are similarly depicted through a stylized regulation of activity that becomes increasingly more cruel and perverse in ratio to the growing supernatural forces: the exorcism of Justine could be a scene in *Salò*. Moreover, a frequent utilization of the free indirect subjective is *Alucarda*'s obsessive use of high-angle long shots. Certainly, the high-angle shot is used to manifest the cinematic cliché of establishing the characters as figures of diminished power, but also reflects the subjective state of the characters. They are constantly represented in a state of being looked down upon, not only suggesting powerlessness but their own subjective perception, or "world-view," of being watched from above, trapped under the omnipotent gaze of an unseen figure looking down on them: a vengeful, punishing God in constant judgment, under whose gaze — the camera — the characters live in perpetual fear and complete subordination.

Ultimately, the convergence of the subjective and objective through the free indirect subjective is far more dramatic than merely obscuring character and camera viewpoints. In *Alucarda*, López Moctezuma's formalist vision becomes integrated with and inseparable from the world-view of his tormented characters, a *collision* rather than a *blending* of points of view.[12] To this extent, Pasolini claimed the free indirect subjective becomes an approach to film that frees it from a "cinema of prose" (narrative) and elevates it to a "cinema of poetry" (imagery):

> The "free indirect subjective" in cinema is endowed with a very flexible stylistic possibility ... *it also liberates the expressive possibilities stifled by traditional narrative conventions,* by a sort of return to their origins, which extend to rediscovering even in the technical means of cinema *their original barbaric, irregular, aggressive, visionary qualities.* It is the "free indirect subjective" which establishes the possible tradition of a "technical language of poetry" in cinema.[13]

As discussed regarding *Mansion of Madness*, it is precisely the *poetic* aspect of Poe that informs López Moctezuma's adaptation: a collection of flamboyant, fragmented, and quite funny vignettes on madness and modernity connected by a threadbare narrative. Attempting to untangle the plot of *Alucarda* will inevitably result in a large degree of disappointment and even frustration for the viewer. While *Alucarda* certainly has a story as such, there is *never* any clarification regarding where madness and the supernatural can be distinguished or even *should* be distinguished. Focusing on *Alucarda*'s narrative coherency — or lack thereof — is to neglect the sheer poetic power of its startling imagery and the film's "barbaric, irregular, aggressive, visionary qualities."

Delirium, Discourse, Dream

Indicative of *Alucarda*'s overall disorientating qualities, the film does not begin with the credits or a stable establishing shot, but a low-angle pan across vine-covered walls and discarded religious statues. A baby's cries are heard off-camera, and a woman emerges from the bottom of the frame, holding a baby covered in blood. The shot cuts to a young woman (Tina Romero, in a dual role) lying exhausted on a bed of straw, having just given birth to Alucarda: a parody of the birth of Christ in the manger, and the first of many times Christian iconography is darkly parodied in *Alucarda*. Alucarda's mother implores the woman to "take her to a convent ... don't let *him* take her away!" Her emphatic statement cuts to a high-angle, extreme long shot of the new mother lying in the straw as the woman flees from the building with the newborn, which then cuts to a high-angle close-up of the visibly frightened woman looking directly at the camera as if it were some malevolent force. Another high-angle, extreme long shot of Alucarda's mother follows, and the camera slowly and inexorably zooms in towards the woman, "closing in" on her as she lies helplessly, still staring in horror at the camera. Fragmented images of the various religious icons are inserted into the zoom-in, and ominous heavy breathing can be heard while the montages are formed. When the zoom-in reaches a close-up of the terrified woman, the shot cuts to a cobweb-covered gargoyle as her screams are heard off-camera.

This brief opening sequence is significant for two reasons. One, the viewer assumes some sort of supernatural, even demonic birth occurred, followed by the death (or murder) of the mother through an unseen yet seeing ominous force — the camera. However, the possible interpretations are only implied by the torrent of imagery rather than explicitly stated. If traditional mexploitation films used a formula where "events are described rather than shown," in López Moctezuma's films "events are *shown* rather than *described*." Various, multiple, and even conflicting meanings are generated by the juxtaposition of *poetic* images, specifically in Pasolini's sense of the "Cinema of Poetry." The shots are striking, compelling, and thought-provoking, yet necessarily vague and abstract; their meanings and messages are conveyed through their singular power and metaphorical associations rather than narrative teleology. Second, the opening sequence establishes the relationship between mental distress, religion, sexuality, and the supernatural; an interaction which becomes more pronounced, and provocative, as the film progresses. It is unclear whether the supernatural force is real or imagined: an actual paranormal power or a manifestation of the mother's guilt and shame for bearing Alucarda out of wedlock in a society of rigid Catholicism. The "him" the mother wants her child protected from could be "Him": the presence of a punishing, vengeful God signified by *Alucarda*'s high-angle shot as a recurring metaphor of the character's receptions of living under God's omniscience, omnipotence, and, above all, judgment.

Following the credits, the scene shifts not only spatially but temporally, although this is not immediately evident to the viewer; there is no explanatory "fifteen years later" subtitle commonly used for such transitions (in the scene at the mausoleum, Alucarda reads the plaque on what is presumed to be her mother's coffin and remarks to Justine that she "died fifteen years ago — our age").[14] A young orphan, Justine, has arrived to live at the convent, this being a reference to Sade's *Justine*: the chronicle of a young girl's initiation to the ways of the world through repeated sexual abuse. López Moctezuma explained, "She was based on Sade's heroine. She's the kind of creature who is always going to look ridiculous when put up against an apocalyptic creature like Alucarda."[15] The two meet; Alucarda mysteriously appears in the shadows of their shared room when a mournful Justine opens a locket containing photos of her dead parents. The dichotomy between the two is quickly established: Alucarda's manic obsessions versus Justine's numbing melancholia. While Justine clings to her locket and nostalgic memories of her parents, the remnants of the holy family, Alucarda produces her own seemingly random collection of found objects full of intensely personal meaning and significance: "These are secrets. Everyday I find a new secret. It comes to me." Giving Justine a small polished stone, she adds, "This, for instance — it means I like you." Rather than a world organized around bourgeois sentimentality, religious order, or even rational significations, Alucarda's world is one of limitless wonderment where myriad signs and objects constitute and reveal their "secrets" to her and her alone (not unlike Dr. Maillard in *Mansion of Madness* and his own "delirious discourses" regarding his asylum utopia, a system which operates perfectly simply due to the fact he imaginatively designs and loquaciously decrees its ideal efficiency). As Foucault suggested, madness is above all "a delirious discourse ... oddity of conduct and conversation" and like the title character freely interpreting the signs and meanings around her, *Alucarda*'s free indirect subjective formalistically reflects a similar method of signification. The "secrets" in *Alucarda* are generated and revealed through an often disjointed series of strange, episodic events. *Alucarda*'s own internal logic is not one of linear narrative deduction, but a "delirious discourse" of poetic images: "delirious with estheticism."

Alucarda leads Justine to the garden outside the restrictive monastery walls, where they observe two identical insects crawling in a leaf. "It's one more secret," Alucarda delightfully exclaims. "One identical to the other. Like two images in the mirror — like you and me." As Alucarda elaborates on how the insects reveal her and Justine's identical nature, the two orphans are shown in close-up crowded together in the frame to exaggerate this closeness and burgeoning interpersonal intimacy. However, while the two are identical "images in a mirror," they are ultimately two very different creatures, even dialectical opposites: Alucarda as an intense, powerful "apocalyptic creature" versus Justine as a deadened, powerless "ridiculous creature." As they frolic in the fields outside the restrictive and claustrophobic confines of the convent, the outdoors becomes a space where they can act spontaneously, reflected by leisurely long takes and mobile camera work.[16] In contrast, the indoors of *Alucarda* (convent), as in *Mansion of Madness* (asylum), is an enclosed, controlled, and regimented space where all activities are precisely arranged in performance and cinematography (as noted, formal strategies essential to Pasolini's *Porcile* and especially *Salò*).

While roaming in the woods away from the safety, or confinement, of the convent, Alucarda and Justine encounter a bearded, hunchbacked gypsy, played by *Mansion of Madness* star Claudio Brook in a dual-role: he also portrays the rational modern man, Dr. Oszek. As "the Gypsy," Brook provides an unabashedly histrionic performance, both eerie and comical as he gesticulates wildly and mangles English, German, and French into statements managing to be cryptic and illogical at the same time (in this way, again comparable to his performance as Dr. Maillard in *Mansion of Madness*). Accompanied by a woman fortune-teller, the Gypsy is a traveling merchant selling "magical" objects, including a dagger which greatly interests Alucarda. In close-up, she holds the dagger vertically in front of her face, and admires it with perverse fascination and erotic interest (in a vulgar Freudian

From left to right: Alucarda (Tina Romero), the Gypsy (Claudio Brook), and Justine (Susana Kamini); the first encounter in the woods in *Alucarda* (courtesy of David Wilt).

sense, the dagger symbolizes a vaginal opening as well as its phallic connotations); this also foreshadows the pivotal role the dagger will play in consummating Alucarda and Justine's "romantic" relationship. In turn, the Gypsy is intrigued with Alucarda's "strange eyes," which immediately cuts to an extreme close-up of Alucarda's eyes, a parody of a patented shot used in countless mexploitation films: an extreme close-up of the eyes when a vampire is engaged in the act of hypnotizing his or her victims. By referencing this filmic cliché, the Gypsy is himself hypnotized by Alucarda's mystery. Moreover, the comment about her "strange eyes" cutting to a close-up of her eyes becomes a literal expression and signal to the audience of Alucarda's psychological state (an effect reminiscent of the literalness of silent cinema). Despite his nearly incomprehensible ramblings, the Gypsy manages to warn Alucarda of a future event: "I can see your dream clearly ... if the dream comes true — I shall be expecting her." The puzzling statement foreshadows Alucarda's growing dementia and the increasing presence of the supernatural, specifically the hallucinatory and ambiguous "dream-sequence" when Alucarda completes her seduction of Justine under the guidance of the Gypsy.

Frightened by the Gypsy's ominous proclamation, Alucarda and Justine flee to the long-abandoned building where Alucarda was born. While Justine is visibly distressed by her surroundings, Alucarda is strangely at ease: "I hear the voices of the past — I feel as if I've been here before." Madness and the fantastic again converge, at once manifesting paranormal forces of the past — ghosts, past lives, reincarnation (suggested by Tina Romeo playing both Alucarda and Alucarda's mother)— and the hearing of voices associated with schizophrenia. Growing increasingly agitated, Alucarda confesses her consuming love for Justine, and Justine will soon love her the same way: "Eternally, with the same blood always flowing through our veins." In this sense, Alucarda's desire for Justine is vampirical, her seduction and domination of Justine expressed through the eroticized exchange and sharing of blood. Brandishing the dagger acquired from the gypsy, Alucarda convinces Justine to make a pact with her. In close-up, Justine's hand slowly enters from the right side of the frame and clasps Alucarda's outstretched hand: a dark parody of Michelangelo's *Adam* reaching for the hand of God. However, before Alucarda can cut her with the dagger, Justine recoils in panic. With her love still unrequited, Alucarda turns and excitedly examines a coffin in the mausoleum, which one assumes is her dead mother. Wrenching it open, Alucarda unleashes a gust of chilling wind and demonic growling; she not only opens a Pandora's Box of past supernatural evil, but unleashes her own internal psychic and psychological "demons."

Retreating from the crypt after the unnerving event, Justine comforts an obviously shaken Alucarda, who simply explains, "I've been dreaming." In *Cinema 2: The Time Image*, Gilles Deleuze distinguishes two representations of madness in the cinema: Expressionism and Artaud. The expressionist film, exemplified by *The Cabinet of Dr. Caligari*, depicted madness as a nightmare world of shadow and darkness, whereas Artaud's screenplays represent madness in the form of the "daydream" in its most literal sense: "Expressionism makes wakefulness pass through a nocturnal treatment; Artaud *makes the dream pass through a diurnal treatment*."[17] In this regard, Deleuze's conception is highly influenced by Foucault: "[D]elirum is *the dream of waking persons*."[18] Thus, Deleuze suggests that the respective figures of the madman are also vastly different in expressionism and Artaud. The expressionist madman is a *somnambulistic* figure: the sleepwalker (*Dr. Caligari*), the vampire (*Nosferatu*), the automaton (*Metropolis*), all wandering in worlds of darkness. Artaud's madman is termed a *vigilambulistic* figure: trapped in the daydream in its most literal sense, the waking hours experienced as the fragmentary occurrences of the dream.[19] In *Alucarda*, Justine embodies the numbed somnambulist, trapped in the nightmare of madness — her seduction and possession by Alucarda in the pitch-black darkness of their room is her entry point to madness. Alucarda is the unrestrained vigilambulist, enveloped in the daydream of madness (the "dream" the

Gypsy warns she will experience, the trip to her birthplace as "dreaming"): the vampire as vigilambulist.

The Agony Is the Ecstasy

Alucarda and Justine's strange experience in the mausoleum shifts to a Catholic mass in progress. The camera slowly pans across the scene: in the foreground, numerous nuns with their backs to the camera stand in regimented order; in the background, a plethora of large crucifixes behind the altar resemble suspended slaughterhouse carcasses as much as sacred religious decorations. A barely visible figure stands amid the disconcerting plethora of crucifixes: Father Lázaro, the oppressive head of the convent. Yet except for this opening shot and a subsequent low-angle, long pan across the altar — both of which emphasize the towering crucifixes rather than the priest — Father Lázaro remains unseen throughout this mass sequence. Instead, he is represented by a stern, booming voice resonating on the soundtrack as he delivers his portentous sermon. Not only does Father Lázaro becomes the voice of God himself, the omnipotent being who is heard but not seen, a verbal rather than a visual force of power and domination, he becomes the tyrannical manifestation of Lacan's "Symbolic Father," the overriding presence and threat of castration under which the whole of the Law is arraigned through the Symbolic Order of culture and language.

Father Lázaro warns, "The Devil enters the body of the person he wants to master and uses the organs of that body for his own pleasure!" Sexual desire and gratification is interpreted as a sign of demonic possession. Yet as Father Lázaro's mass reaches an increased intensity and invective against allowing the body to become a host of evil (sex), tilted low-angle close-ups are inserted of the nuns and orphans as they become more agitated. The fear of demonic infiltration of their bodies is conversely expressed as sexual arousal during the mass: the paradox of Catholic theology's sexual repression and Catholic ritual's violent eroticism, later manifest in Sister Angélica's dream-prayer sequence, the flagellation scene, and, most overtly, the crucifixion-exorcism of Justine (in this way, the immense crucifixes also convey a phallic symbolism). Alucarda and Justine stand next to each other at the mass, dressed as they were outside the convent in the woods: Alucarda in black, thoroughly incongruent with the others; Justine's costume a hilarious parody of Little Red Riding Hood (with Alucarda implicitly her wolf). Overcome by the intensity of the mass, Justine suddenly faints. As Sister Angélica and Alucarda hover over her, the nun glares at Alucarda, establishing and foreshadowing the forthcoming battle over Justine: the supernatural vampire Alucarda and the devout nun Sister Angélica as combatants for Justine's love as well as her eternal soul. They are not only religious rivals, but romantic rivals demonstrating an obsessive lesbian desire towards Justine in two subsequent, hallucinatory sequences of the film: the "marriage" between Justine and Alucarda, followed by the surreal prayer sequence featuring Sister Angélica.

After confining the stricken Justine to her bed, the nuns depart and Alucarda snarls: "Monsters! Spinsters!" Explaining she has again "heard the voices of the past ... beating into me until everything becomes clear," she suddenly begins whirling in circles and careening about the room, invoking the names of demons while unearthly growling and panting can again be heard on the soundtrack. Once more the supernatural and schizophrenia merge, never clarified as to the extent of Alucarda's "oddity of conduct," and whether the ominous sounds are an expression of her mental delirium or demonic possession — or *both*. Understandably reacting with terror, Justine begs Alucarda to stop. When she ceases twirling, the shot cuts to another extreme close-up of Alucarda's eyes as she glares demonically at Justine. However, Alucarda's methods of placing Justine under her power are distinctly less than supernatural; she slaps Justine viciously, sending her into a cowering heap on the floor, and proclaims, "We shall make a pact and seal it with our blood!"

The shot cuts to Alucarda in profile against a pitch-black background, hissing: "We'll make them pay!" Sinister laughter is heard as the Gypsy repeats her line and inexplicably emerges from the darkness and walks into the foreground of the shot, handing Alucarda the dagger she was fascinated with in their previous encounter (however, the film clearly established Alucarda *already* possessed the dagger, suggesting this act, and even the Gypsy's very appearance in the room, is a subjective and symbolic moment as much as an actual narrative event). This cuts to a theatrically staged shot of the bedroom: Alucarda on the left side if the frame, holding the dagger; Justine cowering on the right side of the frame; the Gypsy in the center of the shot. He gestures histrionically and bellows, "But first some rain ... and thunder!" In a parody of theatrical melodrama, lightening flashes off-frame and thunder roars off-camera, as if the Gypsy were the director cuing the special effects department. He continues: "Now call them! Call them! CALL THEM!" Alucarda arches her back, bending over backwards, holding the dagger aloft as she begins to hysterically invoke the names of Satan and other demons while the Gypsy crouches over Justine, shaking her limp body. The shot cuts to the open window of the bedroom, lights flashing and stage fog streaming into the room, and then cuts back to the previous shot, the characters in the same positions — except now Alucarda is completely naked (the effect reminiscent of Pasolini). Beyond the immediate shock of full-frontal nudity, the sequence provides a disorientating break in continuity, with Alucarda having "magically" shed her dress, or inhibitions. In occult vernacular, she has become "skyclad" as the storm outside builds in intensity.

Justine is roughly stripped by the Gypsy, who orchestrates a sexual encounter

The Mexican Cinema of Darkness

"We'll make them pay!" The Gypsy mysteriously reappears to the increasingly disturbed Alucarda (courtesy of David Wilt).

between the two women, placing the highly agitated Alucarda (vigilambulist) and the nearly catatonic Justine (somnambulist) across from each other on their knees, facing each other as the viewer sees them in profile: the antithetical "images in a mirror." Kneeling between the two, the Gypsy raises the dagger, holding it in the center of the shot, and cryptically intones, "You will blend into each other and then blend into me." The scene becomes a Sadean parody of the wedding ceremony, with the romantic union of Alucarda and Justine pronouncing them *master* and *slave*. The Gypsy cuts each woman's breast, wets his finger with the blood, and rubs his finger across their lips. Breasts, lips, fingers, and blood are eroticized and fetishized by the camera through high-angle close-ups of the women's faces as they lick the blood off the Gypsy's fingers as if performing fellatio, particularly Alucarda. More eroticized and fetishistic close-ups follow as the women run their tongues across each other's lips, tasting each other's blood. (In this sense, the scene is quite reminiscent of, and as exploitative as, the whip-duel between Mara and the Woman in Black in *El Topo*.) Two shots of the bedroom window are intercut into the sequence:

the rain, sky, and fog are all now saturated in red hues, with the erotic flow of blood now manifest as a torrential storm in the outside world beyond convent walls. When the shot returns to the Gypsy situated between the two women, he again raises the dagger and abruptly disappears via a jump-cut rather than a traditional dissolve — a technique recalling silent cinema rather than contemporary horror. Professing her love for Justine, Alucarda passionately kisses her on the mouth (the ritual of "kissing the bride") and licks the blood from her lips, chin, and breasts. Alucarda grows more aroused and strident, whereas Justine becomes more visibly horrified as the encounter unfolds, powerless to prevent Alucarda's seduction: vampirical power where the victim is unwilling yet unable to resist as the seducer takes possession of the body, the mind, and the soul — power and sex merging through the flow of blood. Justine is not merely helpless against Alucarda, she is rendered pathetic and even "ridiculous."

The seduction sequence concludes with a close-up of Justine screaming, the only resistance she can summon against Alucarda, and suddenly cuts to a close-up of Sister Angélica anxiously reciting the Lord's Prayer — beginning a new sequence as provocative as the previous one. Shots of Sister Angélica intently praying crosscut with Alucarda and Justine, now mysteriously escorted through a lush forest by a naked witch.[20] Alucarda and Justine are to be the centerpiece of a pagan orgy, and if the previous scene represented a perverse wedding inside the convent, this sequence constitutes a surreal honeymoon outside the convent. During the sequence where Alucarda and Justine are romping in the fields, their playfulness is briefly disturbed by a funereal procession lead by one of the nuns. Alucarda bitterly explains that one of the orphans living in the convent committed suicide and is being punished for her sin by being buried in "unhallowed ground" — the fields outside the boundaries of the convent. In *Alucarda*, the outdoors is unhallowed ground because it is a space where the repressed can flow unencumbered. As Foucault suggested:

> [N]ature, as the concrete form of the immediate, has an even more fundamental power in the suppression of madness. For it has the power of freeing man from freedom. In nature — *that nature, at least, which is measured by the double exclusion of the violence of desire and the unreality of hallucination* — man is doubtless liberated from social constraints ... and from the uncontrollable movement of the passions.[21]

However, Foucault claimed this primal relationship to nature is exactly what must be changed in modern society, and specifically in the treatment of madness. In modernity, nature is transformed from the province of the "savage" (animality, transgression) into a civilized space of intensive physical and mental "labor" (farming, exercise, adventure, introspection): "In short, *an immediate where nature is mediated by morality.*"[22] It is precisely the loss of his mediated relationship to nature which defines Gastón's own madness at the end of *Mansion of Madness*. Gastón, the man of the outside — nature in its controlled, rational form — is ultimately unable to escape from the bizarre workings of the asylum with the realization that the dichotomy between Reason and Unreason, and the spaces represented by Reason (the outside world) and Unreason (the asylum world), are only different manifestations of each other: equally distorted "images in a mirror." Conversely, in *Alucarda* the world of nature — the outside beyond the convent — is a space where "sin" can be expressed in its primordial forms unconstrained by morality and even the rational (the pagan orgy, the rain of blood during the perverse wedding between Alucarda and Justine). It is the constrictive, hermetic world of the convent, the epitome of moral "normalcy," where sexual energies are not repressed as such, but sublimated, redirected, and released in the convent's consecrated, sanctioned, yet perverse religious rituals: masturbatory prayer, masochistic flagellations, and sadistic crucifixions.

The nude witch kneels on the grass and welcomes Justine to the pagan ceremony. This shot crosscuts to a shot of Sister Angélica on her knees praying, forming a montage that associates rather than differentiates Catholic prayer and pagan ritual. As the ceremony continues, the montages grow more pronounced and overt. Sister Angélica writhes on her knees in agony, arms aloft, feverishly praying to God and Christ to protect Justine; similarly, the witch sways on her knees, arms upraised as well, invoking Cernunnos, the Celtic god of fertility. As if caught in her spell, the camera itself sways and tilts from side to side, seemingly hypnotized or seduced by the witch's movements and invocations. These montages associating "nun" and "witch" continue in the next four shots, alternating between Sister Angélica and other naked witches. The positions and postures of the praying nun and chanting witches are closely matched from shot to shot, again suggesting symmetry rather than establishing dissimilarity. But one difference arises in the montages — the shots of Sister Angélica are conventionally framed, whereas the shots of the witches are titled at striking angles which render them diagonal on the screen, recalling and referencing the canted, low-angle close-ups of the sexually aroused nuns and orphans during Father Lázaro's mass.

As Sister Angélica's praying grows more fervent, she begins to cry tears of blood; soon she begins to sweat blood as well. Throughout *Alucarda*, one of the most consistently stunning images is the strange attire of the nuns: copiously bloodstained white gowns rather than the traditional black nun's habit. Resembling heavily bandaged accident victims rather than sisters of the cloth, the heaviest, darkest bloodstains are located in the area of the nuns' vaginas, suggesting not only menstrual blood but that all female bodily manifestations of "wetness" absorbed by their gowns (tears, perspiration, and sexual arousal) are manifest in one form: blood. As in the wedding of Alucarda and Justine (and López Moctezuma's previous *Mary Mary Bloody Mary*), blood becomes the bodily fluid of eroticism in Catholic rites as well — whether by physical beatings and torture (blood flowing from wounds) or paranormal occurrences (crying and sweating blood). When Sister Angélica's prayers reach a "climax," the shot cuts to the lead witch as a vein in her neck suddenly explodes and blood pours down her body. An extended montage is constructed between close-ups of the dead witch and a similarly bloodied Sister Angélica looking upward. In one shot, she betrays a ruthless satisfaction over the killing of the witch; in another, a strong sense of sexual gratification and ecstasy, with her face soaked in the indistinguishable mixture of blood, sweat, and tears. Indeed, the sequence closes with a shot of Sister Angélica literally hovering in the air, bright light streaming through the window with the achievement of rapture — orgasm — in a convergence of religious fervor, the paranormal, and the eroticized release and flow of blood. Rather than pagan religion, Catholicism becomes the site where madness, the fantastic, violence, and eroticism dramatically — and shockingly — converge.

Moreover, these two sequences demonstrate the power of the free indirect subjective. The supernatural events could be symbolic expressions of the characters' intensely troubled psychological states manifest as actual events: onscreen projections of the characters' fantasies, obsessions, and "delirium." Alucarda's seduction and domination of Justine is infused with surreal and subjective images: the Gypsy's inexplicable appearance, the rain of blood. Sister Angélica's experience can be read as a dream sequence, admittedly in a sort of vulgar Freudian interpretation. The pagan imagery and coupling bodies in the field represent her own sexual desires; the striking down of the witch her own yearning to save Justine from sex (or to save Justine for herself); the eroticized violence of prayer/masturbation and its resulting rapture/orgasm being the state of sexual ecstasy achieved in levitation.[23] Yet the issue is not whether events in *Alucarda* actually occur or not, or defining what constitutes a subjective versus an objective moment in the film (as opposed to Jodorowsky's *Santa sangre*, where discerning and eventually distinguishing which events actually occurred in the course of the film becomes vital in understanding the redemption and rebuilding of the main character's psyche). In *Alucarda*, it is not that the subjective and objective moments are ambiguous and therefore demand clarification, but rather that the scenes become subjective and objective *at the same time*, and thus any clarification becomes impossible. The primary importance is *how* the subjective and objective events combine and collide to create poetic moments where narrative ceases in favor of the pure evocative power of the images: the "barbaric, irregular, aggressive, visionary" qualities of the Cinema of Poetry.

The Passion of Justine

The shot of Sister Angelica hovering in sexual-religious ecstasy cuts to a Catechism class. Alucarda and Justine sit whispering and giggling, greatly annoying the nun, who demands they repeat her lesson aloud. Instead, the two begin praising Satan, denying the power of God, and pledging their allegiance to evil. They not only issue their sacrilegious proclamations in perfect unison, but the camera emphasizes and exaggerates their unity by alternating between corresponding close-ups of the two and a medium close-up of Alucarda and Justine closely standing next to each other, directly facing the camera as they perform their precise duet of blasphemy. The camera, through the symmetry, expresses the subjective state of the girls' intense bond — or rather, the state of bondage now existing between the master Alucarda and the slave Justine. The nun orders the rest of the class to flee, captured by an extreme high-angle long shot of the room: another manifestation of the characters' subjective feelings of being perpetually watched over by God (the omnipresent gaze of the camera), and living under His constant vigilance and judgment during a moment of religious crisis. As Alucarda and Justine run about the room in gleeful and disrespectful abandon, it recalls their carefree frolic in the fields, except now the unholy and profane "outside world" has infiltrated the closed system of the convent. Despite being quickly subdued by the nuns, Alucarda and Justine's sudden display of sacrilegious behavior throws the order of the convent into utter disarray.

The scene cuts to a close-up of Justine confined to bed, weak and ashen. A baffling illness is now suddenly sapping Justine's strength — Alucarda's parasitical, vampirical power over Justine draining her life force. At the request of the nuns, Dr. Oszek arrives at the convent to examine Justine. Claudio Brook's dual role constructs an important comparison and contrast between Dr. Oszek and his appearance earlier in the film as the Gypsy. In many classic mexploitation films, science and the supernatural are clear opponents: science representing the benefits of modern progress and enlightenment, the supernatural the dangers of past irrationality — for instance, the mexploitation cult-classic *El barón del terror* (1961, dir. Chano Urueta; U.S. title: *The Brainiac*).[24] In many mexploitation films, the caveat of science is that it must be applied responsibly and for the betterment of society. The reckless pursuit of science can and will result in the creation of monsters: mad scientists creating unspeakable, bizarre life forms, such as Dr. Karol's wax creations in *Santo in the Wax Museum* (Dr. Karol, as noted, was portrayed by Claudio Brook). Equally dangerously, science might *inadvertently* unleash the monsters of the past: hypnosis and past life regression in Rafael Portillo's *Aztec Mummy* trilogy; time travel in René Cardona's *Santo en el tesoro de Drácula* (*Santo in the Treasure of Dracula*, 1968); organ transplants in Cardona's *El horripilante bestia humana* (*The Horrible Human Beast*, 1968; U.S. title: *Night of the Bloody Apes*).

In this context, and despite López Moctezuma's own professed distain for traditional Mexican horror cinema, Alucarda essentially constitutes the classic mexploitation threat to society: the licentious, supernatural female of the past (vampire woman, witch) bringing havoc to the present, although perhaps less as the villain and more as a sympathetic anti-heroine. Likewise, Dr. Oszek, a figure primarily devoted to caring for his blind daughter and the pursuit of modern medicine, is the classic mexploitation supporting stock character of a dedicated father and scientist — the good patriarch and modern man — that becomes tragically parodied in *Alucarda*. By using Brook to play two widely divergent and even oppositional roles — the forces of the supernatural represented by the Gypsy, and science represented by Dr. Oszek — this collision is literally embodied *in the same man,* who eventually abandons rationalism amid the increasingly terrifying supernatural threat of Alucarda by adopting the methods of the film's other increasingly terrifying supernatural threat — the Catholic Church.

While Justine is treated through archaic medical science, Alucarda is subjected to religious persecution and ordered to confess her sins to the intimidating Father Lázaro.[25] Her confession quickly becomes a sacrilegious diatribe, defiantly proclaiming her love for Justine — *"Even enough to kill"*! She taunts Father Lázaro for his judgmental hypocrisy: his shame of the body, his disgust for sex, and his fear of life itself. To emphatically stress her point, she physically attacks Father Lázaro — not to injure him, but to force him to take her sexually (an especially perverse moment considering Alucarda is fifteen years old in the film). Convinced Alucarda's brazen and forbidden sexual advance is a clear indication of a demonic presence permeating the entire convent, Father Lázaro and the nuns engage in an intense bout of flagellation, literally beating the (sexual) evil out of each other, releasing and sublimating their own lust through masochistic sexual practices disguised as religious ritual. This collective flagellation is forcefully depicted by a series of high-angle shots which jump-cut between each other and linger on the bare, bloody backs of Father Lázaro, Sister Angélica, and other nuns as they kneel in submission. One particularly striking shot focuses on splayed flesh and quickly zooms out to a high-angle shot of a beaten nun on her knees, her gown pulled down around her waist to expose her back — an effect recalling the outrageous Eurotrash excesses of Jess Franco. The predominance of high-angle shots in this sequence again suggests the devoutly religious participants' own subjective states of humbling themselves before a disappointed, omnipresent God; it also implies God Himself is voyeuristically enjoying the spectacle.

As the whippings escalate in fury (matched by the increasing tempo of the film editing), the half-naked Father Lázaro delivers another portentous sermon equating sexual desire to demonic possession, and his verbose monologue is punctuated by two extreme close-ups. The first is of his eyes, not only emphasizing his own "strange eyes," but codifying him, within the conventions of classic mexploitation, as a figure of hypnotic evil, with the victims no longer young *chicas modernas* hypnotically attacked by monsters but troubled nuns hypnotically controlled by a priest — "the Father." This is immediately followed by a rather grotesque shot of his mouth as he barks the words, "The Devil!" Responding as a kind of Greek chorus, the nuns repeat "The Devil" several times in astonishment, perhaps as a subtle homage to Russell's *The Devils*. Indeed, *The Devils* (and the nunsploitation genre as a whole) is referenced when Father Lázaro produces a huge book detailing historical examples of demonic occurrences in European convents.[26] Various nuns are forced to read entries, with Sister Angélica, in a touch of dark irony, recounting an incident where possessed nuns began "levitating for hours." Of course, this recalls Sister Angélica's own frenzied praying which climaxed with both a paranormal phenomenon and an orgasm; however, her possession and levitation was the result of divine intervention rather than supernatural evil. Father Lázaro ominously announces that there is an "evil conspiracy against the Church" embodied by two "delicate creatures," and the camera literally circles the room as the nuns chime in about the events in the convent. When one comments on Justine's recent sensitivity to light, Father Lázaro triumphantly proclaims, "That's it! A heliophobic demon — that's a six category devil who hates light!" It is a priceless line that would be equally appropriate uttered by Silva in his role as Chief of Police in *The Brainiac*, where he played a similarly dour — or deadpan — opponent of the supernatural. Finally, the rotating camera returns to Father Lázaro, who portentously declares the dire situation requires drastic solutions: "We must prepare—*an exorcism*!" (perhaps referencing *The Exorcist*). His proclamation is met by another moment of dark comedy as the nuns emit highly melodramatic gasps in unison.

The flagellation is followed by what is perhaps the film's most shocking and outrageous moment: Justine's exorcism. A highly theatrical, precisely orchestrated spectacle, it not only savagely parodies Catholic Mass but the crucifixion of Christ by infusing Christian iconography with melodramatic excess and intense sadism. Alucarda is hauled into the church by a nun, and the camera focuses on her as she recoils in horror; the shot cuts to a zoom-in of Justine secured to a cross at the alter (again, recalling the obsession with camera zooms in Jess Franco's films). Alucarda is also tied to a cross, and both Justine and Alucarda become macabre parodies of the Crucifixion, made all the more noticeable in shots of Justine and Alucarda where huge statues of Christ on the cross can be seen in the background to provide a comparison within the shot. As a close-up depicts Justine in profile, Father Lázaro is seen in the background; his stylized, ornate red robes reference those worn by Silva as the Priest in *Mansion of Madness* as the nexus of pagan and Christian religion, consistent with *Alucarda*'s own dismantling of Christianity versus paganism. Over generic church organ music — used strictly for black comedy — Father Lázaro explains he will expel the demon inhabiting Justine's body, and orders Justine stripped to reveal the "mark of the devil" on her naked body (a mark which, of course, does not exist). Even more so than during the previous sermon, the nuns grow more agitated as they witness the exorcism; they writhe and extend their hands in the air, again suggesting both religious fervor and sexual arousal. Alucarda vehemently protests, defiantly and repeatedly condemning Father Lázaro with blasphemous venom: "*You'll die soon!*" Father Lázaro orders her silenced, and a hooded monk roughly slaps her across the face to render her unconscious. A lengthy, high-angle zoom-in slowly moves from a long shot of the naked Justine on the cross to a close-up of her face; this echoes the early shot of Alucarda's mother after giving birth, where a protracted zoom-in of a malevolent force "closing in" may be God Himself. As Justine is stabbed by long needles by hooded monks under the direction of Father Lázaro, presumably to release the (sexual) evil from her body through the flow of blood, Justine's pale, nude torso is fetishized by the camera as the needles slowly penetrate her flesh, the blood seeping out of the punctures and trickling down her skin. As the exorcism-crucifixion-sexual torture intensifies, the nuns throw themselves onto the floor in the throes of both religious frenzy and sexual orgasm (again, the dark bloodstains on their gowns over the genitals are unavoidable to the viewer). Catholicism, sadism, voyeurism, madness, eroticism, bloodshed, and the exercise of power converge in the unnerving, stylized, vicious, sexual spectacle of the crucifixion-exorcism, which fittingly features López Moctezuma's acknowledged homage to Sade: Justine.

Of course, the exorcism inevitably kills Justine — saving her soul by destroying her body. The ritual of human sacrifice is now the domain of the Catholic Church itself. Arriving too late to prevent Justine's death, Sister Angélica and Dr. Oszek halt the exorcism. Overcome with grief, Sister Angélica falls to her knees sobbing next to Justine on the cross, her unrequited and impermissible sexual longing for Justine expressed by the proximity of Justine's vagina next to her face in the shot. She bitterly asks the Mother Superior, "Where is the love?"— her realization that the convent is not designed for compassion and salvation, but domination and punishment. Horrified and incensed by what has transpired, Dr. Oszek denounces those in attendance for their unenlightened ignorance and archaic cruelty, comparing their actions to the deplorable excesses of the Dark Ages and the Inquisition: "I thought that reason had replaced superstition! This is not an act of faith! This is the most primitive expression of ignorance I've ever seen!" The battle lines between modernity and tradition — science versus superstition — are clearly drawn, with Dr. Oszek designated as the heroic figure of reason against the irrational brutality of Father Lázaro. However, in keeping with *Alucarda*'s complexities, the initial depiction and valorization of Dr. Oszek and the vilification of Father Lázaro is quickly problematized: the two become unlikely, and equally cruel, allies as events grow *more* unexplainable and horrifying.

Trial by Fire

Disgusted with the convent, Dr. Oszek rescues Alucarda from a similar fate as Justine's and takes her to the safety of his home. However, the killing of Justine and removal of Alucarda from the nunnery does not quell the supernatural mysteries; instead, they serve to escalate the terrifying events in the convent. A close-up of Justine slowly zooms out, revealing her dressed in a white shroud on a burial slab. Midway through the zoom, a nun standing next to Justine suddenly faints and collapses in a heap on the floor; it punctuates the somber moment with surreal comedy, not unlike Buñuel. After several seconds examining the scene, the camera slowly zooms in to a close-up of a nun in prayer beside Justine's body and slowly pans left to empty convent space. Suddenly, the shot cuts to Alucarda screaming as she awakens from a nightmare: or, more correctly, a dream proper versus the various states of delirium—"the dream of waking persons" and the "delirious estheticism" of the free indirect subjective—which composes much of *Alucarda*'s startling imagery and bizarre events. Her shriek signifies the unseen violence Dr. Oszek soon learns occurred at the convent. Despite his contempt for the Church after the exorcism, he grudgingly responds to an emergency summons by the Mother Superior: Justine's body and the nun holding the prayer vigil both mysteriously disappeared from the convent. As Dr. Oszek and the nuns argue over how Justine could have possibly vanished, a scream punctuates their bickering. Accompanied by dissonant and overwrought pipe organ music, a dark parody of both church music and the standard organ blast that frequently accompanies such moments in horror films, the missing nun is found dead, unexplainably burned beyond recognition, as if by the very "fires of Hell."

The situation becomes even more ghastly and grotesque when Dr. Oszek is brought to the chapel. The charred corpse of the nun has returned to life, twitching uncontrollably on a table. Quite perplexed, and thoroughly repelled, Dr. Oszek watches Father Lázaro handle the supernatural threat through his own inimitable methods as he decapitates the corpse, repeatedly hacking the neck with a machete until the head careens to the floor in torrents of blood. Shocked and stunned by the events he witnessed, Dr. Oszek—the figure of modernity—concedes defeat and ponders:

> For I studied at the University of Paris, it was proven to me time after time that devil possession was sheer nonsense or the sad result of the workings of an insane mind. They taught me that religion was a farce and a form of slavery, that the time had come to break the chains of superstition, the yoke of lies and falsehood. I'm a man of reason, and now I'm faced with something supernatural, which frightens me.

In this sense, *Alucarda* both expresses yet refigures the tense dialogue between modernity and tradition common in classic mexploitation films. Catholicism, specifically Father Lázaro, is depicted as a primitive and unenlightened force, and Dr. Oszek is repulsed by the savagery of the Church. Yet despite his bitter condemnations, he is also forced to accept and utilize the Church's own barbaric, irrational and even supernatural methods when rationalism cannot explain, yet alone provide a solution for, the strange and terrifying events. Dr. Oszek's own faith in rational science is shattered in the wake of horrific, inexplicable occurrences; it's a metaphor for Mexico's own crisis in faith over teleological modern progress after violent, horrible, and unfathomable events — the massacre at Tlatelolco. While the classic mexploitation films often ended with the triumph of modernity or religious faith over supernatural threats, Father Lázaro (religion, tradition) and Dr. Oszek (science, modernity) represent the limitations of their respective philosophies: *neither* is adequate to address the apparent threat embodied by Alucarda, and *both* tradition and modernity provide solutions to preserving social order which are ultimately as destructive as the actual danger posed by Alucarda.

Now convinced the danger is indeed demonic, Dr. Oszek is aghast to learn that Alucarda, who he rescued from exorcism and took into his home, is also a "receptacle of evil" for the Devil. Realizing the danger Alucarda poses to his blind daughter Daniela (Lily Garza), Dr. Oszek frantically rushes home, only to discover both Alucarda and Daniela are missing, with Daniela presumably the new target of Alucarda's obsessive, sexual-supernatural domination. With his battle against the occult taking on a new and personal urgency, there is a subtle but quite comical shot where Dr. Oszek is seen loading his doctor's "black bag" with religious objects — a cross and holy water — rather than medical equipment. Aware that Alucarda and Justine periodically visited the mausoleum, Dr. Oszek, Sister Angélica and several other nuns investigate. Cautiously walking into the crypt, Sister Angélica opens the coffin of Alucarda's mother: she recoils in horror when she sees Justine lying inside the coffin filled with blood. Justine arises, her naked body also coated with blood. Her murder in the Church, a parody of the crucifixion of Christ, is now matched by an equally perverse parody of the resurrection of Christ as a bloodied, and bloodthirsty, undead monster. She savagely begins to attack Sister Angélica, clawing at her with her fingernails, leaving large abrasions on her cheeks. In two brief shots, the camera assumes the point of view of Sister Angélica, with Justine directly facing the viewer as she hisses and flails with her hand, as if her attack was spilling off the screen and aimed directly at the audience (as noted, a film technique also used in *Mansion of Madness* to disrupt the barrier between screen and film audience). Sister Angélica does not fight back with physical violence, but again invokes the (supernatural) power of prayer, frantically pleading with God to save her and Justine.

It has a sudden, calming effect on Justine, who halts her assault and begins to stare blankly at Sister Angélica. Both relieved and elated, Sister Angélica caresses Justine's face, but unfortunately Dr. Oszek charges onto the scene, now as rabid a combatant of the supernatural as Father Lázaro. Despite Sister Angélica's frantic protests, he douses Justine's back with holy water, searing her flesh, smoke billowing off her body. No longer merely a symbolic liquid of religious faith, holy water becomes a substance infused with supernatural power. Thrown into an animalistic frenzy, Justine pounces on Sister Angélica and tears away at her throat with her teeth, severing her jugular vein. The vampire film motif of biting the victim in the neck is intensified to a much more visceral level, mocking the quaintness of mexploitation or even the slightly more explicit Hammer vampire sagas; it is far closer to the graphic gore of contemporary zombie films (specifically, the work of George Romero and Lucio Fulci). While Sister Angélica pitifully attempts to stop the flow of blood pouring from her neck, Dr. Oszek, oblivious to Sister Angélica's dire medical condition, continues to determinedly pour holy water onto Justine, who writhes in agony before finally collapsing onto the floor and dissolving into a smoking, bloody skeleton. The sequence is highly reminiscent of the ending of *The Brainiac* (specifically, the almost identical high-angle shots of the smoldering skeleton), yet completely parodied. In *The Brainiac*, the monster is destroyed with modern flamethrowers by the rational detectives (as noted, the Chief of Police was played by David Silva). In *Alucarda*, the paranormal power of holy water is implemented by Dr. Oszek, the reasonable man who rejects Reason, to destroy the supernatural threat.

With Justine now eliminated, it suddenly occurs to Dr. Oszek that Alucarda would be in the last place they search for her: the convent (as in Poe's "The Purloined Letter," the best hiding place is "hiding in plain sight"). Indeed, the scene shifts to the convent for the film's devastating climax. As monks, nuns, and orphans mill about the entrance hall, Alucarda, with Daniela in tow, appears at the top of a stairwell, staring down on them vindictively. As Alucarda furiously shouts the names of various demons, fire begins to explode throughout the convent, with several nuns and monks bursting into flames as they attempt to flee Alucarda's supernatural attack. The convent is no longer a place of Catholic sanctuary, but has literally become an inferno — a new Circle of Hell. Periodically inserted into the carnage is an extreme close-up of Alucarda's eye, with a flame reflecting in her iris, which no longer signifies the monster's power of supernatural seduction (hypnotism and the requisite close-ups of eyes), but now designates the monster as an agent of apocalyptic destruction. If the "voices of the past" were audible to Alucarda, Mexico's recent past is manifest as well: Tlatelolco. As the targets of Alucarda's supernatural assault either fall dead or frantically scurry for cover, the slaughter becomes a reenactment of Tlatelolco taking place in a 19th century convent rather than a 20th century public square.

Returning from the mausoleum, Dr. Oszek and the nuns transporting Sister Angélica's body enter the scene of carnage, and are promptly greeted by a wooden chandelier plummeting to the floor in slow-motion. As the walls shake and debris falls from the ceiling, Daniela breaks away from Alucarda and flees, tumbling down a flight of stairs — her fall also captured in extended slow-motion shots (the obvious comparison being Sam Peckinpah). Bursting into tears as her new object of consuming desire forsakes her, Alucarda follows Daniela's path down the stairs. Monks wielding beakers of holy water attack Alucarda; she constructs a wall of fire, and the monks burst into flames. When Father Lázaro appears to confront Alucarda, the viewer fully expects her prophetic remarks that he "will die soon" are about to be graphically fulfilled. However, before she can incinerate Father Lázaro, the nuns carrying Sister Angélica's corpse hoist her body in the air as she assumes (or parodies) Christ on the cross. Becoming disorientated at the sight of the mutilated Sister Angélica as the crucified Savior, Alucarda staggers about as her body begins to smolder until she collapses on the floor and slowly disappears. However, unlike Justine, she leaves no physical trace: she slowly evaporates into nothingness, leaving no bodily remains, her body a mere shell all along. In this respect, the scene suggests that Alucarda may have *never* existed, but was a manifestation of a collective psychosis and explosion of destructive rage: an objective force of inevitable destruction composed of the various characters' distressed psyches and ideologies. In *Alucarda*'s collision of modernity and tradition, and its inevitable disastrous result, Alucarda is both omen and ghost of Tlatelolco.

Ultimately, there is no sense of triumph at the end of *Alucarda*. The final, and quite stunning, long shot depicts the convent's alter and large crucifix saturated in roaring flames. Accompanied by ominous organ music, the camera slowly zooms in towards the burning figure of Christ as the end credits appear.[27] Midway through the closing credits, the zoom-in freeze-frames, trapping the fiery devastation depicted in the final image as a point in time and History which can never be erased or escaped. At the moment the freeze-frame occurs, the music abruptly ceases: the only remaining sound that of crackling fire. Fittingly, the last credit appearing reads, "Directed by Juan L. Moctezuma," as an authorial signature over the film's final, cataclysmic image.[28] In several classic mexploitation films, fire expunges the obsolete and dangerous past to create a modern and secure present: the detectives incinerating the monster with flamethrowers in *The Brainiac*; Santo burning the vampire women in their (vaginal) coffins with his (phallic) flaming torch in *Santo contra las mujeres vampiro* (*Santo versus the Vampire Women*, 1962; dir. Alfonso Corona Blake; U.S. title: *Samson versus the Vampire Women*); Santo waving a large wooden cross, which causes the coven of sexy witches to burst into flames at the end of *Atacan las brujas* (*The Witches Attack*, 1964; dir. José Díaz Morales). In *Alucarda*, the triumph of science or religion is turned on its head. The world in crisis defined by the unreasonable, the unexplainable, and the unsolvable is not salvaged by reason or faith. It is simply and completely obliterated in flames — the apocalyptic collision of modernity and tradition in a perpetual Dark Age.

4

The Filming of the Disaster:
Guyana, el crimen del siglo
(*Guyana, Crime of the Century*, 1979)

We'll set an example for others ... one thousand people who don't like the world the way it is.[1]
— Rev. Jim Jones, November 18, 1978

The Art of Trash

A legend in Mexican cinema, René Cardona, Sr., directed more than 140 films in virtually every genre from 1937 to 1982. He was also instrumental in defining the mexploitation era, directing six *Las luchadoras* ("Wrestling Women") films from 1962 to 1968 and numerous Santo films from 1966 to 1970. Moreover, by the late 1960s, several alternate versions of his *Santo* and *Luchadoras* films intended for international release incorporated topless females and inevitably included the word *sexo* in the title: *Santo en el tesoro de Drácula* became *El vampiro y el sexo* (*The Vampire and Sex*); *Las luchadoras contra el robot asesino* (*Wrestling Women vs. the Killer Robot*) became *El médico loco y el sexo* (*The Mad Doctor and Sex*); *El horripilante bestia humana* became *Horror y sexo* (*Horror and Sex*) — all made in the pivotal year of 1968.

Despite the occasional nudity and stronger violence, most of Cardona's mexploitation films remained quite consistent with their ideological project: a valorization of modern Mexico, represented by *luchadores* (or *luchadoras*), *chicas modernas*, and scientist-father figures, versus enemies of modernity, morality, and social progress, symbolized most often by vampires and mad scientists (*Santo in el tesoro de Drácula* is emblematic of such films). An exception was *El horripilante bestia humana,* which suggested a far more ambivalent study of modern Mexico. Not coincidentally, the screenplay was co-written by Cardona and his son, René Cardona, Jr., whose own films in the 1970s demonstrated a far more pessimistic critique of modernity than his father's films. A pivotal moment in Mexican horror cinema, *Bestia humana* was the last of the *Luchadoras* films, a loose remake of the inaugural film of the series, *Las luchadoras contra el médico asesino* (*Wrestling Women vs. the Killer Doctor*, 1962; U.S. title: *Doctor of Doom*). Released in Mexico a mere four months after the Tlatelolco massacre, *Bestia humana* centers on a young bourgeois man who is transformed into a rampaging monster by the misguided experiments of his scientist-father, a revision of that stock character in many mexploitation films who favorably represents patriarchy and modernity. The human-beast is eventually gunned down by police, serving as a metaphor of the growing divide between an older generation and a radicalized youth culture that culminated in Tlatelolco and its devastating effect on the dreams, hopes, and vision of Mexican modernity.[2]

Juan López Moctezuma demonstrated a strong knowledge of the Mexican horror film tradition, ironically utilizing its filmic conventions, cultural themes, and iconic stars (Claudio Brook, David Silva). However, he did not work in the mexploitation genre proper, specifically the horror-wrestling genre, and explicitly distanced his own work from such films; prior to venturing into horror cinema in the early 1970s, his formative career was divided between avant-garde theater and popular mass media (radio, television). In contrast, being the son of a Mexican cinema veteran undoubtedly facilitated René Cardona, Jr.'s entry into the highly restricted, rigidly bureaucratic, and tightly unionized Mexican film industry. He began his career in Mexican cinema in 1948 as a child actor in his father's films, and in 1963 he directed his first studio film, the romantic comedy *Las hijas de Elena* (*The Daughters of Elena*); he eventually helmed over 100 films until his death in 2000.[3] The younger Cardona was also a leading figure in mexploitation cinema during its peak in the 1960s, and arguably a key influence in its eventual progression into stronger exploitation territory. In 1966, Cardona Sr. and Jr. co-directed the Santo espionage adventures *Operación 67* (*Operation 67*) and *El tesoro de Moctezuma* (*The Treasure of Moctezuma*); *Operación 67* was among the first of many *lucha libre* films that included the requisite topless scenes for international release. In 1970, Cardona, Jr., made *La noche de los mil gatos* (*Night of a Thousand Cats*), an early example of Mexican horror cinema that broke sharply from the current trends in Mexican horror. Instead of muscular wrestlers and anachronistic monsters, *Night of a Thousand Cats* focused on a wealthy serial killer luring sexy young women to his castle to murder them, feed their bodies to his army of cats, and preserve their heads in glass jars. Replete with not only the requisite violence and nudity, but the camerawork and editing techniques of Eurotrash horror films of the era, *Thousand Cats* could easily be mistaken for a Jess Franco film.

Ultimately, René Cardona, Jr.'s notoriety resides in being Mexico's foremost low-budget exploitation filmmaker of the 1970s and 1980s: a dubious honor that earned him the title "the Roger Corman of Mexico." By the mid–1970s, his filmmaking strategy could be divided into two schools of thought. One was blatantly plagiarizing famous films and remaking them on limited budgets with an abundance of sex and gore (which will be discussed further in the next chapter regarding *Birds of Prey*). The other strategy was converting tragic and sensationalistic news stories into quickly-made, low-budget exploitation films. By the early 1980s, John Waters, not surprisingly, hailed the Cardonas as "the top directors in this field ... [and] had the nerve to announce plans to produce *Kill the Shah*, *Boat People*, and *Hostages* (who were then still being detained by the Ayatollah)."[4] In 1975, the Cardonas teamed with a vengeance for the notorious exploitation classic *Los supervivientes de los Andes* (*Survivors of the Andes*), released as *Survive!* for the American grindhouse and drive-in market. It is the grisly account of a true story: in 1972, a Uruguayan rugby team's plane crashed in the Andes Mountains with all presumed dead. Not rescued until over two months after the crash, the survivors resorted to eating the flesh of those who perished during the ordeal. While the Hollywood version of the event, *Alive* (1993), focused on a testimony of the human spirit in the face of incredible duress, *Survive!* posited the appalling dilemma of what occurs when humanity is thrust into a situation where modern conveniences are absent and transcendent ethics and morality becomes irrelevant. Hence, the distinction between the American titles: *Alive* a melodramatic affirmation of human existence; *Survive!* a brutal exploration of human endurance punctuated by an exclamation point. While directed by the elder Cardona, *Survive!* was written by René Cardona, Jr., and is better considered alongside his own horror-exploitation films in that it reflects one of his pervasive themes: the moment where modernity and barbarism converge, and the disastrous effects and aftermath of that moment. Indeed, an unfathomable human catastrophe that shocked the world served as the basis for the younger Cardona's own headline-spawned exploitation epic: *Guyana, el crimen del siglo* (*Guyana, Crime of the Century*, 1979).

White Night

On November 18, 1978, California Congressman Leo Ryan, three journalists (including NBC correspondent Don Harris), and a member of the People's Temple religious sect were shot and killed while boarding a plane in Guyana. However, Ryan's assassination was quickly overshadowed by reports that his murder was connected to a mass suicide at the People's Temple in Jonestown, Guyana. The predictable media frenzy was supplanted by unadulterated shock as conflicting accounts began to reach America. Initial reports of 400 members of the People's Temple committing suicide or being murdered mounted in the following days, and the eventual official death toll at Jonestown reached 913. The almost surreal events at Jonestown, perhaps inevitably, prompted a wave of conspiracy theories from both the Left and the Right.[5]

4. The Filming of the Disaster

The People's Temple, with the Reverend Jim Jones its unquestioned messianic leader, was an established, if controversial, church in California rather than simply a fringe movement of kooks. While his strange amalgam of Marxist rhetoric, Baptist fundamentalism, and Fascist organization confused many, Jones effectively built a congregation drawn mostly from disadvantaged minority groups in the Bay Area. In 1975, Jones was named San Francisco's "Humanitarian of the Year," and the following year the People's Temple represented a sizable enough voting bloc in San Francisco that mayoral candidate George Moscone and even Rosalynn Carter courted Jones during the 1976 elections.[6] In return, Jones was named to the Housing Board after Moscone's victory. However, the People's Temple frequently received highly negative press in California through accounts of Jones' unsettling sermons, reports of mistreatment of church members, and regular rehearsals of the "White Night"—a mass "revolutionary suicide." Numerous investigations into the People's Temple were also launched: welfare and Social Security fraud, tax evasion, child abuse, even allegations of kidnapping and murder. Denouncing the accusations as a conspiracy by the U.S. Government to destroy him and the church, Jones arranged to buy 27,000 acres in Guyana. By 1978, the entire church relocated to realize Jones' vision of a socialist Eden—and avoid eventual legal indictments.

At the request of several constituents fearing for the safety of family members, Leo Ryan and several journalists traveled to Jonestown to investigate allegations of squalor, physical abuse, forced labor, involuntary detentions, and continued mass suicide drills at the settlement. Several members of the People's Temple defected and accompanied Ryan's entourage to the airfield where the ambush occurred. Aware the U.S. Government would take decisive action against the People's Temple, Jones ordered the White Night to be carried out. The shocking, even lurid details became legendary, and lines of people drinking a mixture of cyanide and Kool-Aid became permanently etched in American popular consciousness—a surreal mixture of genocide and tabloid journalism. Jones, who tape-recorded his sermons and pronunciations, provided a lengthy "testament" during the White Night as well: a chilling, rambling, but surprisingly subdued combination of sermon, political manifesto, and pep talk underscored by the screams of the dying.[7] This proved quite useful for screenwriters, and was quoted almost verbatim for the climactic monologue in both *Guyana, Crime of the Century* (henceforth referred to as *Guyana*) and the much more tepid but equally exploitative 1980 CBS docudrama *Guyana Tragedy: The Story of Jim Jones*.

In America, Jonestown's effect on the national psyche was immediate. If the Manson family was used to define the counterculture as unwashed hippies roaming posh suburbs and butchering citizens with kitchen utensils, Jonestown symbolized liberal idealism and the Great Society as the Final Solution. As John Judge noted,

Pete Hamill called the corpses "all the loose change of the Sixties." The effect was electric. Any alternative to the current system was seen as futile, if not deadly.... Religious experiments lead to cults and suicides. Social utopias were dreams that turned into nightmares. The message was, get a job, and go back to church.[8]

Guyana Tragedy, which will be contrasted to *Guyana* in the course of this discussion, went to great lengths to dismiss the People's Temple members as pathetic misfits, and Jim Jones as a sex-crazed, drug-fueled, Bible Belt Rasputin. As unlikely as it would appear, trash cinema *auteur* René Cardona, Jr., provided a study of the Jonestown disaster that went beyond a denunciation of weirdo communes and cults to become, in its own atrocious way, a disturbingly profound study of modern civilization.

"Vile Garbage"

With true exploitation film timing, *Guyana* was completed and released less than a year after Jonestown and immediately targeted for the American grindhouse and drive-in circuit by Universal Studios, who bought the American rights and distributed the film during its initial theatrical run. Retitled *Guyana, Cult of the Damned,* this version added a portentous voiceover narration from a Jonestown "survivor" to provide a sense of documentary authenticity and some socially-relevant commentary. Universal also trimmed *Guyana* from 115 to 90 minutes, primarily to adjust the film to the standard B-Movie running time. However, this version also excised the more disturbing moments, such as the startling opening suicide sequence.[9] While the truncated, version prompted many to complain that *Guyana*'s most offensive component was its sheer boredom, many American critics found much in *Guyana* objectionable, even in its abridged version. Roger Ebert summarized many critical sentiments by denouncing it as "vile garbage ... nauseating and reprehensible ... mixes fact, fiction, and speculation with complete indifference" (these were among the more charitable remarks).[10]

To augment the exploitation component of *Guyana*, especially for its intended American market, Cardona enlisted a veritable all-star cast of second-tier American film and television stars. The primary cast was composed of recognizable actors and actresses who frequently appeared in lower-budget Hollywood films and prime-time television shows of the era: Stuart Whitman as "James Johnson" (Jim Jones); Gene Barry as "Lee O'Brien" (Leo Ryan); Bradford Dillman as Johnson's personal physician and "Johnsontown" medical director "Dr. Gary Shaw" (Dr. Larry Schacht); Yvonne De Carlo as Johnson's press secretary "Susan Ames" (Sharon Amos). Fading Hollywood stars consigned to B-movie status provided cameos, such as Joseph Cotten as "Richard Gable" (Charles Garry) and John Ireland as "Dave Cole" (Mark Lane), the Temple's attorneys. Lesser-known performers better recognized by drive-in patrons rather than mainstream television viewers rounded out the cast: Jennifer Ashley (*The Centerfold Girls*, *The Pom Pom Girls*) as Johnson's personal assistant and mistress "Anna Kazan" (Maria Katsaris); Tony Young (*Chrome and Hot Leather*, *Superchick*) as "NBN reporter Ron Harvey" (NBC reporter Don Harris).

Certainly, one is struck by the cosmetic and almost absurdly minor name alterations of the characters from their actual counterparts. In *Dragnet* fashion, *Guyana*'s disclaimer proclaims:

> The events depicted in this motion picture are based on the real and tragic suicides and murders that took place in Guyana in November 1978. The names have been changed to protect the innocent.[11]

Following this disclaimer, *Guyana*'s first shot is indeed a "shot." During the course of the film, subtitles in typewriter font periodically appear to inform the viewer of specific times and places. "Press Conference ... Modesto California ... March 1979" appears with a close-up of

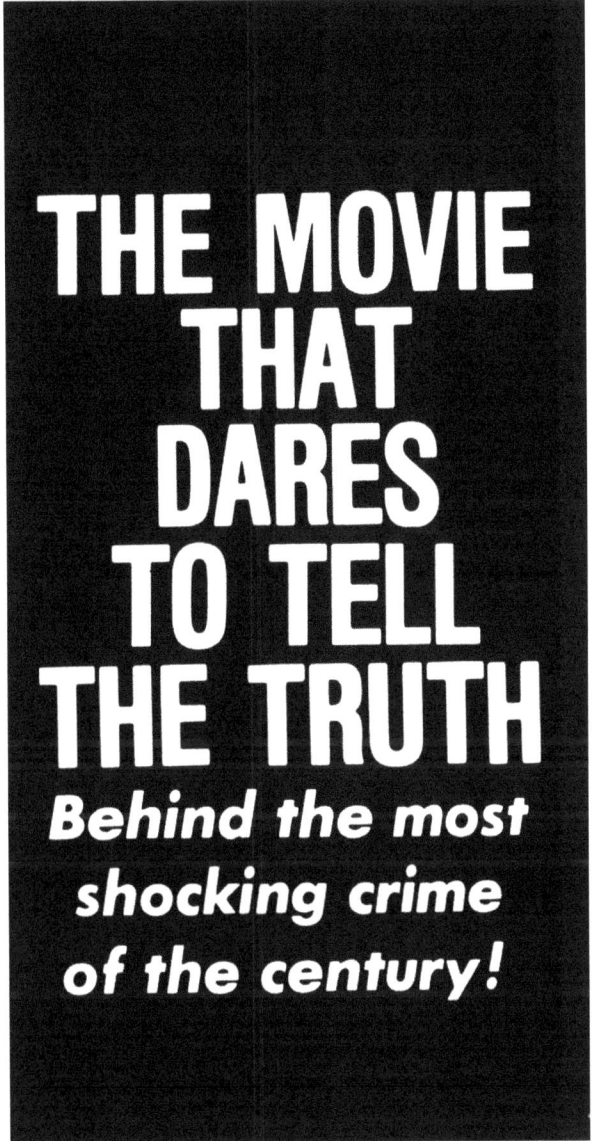

Truth in advertising? Promotional promise from a *Guyana, Cult of the Dammed* lobby card.

a hand holding a pistol. The camera zooms out to reveal an unidentified man as he places the gun against his temple and gazes into the mirror. As a gunshot rings outs on the soundtrack, the shot jump-cuts to an almost identical shot with blood now splattered on the man's reflection in the mirror as he plummets backwards. This incident did occur: People's Temple member Michael Prokes, a member of the Jonestown security force, committed suicide at a press conference in March 1979.[12] However, in *Guyana* it is not the particulars of the press conference and its potential revelations of conspiracy and cover-ups which are the film's focus, but simply the event: the act of suicide itself. While seemingly included simply for the shock value — the man is never identified in the film — it is only when the film *ends* that this seemingly extraneous and gratuitously grisly introduction to the film develops its profundity.

In that the opening "shot" of the film takes place months after the rest of the film, the press conference, the recollection of the catastrophe at Guyana, is manifest by a single definitive gesture: the obliteration of any memory of the event by repeating the event. The man commits suicide while he "reflects" in front of a mirror by shooting himself in the temple (People's Temple). In this context, one of the more enduring images of Jonestown became a photograph of corpses lying next to the patio and chair from which Jim Jones delivered his sermons, including his final testament during the White Night. Behind the chair was a sign inscribed with the aphorism of American philosopher George Santayana: "Those who do not remember the past are doomed to repeat it." *Guyana*'s shocking opening suggests the opposite: "Those who *do* remember the past are doomed to repeat it." In pivotal scenes throughout *Guyana*, Cardona references this sign, but fragments the wording through lighting or framing so the word "*repeat*" is emphasized: the *repetition* of events versus the *recollection* of events. If history serves to teach a social lesson, it does not necessarily provide a moral to avoid future disasters, but a model for reenacting future disasters.[13]

Meet James Johnson

Following the opening "shot" of the film, the credits are shown over stock footage of San Francisco. However, the seemingly innocuous sequence becomes more foreboding than it initially appears due to *Guyana*'s musical score, which primarily consists of a few recurring musical motifs — particularly an ominous, three chord ascending theme — which are used relentlessly throughout the film to underscore the chain of events that culminated in the White Night.[14] The music suggests that the disaster of Guyana is already beginning in the placid American city scenes: it simply has yet to reach its inevitable conclusion. In this respect, the closing shot of the credits depicts an anonymous building as the title boldly proclaims "GUYANA" in the center of the screen, the subtitle "Crime of the Century" in smaller letters underneath. The title fades out and a typewritten subtitle appears over the same shot of the building: "Johnson's Temple ... San Francisco ... early 1977." In effect, while the film begins in San Francisco, Johnson's Temple is already inscribed as being "Guyana" as well.

4. The Filming of the Disaster

    This cuts to a shot depicting the interior of the church from outside, through the front door. The camera slowly zooms in to physically enter the church, seemingly drawn to the vanishing point of the shot—a barely discernable pulpit. While the viewer can vividly hear the sermon (the voice), there is little visual source for the sermon (a body), and the moment the camera enters the church through the door, the voice proclaims the congregation will "pass through the gates of Heaven." The deliberately slow zoom-in and dialogue literalizes the fate of the congregation: from the moment one enters the church, the guarantee is death, if not necessarily an afterlife. A cut to a long pan from left to right has the camera surveying the congregation uniformly sitting and intently paying silent attention to the stern voice. In the background during this pan, the door the camera entered is now being physically closed by an usher. At the moment of entry into Johnson's Temple, one is literally trapped in the church, signified by the fact that the point where the camera and the film viewer entered the church no longer allows any exit or escape.

    As the sermon continues, the speaker's identity remains hidden; the scene is depicted by panning long shots of rapt churchgoers and an overhead high-angle shot of the pews and altar. In this respect, the opening shots of *Guyana*'s sermon are highly comparable to López Moctezuma's *Alucarda* and Father Lázaro's sermon. As in *Alucarda*, the church leader's invective is matched by reaction shots and long pans of intent and even interchangeable parishioners rather than depicting the speaker. However, Father Lázaro is, for the most part, never shown on the screen during the mass but remains an abusive, disembodied voice. Eventually, James Johnson is seen as well as heard after the initial shots concentrating on the congregation; the first shot of Johnson is the clichéd low-angle shot designed to convey his imposing presence as he stands behind the pulpit, with the film audience's view directed upward. As Johnson's protracted sermon continues, the alternation of shots between Johnson at the podium and the reaction close-ups and long pans of captivated (or *captive*) listeners also inevitably invites comparisons to Leni Riefenstahl's *Triumph of the Will*'s juxtapositions of Hitler and enthralled audience members.

    Guyana continues for the next ten minutes with Johnson's ponderous sermon heaping scorn and damnation on his enemies. Certainly, it demonstrates Johnson's paranoia and megalomania, providing an overview of Johnson's convoluted political philosophy as he veers dramatically between the far left and far right of the political spectrum. At one point he denounces the U.S. as a racist empire whose foot soldiers are the Ku Klux Klan. Moments later he condemns the U.S. as a new Sodom and Gomorrah of sex and drugs, a country of "moral angst and contemptible values" (Jim Jones' own adultery, bisexuality, and drug addiction notwithstanding—aspects of Jones' life that *Guyana* implies but were the sensationalized focus of *Guyana Tragedy*). Using a crude map, Johnson explains the impending move to Guyana and consolidates the long history of Johnson's ministry. In this way, the interminable opening sermon in *Guyana* serves the same function as the much more concise introductory narration in *Mansion of Madness:* dramatic monologue used to disguise and condense a substantial amount of plot exposition. With the background provided, and the audience all too aware of the outcome, the film eschews dramatic narrative, character study, and a detailed psychological profile of James Johnson which will provide an explanation for the inexplicable and motivate viewers to contemplate *why* Johnsontown occurred: the case of *Guyana Tragedy*.[15] The lack of narrative and character development is a concession to the fact that *Guyana's* primary interest — and the audience's unspoken interest as well — is not a thoughtful, teleological study of what lead to the horrifying events of Jonestown, but in graphically depicting and expressing the horrors of the unthinkable: the disaster in Johnsontown and its unspoken — and unspeakable — aftermath.

Johnson produces a thank-you list and begins to read the names of the various political personages and agencies instrumental in aiding Johnson's move to Guyana: The First Lady, the Vice President, the U.S. State Department, the former and current mayors of San Francisco. While *Guyana* is dismissed as tawdry exploitation of dubious accuracy, the film correctly notes that the move to Guyana was in part facilitated by Johnson's (Jones') established political connections, including logistical assistance from the U.S. Embassy.[16] However, while Johnson copiously extends his gratitude to his avowed enemies — the U.S. Government — an important event is inserted into the film: a murder. A montage is constructed between scenes of an unconscious man being carried through a railroad yard and placed on the tracks, a speeding train, and the body graphically ground to pieces under the train — all intercut with quick pans of the church members in the pews. The metaphorical implications of the montage is clear: the church members themselves are also inevitably going to be destroyed, crushed under the wheels of an oncoming train — the Johnsontown despotic machine as it careens towards inexorable carnage. To close the sermon, Johnson leads his worshippers in a hymn. As the singing commences he turns his back to them and stares directly at the camera (and film audience) with a sinister, maniacal sneer. The moment becomes pure melodrama: Johnson, the dastardly villain, expressing his contemptible evil to the film viewer. One fully expects Johnson to burst into histrionic, malevolent laughter.

Discipline and Punishment: The Despotic Machine

In *Alucarda,* the title "Father" (Father Lázaro) does not simply denote a figure of religious authority, but one of political and patriarchal authority wielding power through instilling a combination of devotion, shame, and fear in his followers with sexually-infused exercises of power. As his dictatorial reign over the Temple settlement grows more sadistic and irrational, James Johnson becomes a similar figure, whose authoritarian power is manifest in brutal spectacles of discipline and punishment, often with a sexually sadistic component. During a stormy night, three boys are caught in the compound's warehouse stealing food; in a moment of utterly black comedy, one of the boys is seen pilfering packets of Kool-Aid! The congregation is hurriedly gathered in the public square, and the boys brought before Johnson. "Your sons are also my sons, but they have shamed me — they have defied my laws!" One by one, Johnson asks each boy's parent the self-answering rhetorical question, "What shall I do with your son?" Each cedes their (biological) parental status to James Johnson, the community's symbol of definitive patriarchal control; one after another, the parents respond identically: "Punish him."[17] Their inevitable answer is followed by a melodramatic blast of dissonant music and a close-up of their horrified child's face. His anger building, the shot cuts to Johnson standing in front of the sign behind his chair: "Those who do not remember the past are condemned to repeat it." In an act of overkill, he barks out the words on the sign verbatim: a moment where the *written* word, which becomes a point of resistance later in *Guyana*, is subsumed by the *spoken* word. The Law is manifest in the singular, tyrannical voice of the community: James Johnson. Each boy is then punished through tortures more appropriate to South American secret police than a religious community: one tied to the ground and covered with snakes; the second repeatedly submerged in water; the third bound and shocked by electrodes attached to his testicles. Despite their particulars, the process of punishment is almost identical on-screen: brief montages of stripped, screaming boys tied in crucifixion position, with close-ups of each boy's tormented face the only way the viewer can distinguish each victim.[18]

However, the most disturbing shots occur after the torture sequence: a brief close-up of the screaming boy being electrocuted abruptly cuts to a black screen. After a few seconds, the shot is backlit when Johnson opens the doors, revealing the boys in the interior of the Johnsontown detention center. The shot cuts to a close-up of Johnson as he pronounces, "I forgive you, because I love you...." The close-up cuts back to the previous shot, with the towering Johnson standing in the center and the three frail boys kneeling around him — all silhouettes in the doorway. The shot, quite literally, suggests a dark parody of kitsch religious paintings (happy children gathered around Christ), as well as photo images of World War II concentration camps. "...And I will show you my true expression," Johnson concludes. Not only is Johnson's "true expression" completely indiscernible, but each boy is now completely indistinguishable. Individual identity is essential in establishing who will undergo punishment within the community, incidental during the punishment itself, and becomes meaningless in the aftermath of punishment. Johnson's expressions of love and forgiveness for his sons are not acts of benevolence but pure domination. As Horkheimer and Adorno noted:

The Mexican Cinema of Darkness

> The Fascist's passionate interest in animals, nature and children is rooted *in the lust to persecute*. The significance of the hand negligently stroking a child's head, or an animal's back, is that it could easily destroy them. One victim is fondly stroked and the other is struck down, and the choice made has nothing to do with the victim's guilt. The petting demonstrates that *all are equal in the presence of power, that none is a being in their own right*.[19]

The shot of Johnson and the huddled boys cuts to another "true expression" of power in Johnsontown, one that is positively Orwellian. A shot of a loudspeaker is accompanied by a mechanically distorted yet soothing voice of a woman broadcasting an elementary lesson in conversational Russian (Jim Jones was reportedly attempting to relocate the People's Temple to the Soviet Union just prior to Ryan's investigation, and many at Jonestown believed such a move was impending).[20] The shot zooms out to reveal a sign under the loudspeaker: "Johnsontown Agricultural Project." Certainly, the allusions are to Stalinism and the Soviet Union's concentrated efforts at forced collectivization and modernization: Stalin's professed goal of "dragging Russia kicking and screaming into the 20th century." However, when

Hard work is its own reward: uncooperative commune member punished in *Guyana*.

a young man attempts to escape from his daily forced labor, he is chased down by Johnsontown security forces. As he is tackled and restrained, the voice on the loudspeaker recites a Russian phrase and its English translation: "*I love you.*" She repeats the phrase: an act of repetition that augments the savage irony of community love being demonstrated by corporal punishment. As the agricultural project workers gather to watch, the man is held in place and mercilessly beaten from behind with a club (a phallic symbol of Johnson's Law manifest in the everyday practice of social control). Moreover, the scene references another exploitation film genre popular in the 1970s: the plantation film (*Mandingo, Drum*), where a scene featuring the whipping or beating of an escaped slave was as obligatory as a shootout in a Western or car chase in a crime drama. Again, beyond the sheer exploitation value, *Guyana*'s comparability to the plantation films of the era suggests that Johnsontown is indeed a modern plantation: a system of agrarian slave labor where the payment is not being punished. In this sense, Johnson is dragging Johnsontown kicking and screaming back into the 19th century.

Soon afterwards, Johnson sits by himself on his makeshift throne (an effect eerily reminiscent of a man sitting in an electric chair), and assorted members of the congregation bid him goodnight, presumably after yet another White Night rehearsal. However, Johnson observes a young couple in the nearby bushes having sex, electing to express their libidinal energy through sexual intercourse versus a demonstration of simulated self-destruction proving devotion and subordination to Johnsontown's (founding) Father. Both naked, the couple is forced to kneel before Johnson in the public square, in full view of the reorganized congregation. Three reaction shots follow: one of Dr. Shaw, and then two shots of the parents whose children were previously punished by Johnson. Their stunned and shamed expressions are not merely identical to the previous scene; it is the *same* footage recycled from the previous scene, literally suggesting the rituals of punishment in the Johnsontown community are constant and invariable. Pointing menacingly off-camera, Johnson loudly beckons: "Lázaro!" *Guyana* references Father Lázaro, the authoritarian enforcer of sexual discipline and punisher of sexual impropriety in *Alucarda*. A hulking African-American male pushes his way through the crowd, a low-angle camera shot accentuating his imposing size. Glaring at the young man on his knees before him, Johnson pronounces his punishment: "You will perform a sex act on another man! The entire community will be your witness!" Lázaro strips off his t-shirt and lecherously stares at the off-frame victim, now recalling another plantation-film genre staple: sex between races. This shot cuts to the naked young woman, her mouth agape but unable to even scream — to *voice* protest — as she vainly attempts to cover her face with her hands. The scene concludes by way of an utterly perverse montage derived from Alfred Hitchcock, a frequent source of material for the younger Cardona (to be discussed further regarding *Birds of Prey*). The montage of Cary Grant and Eva Marie Saint kissing in a sleeper car cutting to the train entering the tunnel, and its obvious metaphor for sexual intercourse, which concluded *North by Northwest* is harshly parodied in *Guyana*: the close-up of the woman's horrified reaction to the off-frame homosexual rape abruptly cuts to a streetcar plowing up a hill in San Francisco.

These sequences in *Guyana*, beyond generating the requisite moments of exploitation film shock value, become disconcerting essays on the function of punishment and power in society. Punishment must be a cycle of repetition as public spectacle in order to become entrenched in public memory and consciousness. It must be necessarily witnessed by the public, whose role is as vital to the spectacle as the person(s) imposing the punishment and the punished person(s). To witness punishment is to indirectly participate, and the passive spectator who does not intervene inherently sides with the punisher. Describing the function of public executions in *Discipline and Punish*, Michel Foucault wrote: "Not only must people know, they must see it with their own eyes. Because they must be made to be afraid; but also because they must be the witnesses, the guarantors, of punishment, and because they must to a certain extent take part in it."[21] Punishment serves to inflict a moment of indelible trauma on both the condemned person and the community as a whole. All punishment in Johnsontown is witnessed by the community, who must both endorse the practice and empathize with the victim, if only to the degree that they realize and are reminded they also can, and will, be the punished for breaking the law (the Law). The spectacle of public punishment becomes a sign of implied consent with the order, ingraining itself into each member of the community's psyche as a horrific memento of what occurs when the social code is violated. In punishment, one is reminded of the brutal consequences of both a *past* transgression and any *future* transgression.

After the public rape and a brief plot exposition constructed as an interview with reporter Harvey and Temple lawyer Gable, the scene returns to Johnsontown for their most important political ritual: a rehearsal of the White Night. In *Civilization and Its Discontents*, Freud contended that civilization is locked in a battle between Eros (love, sex, family, community) and Death (aggression, destruction):

> [C]ivilization is a process in the service of Eros, whose purpose is to combine single human, individuals, and after that families, then races, peoples, and nations, into one great unity, the unity of mankind.... These collections of men *are to be libidinally bound to one another*.... Man's natural aggressive instinct, the hostility of each against all and all against each other, opposes this programme of civilization. This aggressive instinct is the derivative of and the main representative of the death instinct ... the evolution of civilization is ... the struggle between Eros and Death, between the instinct of life and the instinct of destruction.[22]

However, Freud's dialectic between Eros and Death reaches synthesis in modernity often with dire consequences, as noted by Herbert Marcuse: "Only a strong

Eros can effectively 'bind' the destructive instincts. And this is precisely what the *developed civilization is incapable of doing* because it depends for its very existence on intensified regimentation and control."[23] Thus, Marcuse observed, "Civilization is plunged into a destructive dialectic: the perpetual restrictions on Eros ultimately weaken the life instincts and release the very forces against which they were 'called up'— those of destruction."[24]

As Johnson explains the U.S. Government's plan for "racial genocide" directed at the Temple, the congregation must be prepared to commit a "revolutionary suicide" in protest. The only way to prevent being destroyed is through destroying itself as the ultimate expression of community love: the libidinal force of Eros expressed and binding the entire community through its antithesis, the Death Instinct (and, to reiterate, the vital importance of publicly punishing the young lovers caught having sex instead of participating in the White Night ritual). As his worshippers listen, Johnson stands on his makeshift patio-altar-throne and reminds them, "We have rehearsed this night many times before." The medium long shot of Johnson is framed so the viewer can only read the bottom line of the sign behind him: "— *To repeat it.*" Through the continual rehearsal of the White Night, power is kept at the virtual. Johnson's power can be continually acted out as a form and forum of public spectacle where the religious revival and salvation show becomes a grotesque "community theater" of self-annihilation. Johnson's ultimate sovereignty, the power to determine the life and death of his subjects, can be continually exercised without being exhausted — in that the White Night can obviously only be actualized once. In this way, Cardona Jr.'s depiction of power manifest through ritual demonstrations and spectacles also recalls Pasolini's *Salò*, where power is expressed through elaborate and orchestrated performances of power that humiliate and debase the victims. However, very few are killed in *Salò* until the final exercise of power: the final solution as the final act of the theater of domination in an orgy of violence when all the victims are summarily and finally murdered while the torturers nonchalantly watch from a balcony with opera glasses. In *Salò*, torture and punishment becomes an elaborate, inexhaustible theater of power as long as it remains *virtual*: the moment one of the torturers places an unloaded pistol to one of the victim's head, pulls the trigger, and laughs, "We'd want to kill you one thousand times!" Likewise, when James Johnson asks, "Raise your hand those of you who will die for me," and leads his flock to their *faux* cyanide communion, the congregation can demonstrate their willingness to die for their father *ad infinitum* until the White Night inevitably becomes a horrible reality.[25]

Johnsontown becomes a brutal parody of the body-politic theorized in Thomas Hobbes' *Leviathan* (1651). Hobbes argued that the mutual fear of death motivates individuals to enter the social contract and form the body-politic under a sovereign power all obey: all men are created equal based on their potential to kill one another. As Giorgio Agamben noted, "The great metaphor of the Leviathan, whose body is formed out of all of the bodies of individuals, must be read in this light. The absolute capacity of the body to be killed forms the new political body in the West."[26] In *Guyana*, the "absolute capacity of the body to be killed" no longer forms a body-politic through the *fear of individual death* but the *promise of collectively dying*, to "hold hands and die" in a White Night. Johnsontown as a metaphor of the body-politic or a social machine's regression is not simply its degeneration into totalitarianism, but collective self-destruction: a truly "fascist state" that does not make power its goal, but inevitable and total destruction—above all, its *own* obliteration. In *A Thousand Plateaus*, Gilles Deleuze and Félix Guattari contended:

> [I]n fascism, the State is far less totalitarian than it is *suicidal*. There is in fascism a realized nihilism. Unlike the totalitarian State, which does its best to seal all possible lines of flight, fascism is constructed on an intense line of flight, which it transforms into a line of pure destruction and abolition.[27]

In this respect, Jim Johnson becomes a far more important figure than Ebert's glib appraisal as "Hitler meets Elmer Gantry."[28] In effect, Johnson is "the despotic signifier"—the centralized point from which all power and social organization emanates in a despotic "social machine." In *Anti-Oedipus*, Deleuze and Guattari formulated the evolution of Western civilization around the coding of "flows of desires." The first stage, "the Primitive Territorial Machine," is the structure of clans, tribes and nomads, characterized by the coding of desire and the construction of essential taboos: cannibalism, incest, and murder. As empires became established, the primitive machine evolves into the ""Barbaric Despotic Machine," the regimes of emperors and kings in which codes become "overcoded" through the central single ruler: a sovereign invested with surplus power to determine all law, conduct, and even give and take life itself. In turn, this despotic machine evolves into "the Civilized Capitalist Machine," where overcoded flows, stemming from the despotic signifier, become dispersed and disseminated into a system of coding and decoding flows of desire: multiplicities of capitalist exchanges determined by social contracts instead of sovereign decrees, and governments structured on physics (action and reaction, cause and effect, "checks and balances") rather than a sole figure or lineage of figures ordained by God.[29]

Defining modern authoritarian regimes as "regressive" is quite correct to the extent that the modern social machine, "the Civilized Machine," reverts to its previous stage, "the Despotic Machine"—the paradox of modernity, epitomized by Nazi Germany, where humanity progresses technologically and degenerates socially into modern barbarism. Rather than the absurd caricature of modernity constructed in the confines of the asylum in *Mansion of Madness*, Johnsontown represents the regression of modern civilization into a despotic and ultimately fascist-suicidal social machine. "Socialist utopia" becomes a system of the most obsolescent and brutal mode of production: slavery and forced labor (plantations, forced collectivization, and concentration camp). The methods of social control favored by Johnson — public spectacles of discipline and punishment — are themselves anachronistic according to Foucault, who claimed discipline and punishment are now effected in modernity by procedures of *surveillance* (prisons, asylums) rather than *spectacle* (Roman Circus, public executions).[30] As the despotic signifier in a perverse Leviathan, the single point through which *all* codes of desire within society must circulate (sex, love, family, work, and, finally, death), James Johnson is endowed with the privilege of inflicting punishment on the bodies of his congregation at his own discretion and slightest provocation. As Deleuze and Guattari contended:

> Overcoding is the essence of the law, and the origins of new suffering on the body. Punishment has ceased to be a festive association, from which the eye extracts a surplus value.... *Punishment becomes a vengeance*, the vengeance of the voice, the hand, and the eye now joined together on the despot.[31]

Pressing the Issue: Inside Johnsontown

While *Guyana* begins by depicting the situation in Johnsontown veering towards the already-known catastrophic outcome, and concludes with a harrowing depiction of the White Night, the middle portion of the film focuses extensively on Lee O'Brien's steadfast intentions to investigate Johnsontown, despite the objections of Johnson's representatives, the U.S. State Department, and even his own hesitant secretary, "Leslie Stevens" (a pseudonym for Jackie Speiers, played by German actress Nadiuska). The remainder of *Guyana* is spent constructing the confrontation between Johnson and O'Brien through an endless string of scenery-chewing monologues, melodramatic discussions, speculative ruminations, cryptic foreshadowing, and astringent subplots which are not introduced to provide dramatic tensions, narrative impetus, or even coherency. Ostensibly, many of these scenes appear designed to simply consume film time until the final tragedy at Johnsontown occurs; O'Brien's ill-fated arrival in Guyana is padded with several tedious minutes of travelogue-style footage as he drives through Georgetown, Guyana, before his contentious meetings with Johnson liaison Susan Ames and U.S. Embassy officials to demand access to Johnsontown. If *Guyana* becomes something of a test for the viewer's patience, it does so in part because the audience not only knows that conclusion of the film, but expects *Guyana* to provide a climactic, grisly depiction of the mass suicides: a resolution the audience awaits with impatient anticipation rather than dread as the film inescapably, if interminably, proceeds towards that goal.

O'Brien's decision to investigate Johnsontown is spurred by Johnson's refusal to return a child, in defiance of a U.S. court order: another plot point that allows Johnson, in a wonderfully histrionic speech by Stuart Whitman, to proclaim his self-appointed status as Father, God, and the Law of the Johnsontown body-politic. A long discussion decision Johnson and Shaw implies that Johnson is terminally ill, a reason behind his drug addiction and eventual decision to lead his followers to suicide: "If I die, what will happen to my children?" While the custody dispute did occur (it was a primary factor in Ryan's between to investigate Jonestown), Johnson's medical condition is pure fabrication on Cardona's part.[32] *Guyana*'s amalgam of "fact, fiction, and speculation" merges for a key reason: to reiterate the depiction of Johnson as the mad patriarch or "founding Father" of the community. In this respect, *Guyana* subverts the docudrama by violating the essential rule of the genre: not only to depict *what* happened but to offer some reasonable or moving explanation of *why* events happened, be it in the simplistic biographical study of *Guyana Tragedy* or the abundance of conspiratorial intrigue offered by the films of Oliver Stone (*Salvador, JFK*). *Guyana* offers an *expression* of the catastrophe of Guyana rather than an *explanation* or the antithesis of "social realism." The unanswered and unanswerable questions that November 18, 1978, inflicts on the viewer can only be addressed in the disconcerting spaces of *Guyana*'s text: the glaring plot holes, the lack of character development, and, above all, the waiting for the catastrophic conclusion. Rather than inept filmmaking, *Guyana*, even if unintentionally, manifests the inherent limitations of a text to adequately articulate, rationally explain, and fully comprehend a historical moment of disaster.[33]

Rather than government bureaucrats, O'Brien enlists a team of intrepid news reporters to accompany him, a strategy that *Guyana* implies was a conscious and somewhat opportunistic decision by O'Brien to sidestep the U.S. Government stalling his investigation by bringing his case directly to the American public through the power of the press. When O'Brien meets with uncooperative U.S. Embassy official "Alex Dressler" (a pseudonym for Richard Dwyer), the media presence becomes a major source of Dressler's concern (read: irritation).[34] Certainly, as a product of the late 1970s and the aftermath of Watergate, this depiction of crusading journalists against corrupt politicians was not uncommon (specifically, the Watergate docudrama *All the President's Men*). Several minutes of *Guyana* are comprised of the initial meeting between O'Brien and the reporters, or another "press conference," one that brings together O'Brien and the journalists so they can eventually die in Guyana: their investigation will not culminate with a sound explanation of events, but gunfire and death. Indeed, this press conference is soon followed by three scenes of separate reporters that foreshadow with heavy-handed melodrama the inevitable and deadly result of their investigation: one reporter tells his wife and children that this is the first assignment he is afraid to pursue; Harvey places his teenage son in charge of the home until he returns from Guyana; a worried father makes a special trip to see his photojournalist son one extra time before he departs in the event anything unforeseen occurs.

This preliminary meeting is also used as a platform by O'Brien to explicitly

4. The Filming of the Disaster

debunk the conspiracy theories involving Johnson and his ties to important figures in the U.S. Government and local Bay Area politicians as mere peripheral relationships established in the normal workings of city politics and the 1976 elections. While *Guyana*'s own stance on the issue of conspiracy is decidedly mixed, the apparent message of the film as expressed by O'Brien is that conspiracy is not the domain of legitimate politics (Watergate notwithstanding), but the rhetoric of pathologically paranoid cult leaders (James Johnson) and arrogant activist lawyers (Dave Cole): the real dangers to America. On a surface level, this is consistent with *Guyana Tragedy* and the message of Jonestown constructed in American public memory: any departure from mainstream American politics unavoidably leads to disaster. In this respect, *Guyana* also commits a glaring historical inaccuracy. Many of Johnson's followers are depicted as white and presumably from middle-class origins; in fact, with the exception of his elite inner circle, Jim Jones's People's Temple congregation was overwhelmingly composed of poor, African-American women and children.[35] By skewing the race, gender, and class composition of Johnson's congregation, the (false) impression is created that the victims at Guyana were not disenfranchised Americans whose circumstances quite unfortunately drew them to a Jim Jones, but hoodwinked, everyday citizens from the white middle-class suckered into the 1960s dream of a Great Society devoid of racial and economic inequality.

Prior to the film's conclusion, there is another press conference: an unsettling interview with Johnson by Harvey and the other journalists. Disconnected and distracted, Johnson stammers and fidgets in his chair, with Whitman's performance reminiscent of Humphrey Bogart's imploding petty fascist Captain Queeg on the witness stand in *The Caine Mutiny* (1954). The confrontational questions are met with Johnson's meandering contradictions, such as the issue of disciplinary tactics at Johnsontown: "I reject corporal punishment ... uh, we don't do that anymore." Asked about his critics in the U.S., Johnson responds with conspiratorial ramblings about the CIA attacking him for being a socialist, and Harvey's incredulous doubletake in response to the incoherent answer is priceless. While the seasoned, sensible politician O'Brien persuasively dismisses the idea of conspiracy for the viewer with cogent, logical arguments, the irrational cult leader Johnson can only articulate politics in terms of vague, paranoid diatribes. A question about the boy whose parents left Johnson's Temple and now demand his return is met with a bizarre response. Johnson orders the boy to stand next to him and Johnson pries the boy's mouth open to show them his teeth, as if he were displaying him at a dog or cat show ("the Fascist's passionate interest in animals, nature and children"). Johnson proudly exclaims: "See how much he looks like me?" The next question regarding Johnson having the sole privilege of unregulated sex in the church is met with an indignant response: "Oh, that's *bullshit*! We had thirty babies born here last year!" Not content with displaying his prized pet — his adopted son — he now extols his successful Johnsontown breeding program. Beyond the surprising, off-color language used by a minister (in fact, Jones' sermons were frequently punctuated with profanities), one can recall the punishment of the couple caught making love and wasting libidinal energy on sexual pleasure rather than conceiving children and producing new material for the body-politic. All sex must flow through Jim Johnson in order to maintain and perpetuate control of the community, the man who is every church member's "father" (in one scene where O'Brien interviews two young girls about their parents, they blankly respond that their father is "James Johnson" and scamper away). Moreover, given his own status as the only person who can and does have sexual relations at will, the regulation of sex in Johnsontown revolves around, for lack of a less vulgar phrase, "James' 'johnson.'" His own unrestrained libido and symbolic status as the sole male procreator becomes the symbol of unlimited phallic and patriarchal power in the community.

With the investigation set to close the next morning, there is still a lack of concrete evidence concerning alleged abuses. However, as the reporters are being escorted off the Johnsontown premises for the evening, Harvey is surreptitiously handed a note by one of the Temple members: a hastily scrawled plea to help them escape Johnsontown. When O'Brien first arrives at Johnsontown, he delivers an impassioned and somewhat overconfident speech, imploring, "Does anyone have anything they want to *tell* me?" (emphasis added). He is met with a long, uncomfortable silence for his answer as Johnson looks on assuredly. It is a desperate gesture of *writing* rather than *speaking* that begins the cycle of events that lead to the White Night. (In an odd moment of comedy almost parodying the Hope-Crosby *Road* films, Cole and Gable eventually escape the carnage by fast-talking the armed guards and convincing them they must be allowed to leave Johnsontown so they can *write* about the event and preserve its historical significance for future generations.)[36] No one may speak out against the Symbolic Father, the sole voice of authority. And ultimately, *Guyana* suggests the impossibility to adequately speak about the disaster in Guyana at all: before or after November 18, 1978.

The Last Day

A shot of the sun just above the horizon is underscored by the subtitle "Guyana, November 18, 1978.... The Last Day." The journalists return to Johnsontown; now armed with the note as material evidence of community dissent, their investigation becomes much more determined. Two reporters are refused entry to the locked barracks, the "Jane Pittman Place"—another allusion to plantations and slavery—and are threatened at gunpoint by a guard. Gable and Cole convince the guard to let the reporters investigate, and even Johnson's lawyers are shocked by the rows of emaciated people crowded into bunks—the shots again modeled on photos of Nazi concentration camps. In his final interview with Johnson, Harvey confronts him with the note, producing another rant by Johnson against a conspiracy of enemies attempting to orchestrate his downfall. Encouraged, several church members now "speak up" and announce their wishes to leave with O'Brien, which emboldens O'Brien to offer all church members the chance to leave with him. Johnson, growing more disturbed (in both senses of the word), unleashes another diatribe at the traitors and liars who have infiltrated Johnsontown. As arguments between the congregation members erupt, O'Brien realizes that the situation is quickly escalating out of control, and he hastily gathers his entourage and the defectors. However, a thin, bushy-haired man joining them is explicitly pointed out to O'Brien: "He's not really leaving. He's one of *them*." (Unnamed in *Guyana*, this was long-time People's Temple member Larry Layton.)

The scene shifts to the airfield, where O'Brien and the others frantically start boarding charter planes. A group of unidentified soldiers gravitate around a small tent next to the runway (not surprisingly, their mysterious presence is never explicitly addressed in *Guyana*).[37] A tractor towing a tarp-covered trailer also slowly approaches. Amid the confusion, Layton boards one of the planes, draws a pistol, and begins to indiscriminately fire before quickly being disarmed. Layton's initial attack is quickly followed by a group of men rising from the trailer armed with rifles, firing indiscriminately into the crowds gathered around the planes.[38] As the gunmen determinedly walk towards the runway with rifles blasting, the solders inexplicably retreat from the airstrip. Shown in long shots as they withdraw from the scene, they are rendered as ineffective figures, retreating not only from the gunman but from one of the individuals on the runway desperately seeking help. A dark parody of the classic Western or action-film shootout sequence ensues; it also constructs more explicit comparison in *Guyana* between the camera and the gun: the reporters begin shooting the attackers with their cameras, while the gunmen shoot the journalists with high-powered rifles. One montage depicts a reporter with a camera frantically shooting photos, cutting to a gunman deliberately aiming his rifle, and cuts back to the reporter being leveled by a bullet. Another reporter with a video camera is similarly mowed down as he attempts to film (or shoot) the scene as well. As others attempt to escape, montages are constructed between gunman seemingly pointing their guns at the camera and hand-held camera shots of the fleeing victims shown from behind, with the camera adopting the point of view of the gunmen — or even the rifle itself. After the gunmen depart from the scene, one wounded reporter staggers back to the fallen bodies: his first act is to pick up a discarded camera and take more photos. To be shot — by the camera or by a gun — in *Guyana* is invariably connected with dying. While the camera is endowed with the power to record the bloodbath, it is ultimately powerless to prevent it: precisely the situation the film viewer will soon be placed in when they are subjected to the horrifying depiction of the White Night, which they can only uncomfortably watch unfold as witnesses, or even passive participants, to genocide.

The final shot of the ambush sequence tracks O'Brien's sobbing secretary, Leslie Stevens, wounded in the hip, staggering down the runway until she locates and kneels over O'Brien's body. Two of the unexplained soldiers who fled during the assault now indifferently walk into the frame. They casually circle Stevens and O'Brien's corpse; shown from only the waist down, they are defined by military boots, crotches, and dangling rifles. With abject horror, Stevens surveys the scene, seemingly awaiting and even expecting her potential execution. However, the scene abruptly cuts away, and this final edit is perhaps the most disturbing moment of the ambush because any resolution of the massacre is left unanswered. Like the dumbfounded Stevens, the film does not determine if the slaughter has concluded, or is about to resume with a new set of faceless gunmen.[39] Instead, the scene suddenly cuts from Stevens and the airfield to a long shot of the tractor as it lumbers into the foreground of the shot, a picturesque sunset on the horizon in the background. As the gunmen dismount from the trailer and exit off-frame, one silhouette remains behind, standing stoically next to the tractor with rifle in hand and the setting sun behind him: another morbid parody of the Western.

The remainder of *Guyana* is (finally) devoted to an utterly nightmarish depiction of the mass suicides. Johnson begins a long speech; as noted, much of it is taken from the audio tape Jones made during the White Night. Entire sections are not only quoted but recreated aurally through Whitman's restrained but rambling oratory and the plethora of disembodied screams in the background as the film grinds towards its protracted, tormenting conclusion. Visually, the White Night is depicted in two primary ways. One is a relentless series of unnerving, wide-angle close-ups taken by a hand-held camera: equal parts surreal horror and home movie. These shots capture various members of the church, many of whom were introduced as ancillary characters throughout the film, lining up to drink the lethal Kool-Aid. Some willingly place the cup to their lips and drink, such as the young couple publicly raped for engaging in unauthorized sexual activity; they share the cup of poison with a sense of resignation rather than fear or jubilation. Others are less cooperative, and are held by the arms as the poison is poured down their throats — either with cups or with syringes. Particularly distressing is a shot of two children being administered the poison, the second of whom is one of the girls previously seen interviewed by O'Brien. She is dispassionately fed the cyanide-laced Kool-Aid as though she were obediently taking some slightly distasteful medicine. These disturbing close-ups are crosscut with long shots of church members staggering through the compound or huddled into rows of dead bodies. In one evocative shot, with numerous dying church members lurching in the darkness, the effect is highly reminiscent of the zombie film genre: the congregation as the (*White*) *Night of the Living Dead*. Moreover, in the background of this shot, one of the towering fence posts is intersected near the top by a large, florescent lighting rig: a sort of electrified, neon burning cross is formed, suggesting the

4. The Filming of the Disaster

White Night: James Johnson (Stuart Whitman) orchestrates the mass suicides at the conclusion of *Guyana*.

nighttime rallies of the Ku Klux Klan (with Jim Johnson the congregation's "white knight").

In this way, the depiction of the White Night — close-ups of the followers and longs shots of the scene, becomes a gruesome parody of the narrative formula Bill Nichols suggested D.W. Griffith employed in his melodramatic historical epics (*Birth of a Nation*) and John Ford in his Westerns (*Stagecoach*): "Long shots to convey the epic sweep of historical events, and close-ups to individualize those characters whose destiny we will follow."[40] Yet Griffith and Ford used these formal techniques to dramatize American history and articulate the mythic components of the Civil War, the American West, Manifest Destiny, and the American Dream. Cardona savagely parodies these same techniques to focus on individuals and their destiny (the close-ups) and convey an epic sense of history (the long shots) in order to depict the "death of a nation" through its self-destruction: the utopian dream of a racially and economically equal society — the Great Society of the 1960s — turned into a hellish nightmare, and the manifest destiny of Johnsontown a preordained course of mass suicide.

113

As the White Night progresses, there is a low-angle medium shot of Johnson: a long take where he faces the camera, urging his followers and extolling their actions. Almost immediately, the shot becomes saturated with a blood-red tint as a superimposed, photographic negative image appears over Johnson, matching his gestures but moving several seconds ahead of them. The voice grows distorted and almost unintelligible. Given the hallucinatory quality of the shot and sound, and the position of the camera looking up and facing Johnson, it suggests a point-of-view shot from the perspective of a disorientated, dying follower. However, it is also comparable to the closing shot of *Mansion of Madness* and the tinted negative of the asylum grounds: the world of reason darkened and reason dazzled. In *Guyana*, reason is similarly darkened and dazzled — with the color of blood. Moreover, the obvious implication of the shot is that Johnson is no longer an (overcoding) vengeful God, but now Satan himself; by extension, Johnsontown has now literally become Hell on Earth. As the overwhelming red tint fades, Johnson suddenly stops, his agitation replaced with a sense of relief, calm, and even gratification; he even absentmindedly removes his omnipresent sunglasses. The frenzy of orchestrating and actualizing the White Night becomes a source of intense sexual excitement for Johnson, who has achieved the pinnacle of sexual climax during the horrific proceedings where Eros and Death finally become indistinguishable: what Marcuse termed *the nirvana principle*, "the terrifying convergence of pleasure and death."[41]

Drawing to a close, the White Night grows more chaotic. As more individuals attempt to flee, they are gunned down by Johnsontown security forces. Anna Kazan is shown stuffing money into suitcases and planning an escape rather than joining her fellow church members in revolutionary suicide. Johnson's own wife and adopted son determinedly walk to the Kool-Aid stand and drink the poison; as a final gesture of devotion, she hands her lecherous husband a cup of poison before she falls to the ground. Johnson holds the cup and raises it to his lips, pausing several seconds before declining to take his own life. Suddenly, several gunshots explode on the soundtrack, accompanied by a montage of shots: a close-up of Kazan careening backwards on the edge of her bed and hanging upside down jump-cuts to an almost identical shot from a farther distance, with Kazan and her accomplices all dead in the office. Another gunshot is heard and the camera-shot cuts to a cup falling between a pair of staggering tennis shoes, which quickly cuts to a medium close-up of Johnson clutching a bullet wound in his neck (like Kazan, Johnson is shot by unseen and unknown assailants from off-frame).[42] He falls on his back and begins flailing on the ground; and like the death of Kazan, the shot of the mortally wounded Johnson cuts to the same shot from a greater distance as Johnson continues to writhe in agony. However, this cuts to a shot of Johnson lying face down on the ground, obviously dead, and *then* cuts back to a shot of Johnson on his back as he ceases convulsing. While the editing could be dismissed as mere continuity error, the act of being shot by the camera-gun and the process of dying also becomes another cycle of filmic repetition: the viewer sees Kazan die *twice*, and Johnson *three* times.

With Johnson's death, the camera slowly pans right, surveying the piles of dead bodies, the soundtrack noticeably silent. This cuts to another long shot that pans left across the carnage. Tall, vertical fence posts intersect with horizontal planks slightly above the ground: they become a series of connected, inverted crucifixes to symbolize Johnsontown's (de)evolution into Hell. Slowly, the camera zooms in to the sign behind Johnson's altar, now barely discernable in the shadows and darkness: "Those who do not remember the past are condemned to repeat it." However, the only readily identifiable words are *condemned* and *repeat*. The truncated version of the maxim again suggests the contradiction of history as preventing a repeat of the past and history as the inevitable reliving of the past, the paradox embodied by the man's suicide at the press conference in the first "shot" of the film: the moment of "reflection" and the memory of the past is matched by a gesture that replicates and reiterates the horrors of the past. Thus, the film comes "full circle," beginning and ending with a gunshot and bullet holes, and the credits appear over a freeze frame of another blood-red circle: the recycled shot of the sun suspended in the sky on the horizon that announced the Last Day. The sunrise that began the Last Day — the day Johnsontown became a "Circle of Hell" — has now become the sunset on the White Night. The all-too-familiar musical score begins again: the themes used to continually foreshadow the already-known outcome of November 18, 1978, now also serve as a lament, a eulogy, and a reminder of the White Night and the Last Day.

Whereas the freeze-frame of *Alucarda* depicted social order eternally engulfed in flames, in *Guyana* the world itself becomes frozen in time, locked in a perpetual apocalyptic sunrise/sunset on civilization; indeed, the final freeze-frame resembles a generic landscape photo one might find on a postcard, greeting card, or, more perversely, a condolence card. The Last Day/White Night becomes a moment of unforgettable and unfathomable horror seemingly destined to be continually repeated as an endless cycle of self-annihilation: recalling the disaster that occurred and foreshadowing the next catastrophe to follow. As Maurice Blanchot suggested, the moments of disaster in the modern era — World Wars, the Holocaust, the A-Bomb, genocides, ethnic cleansings, and one could easily add Tlatelolco and Jonestown — become so devastating on the psyche of humanity because they do not represent the exceptional, catastrophic breakdowns in modernity, but moments of the disastrous potential inherent in modernity that become the Rule: "The 'disaster,' a rip forever ripping apart, seems to say to us: there is not, to begin with law, prohibition, and then transgression, but rather there is transgression in the absence of prohibition, which eventually freezes into Law, the Principle of Meaning."[43]

5

Lines of Flight, or Death from Above: *Ataque de los pájaros* (*Attack of the Birds*, 1986)

> *The revolutionary war is a war of the masses.*
> —Mao Zedong,
> *The Little Red Book*

A Remake for The Birds

When a ghastly headline could not provide a screenplay, Rene Cardona, Jr., simply "borrowed" the scenario from a popular or well-known film without any pretense of postmodern "homage" and remade it with less money and more sex and violence; *Tintorera!* (*Tiger Shark!*, 1976), for instance, was a shameless, low-budget copy of Steven Spielberg's *Jaws* enhanced with nudity and graphic if unconvincing violence. However, Alfred Hitchcock was most often the recipient of Cardona's "King Midas-in-reverse" touch. *Ciclón* (*Cyclone*, 1977) was a gore infused copy of *Lifeboat* (1944), with a laborious pace that made Antonioni look like an action-film director. Focusing on a group of individuals marooned in the ocean on a tourist boat after a hurricane, Cardona dispensed with the stagy banter and U-Boat threats in favor of cannibalism and a rousing finale of shark attacks which kill off most of the cast just as the rescue planes arrive. In 1986, *Ataque de los pájaros* (*Attack of the Birds*) took Hitchcock's *The Birds* to the point of the Theater of the Absurd: birds begin attacking the world, they stop, and they may or may not start again. The film subsequently appeared in American drive-ins, grindhouse theaters, and the burgeoning home video market under a variety of fairly generic titles—*Beaks: the Movie*, *Evil Birds*, and *Birds of Prey* (the version to be discussed, and henceforth the film will be referred to by that title). While the film's strained rationale is provided by some fairly explicit ecological messages, consistent with several horror and science-fiction "nature's revenge" films of the ecology-conscious 1970s (such as the

1972 AIP classic *Frogs*, dir. George McGowan), *Birds of Prey* is far more than environmentalist lip service. It is a sly parody of Hitchcock, a sardonic study of the horror genre, and a complex theorization of politics.

One of the more confusing and frustrating aspects of *Birds of Prey* is its narrative construction. Many horror films — the haunted house film and the slasher film subgenres in particular — focus on a specific, frequently isolated location; a select group of imperiled characters within that site; and a determinedly teleological series of events which usually eliminate various characters in the course of the protagonist(s) defeating the malevolent force. (This is not to say that most horror films offer definitive conclusions; most opt for open-ended resolutions, often to allow for a sequel or potential series of films.) In the case of *Frogs*, the locale is a mansion in the Florida Everglades, and the cast is a small group of characters revolving around a provincial, abusive landowner and family patriarch, Jason Crockett (Ray Milland). In *Frogs*, the attack is specifically directed against Crockett, his family, and associates; and those who do not flee the property are dispatched one by one by a variety of animals (snakes, alligators, fish, and, of course, frogs). However, there is little sense that the battle is anything beyond a local feud.[1] In *The Birds*, the bird attacks not only center on a specific group of people, but concentrate on a select individual: Melanie Daniels (Tippi Hedren).

Conversely, *Birds of Prey* freely veers between various characters and locations across the world. Scenes are abruptly truncated, interrupted, and alternated to the point it seems the film was either edited at random or with a deliberate attempt to subvert any and all continuity and narrative cohesion. As a result, *Birds of Prey*'s narrative is essentially a set of independent subplots connected by the film's central premise of a sudden, global attack on humans by birds. Limited continuity is provided by the film's two American stars, Michelle Johnson as journalist "Vanessa Cartwright" (a parody of actress Veronica Cartwright, who appeared in *The Birds*) and Christopher Atkins as her cameraman and boyfriend Peter. As the bird attacks multiply, the duo travel to various locations and report on the strange events through mock news broadcasts and interviews with other characters (with "mock" used in both senses of the word); they are also caught in a massive bird attack at the conclusion of the film. Other characters include a contentious married couple, Carmen (Sonia Infante) and Joe (Salvador Pineda), vacationing in Puerto Rico with their children; a Spanish farmer and his wife, Arthur and Olivia Neilsen (Aldo Sambrell and May Heatherly); an elderly Spanish hunter, his daughter Sharon, and granddaughter Kathy (the name of Veronica Cartwright's character in *The Birds*); tourists in South America seen early in *Birds of Prey* to provide some expository logic for what will unfold, courtesy of a tour guide's monologues; and two horny teenagers introduced into the film so, in keeping with 1980s horror film logic, they can be killed or maimed after they have sex.[2]

"Trash" Cinema

The current state of the horror genre, specifically in the wake of Wes Craven's *Scream* (1996), has been a preponderance of "self-awareness," or horror films *about* the horror genre as much as being horror films; a situation which quickly reached the ultimate level of self-reflexivity in Craven's *Scream 2* (1997), where a new set of murders revolve around a film ("Stab") based on the events of the first film, itself an ironic study of the slasher-film genre. However, more often the "self-aware horror film" is simply a collection of plot points and scenes borrowed from other films, justified by a continuous, self-conscious referencing of the genre — as epitomized by *Final Destination* (2000, dir. James Wong). Most of *Final Destination's* character surnames are derived from important producers, directors, or actors from classic horror films ("Alex Browning," "Ms. Lewton," "Billy Hitchcock," "Larry Murnau," the FBI Agents "Wiene" and "Shreck," etc.). *Final Destination's* plot is itself a loose conflation of two *Twilight Zone* episodes: "Twenty-Two," where a woman escapes death in a plane crash due to a premonition; and "The Hitchhiker," where a woman is pursued by Death after she fails to realize she has already died in a car crash. These plot devices are coupled with a series of supernatural killings which appear to be gruesome accidents derived from films such as *The Omen* (the death of Billy Hitchcock, decapitated by a piece of metal debris hurled by a passing train, is markedly similar to the death of Keith Jennings in *The Omen*, decapitated by a glass windowpane thrown from a passing truck). At its worst, *Final Destination* becomes little more than a contest between the film and audience as to who can outguess the other in the constant juxtaposition of shock and red herring plot manipulations, and who can outshine the other in horror film literacy.

To say *Birds of Prey* does not take itself seriously would be a gross understatement: its emphasis on self-reflexivity and inner commentary borders on pure self-ridicule. While *Birds of Prey* demonstrates a self-awareness that rivals any recent horror film commenting about its own status as a horror film, it is not a postmodern exercise in cultural referencing and demonstrating genre fluency, but rather an application of Bertolt Brecht's theatrical aesthetic of a "direct changeover from representation to commentary."[3] In the opening credits, a brief series of shots depicts birds flying around and feeding in a garbage dump. Certainly, this is included to reinforce the environmentalist implication of the film: nature literally reduced to existing on the garbage which natural resources become in modern economies. Unlike the other transitional establishing shots of the film, there is no explanatory subtitle to provide the viewer any information as to where this scene is specifically occurring: the garbage dump is a generic space that serves as metaphor for the modern world as a whole. However, it is within this credit sequence that the names of the two Hollywood stars appear: Christopher Atkins and Michelle Johnson. Moreover, they are the *only* two cast members whose names appear in this garbage dump

5. Lines of Flight, or Death from Above

sequence; the remainder of the credits are shown over footage of South American landscapes, villagers, and the plethora of visiting foreign tourists (a metaphor for the Latin American production core and the various international producers and actors involved in the film). While Atkins and Johnson possessed a degree of name recognition for U.S. viewers in the mid–1980s, this was primarily due to their inauspicious film debuts. Atkins achieved a modicum of fame by starring opposite Brooke Shields in the soft-core, teen-porn version of *Robinson Crusoe*, *The Blue Lagoon* (1980). Johnson's first major movie role was in the much-maligned Hollywood comedy *Blame It on Rio* (1984), portraying the Lolita-like teen sexpot and love interest of Michael Caine. By featuring the names of the film's marginal U.S. box-office draws over shots of a garbage dump, Cardona readily concedes, even delights in, the fact that the stars of the movie are literally appearing in trash — or that Atkins and Johnson are themselves the trash in the film.

Despite his top billing, Atkins is regulated to sidekick and comic-relief status as Peter; his primary purpose in the film is to provide sophomoric sex jokes and sarcastic asides about the film's events. While Atkins tends to shamelessly overact and hammer the material into the ground with little comedic discretion, Johnson is bland, stiff, amateurish, and miscast as a seasoned, globetrotting journalist (Johnson was 20 when the film was made, and looks substantially younger). However, to say Johnson's performance is unconvincing or that Vanessa is not a believable character is not critical disparagement, but rather suggests that she is a key component to the complete lack of verisimilitude manifest in *Birds of Prey*. In her on-location news reports that punctuate the film, Vanessa becomes a character-as-commentator who serves as an intermediary between the movie and the audience as she explains key points in the film and editorializes about their significance, often times speaking directly to the viewer via the camera (the movie camera assuming the point-of-view of the news camera). Her monologues are at once melodramatic, portentous, and self-referential: a mixture of ominous descriptions, woeful jokes, and sardonic commentary on the premise and status of the film.

Early in the film, and much to her displeasure, Vanessa is given the assignment to interview Arthur Neilsen, a farmer recently and inexplicably attacked by his chickens. "This is ridiculous ... a story about attacking chickens," she complains, one of her many commentaries about the implausibility and outright absurdity of the film. (Later, during her interview with the elderly hunter partially blinded in a bird attack, she interrupts his grim ruminations about the impending "war" between humanity and the birds by sarcastically remarking, "I'm having a hard time believing this!") Her report about the "attacking chickens" begins like a standard TV news story: a long take of Vanessa talking into a microphone as she walks through the Neilsen farm, providing a ludicrous monologue disguised as a journalistic report that sets the stage for the film as it escalates in both grisly violence and sheer absurdity:

It happened here. These coops are filled with happy chickens. Happy creatures: or so it would seem. Then one day, and for no apparent reason, they launched an attack on their owner. The feathered mutiny spread and these turkeys joined the fray—and it's not even Thanksgiving. This would have been dismissed as a sick ... as a *single, freak* incident—except for one thing. We'll be right back to tell you about it. Stay tuned! Cut!

When Vanessa says "a sick ... a single, freak incident," she pauses after saying "sick" and then over-enunciates the words "single" and "freak." It appears Johnson badly flubbed the line and Cardona simply did not bother to re-shoot the scene. While this may be true, or whether the misspoken line was intended (perhaps to create a sense that Vanessa is "winging" her report), the effect is the same—it momentarily but effectively disrupts any verisimilitude in the film, with the audience startled that the lead actress appears to have badly stumbled over her dialogue and it was left in the finished film.

In filming the report, the news camera and the movie camera are initially undifferentiated; Cardona does not film the news story footage to make it appear to the audience that it was filmed by a mobile news camera (using video tape or different film stock). Rather, the distinction between the two cameras comes when Vanessa closes her report by inviting the viewer to "Stay tuned!" and the film camera pulls back to include Peter within the shot: filming Vanessa with the news camera. What was thought to be a point-of-view shot from Peter's news camera is revealed to be a shot from the film camera when Peter and his camera actually appear in the shot, breaking the filmic illusion by making the viewer conscious of the camera they assumed was filming Vanessa. In this respect, the various news reports that punctuate *Birds of Prey* not only feature Vanessa in her journalist-as-commentator role, but alternate with shots of Vanessa being filmed by Peter within the shot, as well as shots of Peter holding the camera and at times seemingly pointing it directly at the film camera (and the film viewer). The camera within these news reports, and internal commentaries, overtly announces its presence to the viewer, reminding the audience that they are not only watching a film, but, in effect, watching the film being filmed. The degree the camera is made conspicuous to the viewer within the film is taken to a level comparable to Godard.[4] *The Birds*, despite its implausibility, is nonetheless a thoroughly believable on-screen world: at times, *too* harrowingly realistic.[5] At no time in *Birds of Prey* does the audience buy the premise, characters, or events—nor does the film allow any kind of audience engagement beyond a detached bemusement.

Back(lash) to Nature

Following the initial bird attack which begins the film (to be discussed at length shortly), the opening credits begin where, to restate, the American stars appear over shots of a garbage dump. The lengthy credits sequence continues with a shot inside the cockpit of a passenger jet as it approaches an airstrip; the subtitle designates the location as "Cuzco, Peru." The association between human and avian forces is manifest in a long (and rather unsubtle) montage alternating between the jet landing and slow-motion shots of a bird descending from the air and landing on a rock, signifying the impending territorial conflict in which birds will not only challenge humanity invading its airspace, but take the offensive and attack humanity on the ground. As the credits continue, the location shifts to Inca ruins, the subtitle now designating the location as "Machu Pichu, Peru." A group of tourists wander through the site while the tour guide relates the myth of how the Incas created their cities in the mountains with the help of giant birds, who transported the enormous rocks. After their task was completed, the Incas "made war" against the birds, who returned to the heavens and one day "will return as birds of fire to punish man." The scene cuts to another shot depicting a new location: a small charter plane flying over mountains, and the subtitle "Enigmatic 'signs' of the Nazca 100 B.C.—Pre-Inca Culture of Peru." The plane becomes yet another intrusion into the birds' airspace. The same tourists fly over the famous, mysterious ancient markings: expansive shapes and drawings that can only be seen and deciphered from the air. The tour guide explains that these markings may have been made as "beacons" thousands of years before the invention of flight and could somehow be connected to the myth of the great birds—or, as a young girl excitedly proclaims, "Spacemen!"[6] Theories of "ancient astronauts" aside, the signs are introduced as evidence of a strange and unexplained historical *past* between humanity and avian life, and the tour guide's reminder that "man's *future* was linked to the arrival of the fiery birds that come from the heavens," with the birds one day exacting their revenge. In *Birds of Prey*, the Inca myth not only provides a thin attempt at narrative inner logic, but, more importantly, reinforces a key theme of the film: nature's eventual retribution for its continual exploitation by humanity, specifically manifest in the exploitation of the *labor* of the great birds, and the Incas who "made war" against them when their services were no longer required. Shortly afterward, in a brief sequence jarringly inserted into the film (lasting less than thirty seconds), the tourists are in a powerboat off the coast of what is designated "Ballestas Islands, South America"—the sequence intended to simply point out a specific site where "pollution and contamination threaten these animals with extinction." Not only is the relationship between humanity and nature defined by exploitation of animal labor as "beasts of burden," but by the disregard for their habitat as a usable and disposable resource.

    The location shifts to "Villanueva del Pardillo, Spain," featuring an old hunter at his estate attended to by a nurse, presumably recovering from a health crisis; the walls of his den are decorated with numerous skulls of animals—trophies of his former efficacy as a hunter. He is promptly attacked by an owl and partially blinded (the importance of which will be addressed shortly). This is followed by the first news story by Vanessa and Peter, reporting on a famous marksman. In a morbid in-joke relating to the previous scene, the marksman has achieved fame because he is capable of shooting birds in flight while *blindfolded*. The reporters are disgusted by the sharp-shooting display. Vanessa's news report, delivered directly to the film viewer, is infused with indignant sentimentality about the abuse of the birds, while Peter incredulously confronts the esteemed marksman. Asking him why he does it, the marksman issues a terse, one word reply: "*Pleasure.*" The domination of nature is no longer limited to exploitation of labor and resources, but destroying nature for sadistic satisfaction.

Later in *Birds of Prey*, when Vanessa and Peter are driving between location reports, a news bulletin on the radio recounts two recent bird attacks: the couple assaulted by an eagle in Acapulco (which opens the film), and a priest drowned by ducks while he was fishing (a moment not depicted in the film, but one which could have easily been a scene out of a Buñuel film). While their skeptical reaction epitomizes *Birds of Prey*'s brand of acerbic self-commentary, it also suggests another important aspect in the growing battle between mankind and the birds:

> PETER: Shit, the whole world has bird fever! They're becoming star material! (Peter imitates a B-movie trailer voiceover) Ladies and gentlemen, just what you've been waiting for — brought to you direct from everywhere! BIRDS!
> VANESSA: Shut up — I'm trying to hear this.... This has to be some kind of weird joke: chickens, canaries, ducks — give me a break!
> PETER: Look at those chickens over there — (A shot of Vanessa and Peter in the front seat from the front of the car, through the windshield, cuts to a slow zoom-in of chickens being cooked on a roaster in a store window)
> PETER: Now, if they were my buddies being roasted skew [sic] — with a skewer ... with a skewer up my ass, I'd be a little upset, too!

Beyond the strained attempts at humor and the in-jokes — the birds "becoming star material ... brought to you from *everywhere* (the film's baffling and constantly shifting locations) — it appears Atkins also flubbed his last line and it was simply left in the film. More importantly, the scene adds another element of war between humanity and birds: the exploitation of nature not only through labor, pollution, and sadism, but as food for humans — the bodies of animals, as well as natural resources, become objects of consumption.

A Peck on the Cheek, a Poke in the Eye

Birds of Prey begins with a crucial, three shot montage. A close-up of an eagle is followed by a couple kissing on a moonlit beach with the subtitle "Acapulco, Mexico" — information not only provided to designate the first of numerous shifting locations in the film, but referencing a popular romantic getaway for honeymooners and lovers. In turn, the shot of the couple cuts to a long shot of the city streets at dusk where birds have massed on the electrical lines weaving through the city; they are mobilized and lined up as if in a sort of military formation (close inspection of troops). Two key themes of *Birds of Prey* are established. One is how *Birds of Prey* treats sex and violence beyond the usual parameters of the horror film — both as dark comedy and as sweeping politics of sexuality beyond psycho killers and dead cheerleaders. The opening montage and association between the bird(s) and amorous couple suggests that the kiss is not a romantic gesture but a precursor to rapacious violence. This, in turn, leads to the film's second and perhaps most ambitious theme, to be discussed at length shortly: the "nature" of historical and political transformation through the forces of the mass movement.

As the credits sequence begins, the opening shots are essentially repeated: now daytime, the close-up of the eagle forms a montage to a couple kissing before they venture of a cliff in their hang-gliders: a "lover's leap" where they take to the air with large, artificial wings. They become human-birds, and their action constitutes an invasion of the birds' domain and territorial space. As the scene unfolds, several shots alternate between lengthy shots of the couple soaring in the air and close-ups of the eagle, who almost seems to register a sense of palpable anger at the couple (the cynic might suggest the eagle is the most emotive actor in *Birds of Prey*). Eventually, a slow-motion long shot of the eagle taking flight to inaugurate the war between humanity and birds coincides with the credit "A René Cardona, Jr. Film" appearing over the shot. The bird of prey, the source of the film's violence, is explicitly linked to the name of the director. Later in the credits sequence, precisely when the tour guide utters the words "to punish man," it is not coincidental that the final credit appears on the screen: "Directed by René Cardona, Jr." The equation of the director, the birds, and punitive violence is played out as macabre comedy in a recurring motif throughout the film: the birds' aggression specifically directed against victims' *eyes*. In this context, one can compare Hitchcock's legendary and often highly symbolic cameos in his films, specifically *The Birds*. In the opening sequence, Melanie is startled by a flock of birds. Then, as she enters a pet store, she passes Hitchcock leaving the pet store with two poodles. Shortly thereafter, Mitch Brenner (Rod Taylor) enters the pet store to buy two lovebirds, establishing the film's "couple logic" between Melanie and Mitch. The inherent and unconscious violence in the couple's relationship is manifest by the presence of the birds (both the wild birds and caged lovebirds), with Hitchcock designated as having master status over the couple, both as characters in the film and as actors working under his direction. Keeping in mind Hitchcock's notorious comment that actors were "cattle," in *The Birds* they become his own couple of pet poodles, which he literally keeps on his leash and at his whims.[7] In *Birds of Prey*, the film's source of violence is specifically connected with the director, and his stars literally consigned to the garbage dump.

One of the more infamous aspects of *Birds of Prey*'s opening sequence is that the first five minutes of film time is consumed by endless aerial shots of the hang-gliding couple and the bird circling them. The viewer quickly surmises what will eventually occur — a violent attack by the bird — with emphasis on the word *eventually*. The initial attack becomes a parody of Hitchcock suspense: waiting as events develop only to have them resolved in a completely unpredicted way (the master stroke of *Psycho*'s killing of the star a third of the way into the film); not wondering what will happen, but *knowing* what will happen and waiting to see when and how it occurs (in *Psycho*, the revelation of the killer's identity); including red herrings into the plot, or what Hitchcock termed "the MacGuffin" (the stolen money in *Psycho*). In *Birds of Prey*, suspense is negated by being drawn out to the point of sheer tedium. When the bird attack finally occurs, it does not come with a sense of tense anticipation, but a sense of relief that the protracted waiting is over and the fully expected has finally occurred.

The bird first swoops in to slice the man's throat with his beak and then tears out the man's left eye with its talons. As alluded to, the film's emphasis on birds gouging out the victims' eyes becomes a running commentary about the horror genre throughout the film; as Carol J. Clover noted, "Horror privileges eyes because, more crucially than any other kind of cinema, *it is about eyes*."[8] As much as sex and violence, horror films are obsessed with *seeing* (particularly Hitchcock films such as *Psycho* and especially *Rear Window*).[9] In *Birds of Prey*, the bird — the figure of violence explicitly matched with the name of the director — begins its eventual assault on the helpless hang-guilder pilot suspended in midair, who represents the audience held in suspense, or incessant waiting. The bird forces the victim to "hang around" for what seems an endless amount of time before literally "going for the jugular" and then gouging out the eye: a sardonic metaphor of Cardona's treatment of the film viewer.[10] Ocular assault becomes a kind of wicked running joke in *Birds of Prey*. The film's second bird attack is essentially a repeat of the first. When the elderly hunter walks onto the balcony for some fresh air, an owl perched in a tree suddenly flies towards him in slow motion. The shot cuts to a close-up of the man staring in horror, and directly at the camera, and quickly zooms in to an extreme close-up of his eye. This shot abruptly cuts to a medium close-up of the man's face as he reaches to cover his eyeless socket gushing blood as the bird flies away, the eye now grasped in its talon. To add insult to injury, the owl simply returns to its perch, seemingly oblivious, even contemptuously indifferent, to the horror it has inflicted. In a subsequent attack, Vanessa and Peter film an interview with Arthur Neilsen inside a church — the large, stained-glass window behind the altar ironically depicting a dove. After he recounts the strange incident when the denizens of his poultry farm turned against him, Vanessa releases a canary from a bird cage. The tiny bird immediately swoops to assault Neilsen and narrowly misses his eye, instead gashing him just below the eye socket: a moment of black comedy where a bird attack indeed becomes "a peck on the cheek"— referencing the opening montages of the kissing couple and the vengeful bird(s). Ultimately, the war between the birds and humanity is a matter of survival, and one of the essentials of survival is sexual reproduction.

Animal Husbandry

To reiterate, *Birds of Prey* begins with a three-shot montage of the close-up of an eagle, a couple kissing on a moonlit Acapulco beach, and a mass of birds mobilized in the city— associating an onslaught of impeding animal violence with the romantic couple. This dark undercurrent contained in the sexuality and relationship of the couple is also a central theme in *The Birds*, even if it's not as overtly misogynistic as other Hitchcock films such as *Psycho* or especially *Frenzy* (1971), which is little more than a filmed series of rape and murder fantasies. In *The Birds*, the first bird attack occurs in an almost archetypal Hitchcock scene. Melanie, intrigued by Mitch after the pet store meeting, decides to surprise him and pursue a potential relationship by buying his sister Cathy two pet lovebirds for her birthday. As Mitch watches Melanie approach his waterfront home by boat through his binoculars, Melanie is attacked by a seagull: a material manifestation, or symbol, of Mitch's unconscious masculine rage and revenge against women. In one sense, it his reaction to Melanie's intrusion and the possibility of being trapped as a "caged lovebird"; in another sense, it represents his own desire to punish and tame Melanie, his own potential "pet."[11] Misogyny becomes most directly expressed in *The Birds*' finale, the protracted assault on Melanie after the birds trap her in the attic: Hitchcock's deliberate and systematic filmic depiction of tearing the modern, sophisticated woman to shreds, a metaphorical gang-rape infused with an excess of sexual sadism where even the beaks pounding through the wood of the attic door become signifiers of repeated vaginal penetration.[12]

Like *The Birds*, *Birds of Prey* is steeped in sexual politics. The film's Spanish title *Ataque de los pájaros* can be read with *pájaros* as a pun on the world *parejas* ("partners" or "couples"), and could be rephrased as *Ataque contra las parejas: Attack on the Couples*. Throughout *Birds of Prey*, relationships between the main characters center on the primacy of the heterosexual couple: Vanessa and Peter, Carmen and Joe, Arthur and Olivia Neilsen, the amorous teenagers, even the old hunter and his attending nurse. Moreover, it is the couple that is a primary object of attack by the birds (*pájaros* versus *parejas*). The victims in *Birds of Prey* are either the male component of the couple or both members of the couple, as opposed to the woman who is ultimately singled out for prolonged punishment in *The Birds*. In the aforementioned opening hang-gliding sequence, the boyfriend is blinded and killed while his girlfriend successfully fights off the attacking bird. Joe and Carmen's children discover the mutilated body of a young man hanging on the door of the mobile home like a hunting trophy, killed after he and his girlfriend had sex; his injured girlfriend survived the attack and joins forces with Joe and Carmen's family. Conversely, the old hunter and his nurse are both killed, as are the aging Neilsens, who are savagely ripped apart by birds in their small home in a long, blood-spattered, slow-motion sequence which could be described as *The Birds* directed by Sam Peckinpah rather than Hitchcock.

The exception is the relationship between Vanessa and Peter, which is played out as a parody of the sophomoric, teen sex–comedy genre. Johnson's nude scenes are obviously done by a body double, and done in such a way that the nudity cannot be seen as anything more than blatantly and excessively gratuitous. When Vanessa leaves the shower, Cardona inserts a brief, full-frontal nude shot with the body double's head cut off at the neck by the top of the film frame in order to obscure her identity: the cardinal signature of bad photography via cropping the head of the person in the photo. Moments later, when Vanessa leaves the hot-tub to answer the phone, Cardona simply recycles the *same* full-frontal shot of the body double, providing an effect more disorientating and hilarious than erotic or titillating. Of course, the name "Peter" has its inevitable allusions to the penis, none-too-subtly reflected when the sexually aroused Peter is left alone in the soapy water and laments the situation after he learns the phone call is a breaking news story they have to cover. Mugging like a bad burlesque comic, he engages in a rhetorical discussion with his genitals: "Well, buddy, better luck next time!" His comment is also directed at the male spectator denied the obligatory and much-anticipated sexual tryst, who will also need to have "better luck next time" when watching a low-budget horror film and expecting an abundance of sex and nudity.

Cardona's *Night of a Thousand Cats* and *Los placeres ocultos* (*Hidden Pleasures*, 1988; U.S. title: *Playback*) are films about "couple politics" expressed through disturbing studies of the power dynamics of sexuality (rape, murder, sadism, masochism) in the genre context of horror (*Thousand Cats*) or erotic thriller (*Playback*).[13] *Birds of Prey* explores the question of sex and couple logic in terms of sexual reproduction — specifically, the reproductive power of the birds being threatened by both the destruction of their breeding grounds and their placement in captivity. When Vanessa initially is given the assignment of investigating the bizarre wave of bird attacks, she complains that she went to college for "journalism, not animal husbandry." Midway through *Birds of Prey*, Vanessa and Peter film a news report at a zoo, and the crux of the report is an interview with the zoo's resident bird expert, Dr. Murayama (Kunio Kobayasy), intended to provide some narrative rationale, environmentalist editorial, and exploration of a crucial thematic element of reproduction and its political implications within the film. Dr. Murayama explains that birds in captivity "react in an entirely different manner" than birds in the wild, often demonstrating "the unwillingness to mate." In this sense, the birds' refusal to reproduce becomes a political gesture and protest against captivity: a sort of revolutionary suicide and an attempt to end the cycle by not producing new birds doomed to exist in confinement — the space of the zoo, where birds are displaced trophies in the course of modern progress, subsisting as souvenirs and objects of curiosity to tourists. The prospects are equally bleak for the birds in their natural environment, where their migratory cycles and nesting grounds are being destroyed by pollution, urban growth, the appropriation of and consumption of natural resources and animals, or simply by Mankind dominating and destroying nature for pleasure. Cryptically, Dr. Murayama observes, "Many birds are subject to extinction; that is, of course, *if man does not destroy himself first*" (emphasis added).

This theme, the inherent danger of modern progress as a means for humanity to destroy itself, was very much a concern in the classic mexploitation era of the 1960s, despite the often otherwise idealistic vision of Mexican modernity embraced by these films. These ranged from the general threat of misapplied science (notably *El horripilante bestia humana*) to the specific danger of nuclear war strongly voiced in *Santo, el Enmascarado de Plata contra las invasión de los marcianos* (*Santo, the Sliver-Masked Man versus the Invasion of the Martians*, 1966; dir. Alfredo B. Crevenna) — a theme most appropriate for the Cold War era.[14] In the 1980s, with the resurgence of pre–1960s ecology movement attitudes towards nature (Ronald Reagan's famous comment that "trees cause more pollution than nuclear energy"), Dr. Murayama's warning suggests that the possibilities for mankind to destroy itself is indeed potentially limitless — be it with the proliferation of devastating atomic bombs or teeming garbage dumps.

As with the "chicken attack" report, the zoo sequence begins with the film camera assuming the viewpoint of Peter's new camera. During Vanessa's report, the long take of Vanessa talking and wandering through the paths of the aviary abruptly cuts to a shot of Peter not even filming her, but instead recording the antics of flamingos in a nearby pond; again, it disruptively differentiates the news camera and the film camera, which initially appeared to be the same camera. Moreover, Vanessa constantly breaks the somber mood, and filmic illusion, of the sequence by frequently yelling at Peter to pay attention when his camera wanders. Like her other reports, Vanessa's news story functions as a disguised combination of plot exposition, social commentary, and ironic self-reference:

> Here we are surrounded by different and beautiful birds ... this wonderful habitat, where birds appear to live in relative freedom. As you can see, we can share the same space with these wonderful creatures, and one gets the impression of being in some kind of paradise.

Of course, the dark comedy and satirical commentary of the report is manifest by the fact that the birds live in "*relative* freedom," and "we can share the same space with these wonderful creatures" by keeping the birds at levels of manageable confinement in captivity. Several close-ups of birds in the aviary are taken from outside the cage where they are literally tapped in the confines of the frame by a wire fence running across the screen and in the background. Nor is it coincidental that the birds allowed the greatest freedom in the zoo — ostriches, peacocks, and flamingos — are flightless birds or birds whose capacity for flight is severely restricted (the case of flamingos, which require expansive spaces in the wild to implement their ability to fly). As the sequence concludes, Peter films the tranquil, flightless birds wandering the grounds before he pensively observes a flock of birds flying over the zoo, augmented by over-amplified flapping wings and excessively ominous music. The "shared space" between humanity and nature becomes a harmonious "paradise" only if nature can be constrained, contained, and controlled.

A Thousand Pájaros: Macrohistory, Mass Movements, and the War Machine

In his reading of *The Birds*, Slavoj Žežik suggests that the title characters are "a massive, oppressive, material presence ... a mute embodiment of an impossible *jouissance*."[15] While *The Birds* is frequently interpreted in psychoanalytic terms, with the birds as manifestations of raging unconscious impulses (misogyny, irrationality, pleasure, *jouissance*, transgression), in *Birds of Prey* the birds as "a massive oppressive, material presence" represent the unrestricted forces of political and historical transformation. In *A Thousand Plateaus*, Deleuze and Guattari posit two levels of history: *macrohistory* and *microhistory*.

> On one hand, *masses* of *flows*, with the mutations, quanta of deterritorialization, connections, and accelerations; on the other hand, *classes* or *segments*, with their binary organization, resonance, conjunction or overaccumulation, and line of overcoding favoring one line over the others. The difference between macrohistory and microhistory has nothing to do with the length of the durations envisioned, long or short, but rather concerns *distinct system of reference*, depending on whether it is *an overcoded segmented line* or *the mutant quantum flow*.[16]

Macrohistory is defined by "mutant quantum flows" of mass movements; microhistory is defined by "overcoded segmented lines" of class and national conflicts. However, as Deleuze and Guattari suggest, "The rigid system [microhistory] does not bring the other system to a halt: the flow [macrohistory] continues beneath the line, forever mutant while the line totalizes."[17] While the macrohistorical flows and microhistorical lines are "distinct systems of reference," the two are necessarily intertwined: macrohistory is always manifested in microhistorical moments or events; microhistory is always propelled by the underlying macrohistorical force or flow.

5. Lines of Flight, or Death from Above

By way of comparison, D.W. Griffith's silent epic *Intolerance* (1916) juxtaposes pivotal microhistorical moments of civilization in crisis, underscored by the macrohistorical flow: the Fall of Babylon, the crucifixion of Christ, the St. Bartholomew's Day Massacre in France (1572), the United States of America in the era of World War I and the impending Russian Revolution (in one scene where striking workers are machine-gunned by solders, a billboard reads, "The same today as it was yesterday"). However, while the previous three microhistorical segments end in ruin and devastation, the contemporary American microhistorical segment manufactures a melodramatic happy ending and ultimately arrests the macrohistorical flow itself: the U.S.A. as a utopian end of all History. In *Birds of Prey*, the macrohistorical force — the birds — assumes predominance as the sheer speed and power of the mobile and mobilized mass that affects and disrupts the sedentary and segmented microhistorical line:

> Mass movements accelerate and feed into one another (or dim for a long while, enter long stupors), but jump from one class to another, undergo mutation, emanate or emit new quanta that modify their class relations, *bring overcoding and reterritorialization into question, and run lines of flight in new directions. Beneath the self-reproduction of classes, there is always a variable map of masses.*[18]

The macrohistorical surge in *Birds of Prey* is antithetical to *Intolerance*: macrohistory is not categorized and "pigeonholed" into microhistorical eras in which it periodically surfaces, and eventually reaches its teleological resolution with the United States in the early 20th century. The birds represent the very moment the seething force of macrohistory surfaces to subsume the Earth as a whole, reflected in the abrupt and often bewildering narrative shifts between the numerous characters in various parts of the world, only related by recurring images of large flocks of flying birds: "lines of flight" underneath the segmented subplots all experiencing and being disrupted by the exact same and harrowing event — the "massive, oppressive, material presence" of the birds first depicted in the third shot of *Birds of Prey*, with the birds converging on the city and perched on the electrical lines *en masse*. The mass movement no longer fumes "beneath the line." It literally becomes a material presence *on* the line in full force.

Throughout *Birds of Prey*, the struggle between humanity and the birds is explicitly stated to be a "war" through portentous observations peppered with black comedy. Shortly after being attacked, the old hunter is interviewed by Vanessa and Peter. With his missing left eye heavily bandaged and inevitably drawing the viewer's attention, he gazes out the window and ponders: "I get the feeling I'm being — [long dramatic pause] — *watched*!" Following the gruesome in-joke, he adds, "It seems organized ... these birds seem to be in a rush to prepare a war ... billions of birds at war with mankind." After the Neilsens are killed on their farm, Vanessa provides a typically ironic news report: "The scene is macabre. The bodies of Arthur and Olivia Nielsen were found bloodied and mutilated. The victims of doves; the same white doves that have been a universal symbol for peace, and they have now declared war, a mysterious war against mankind." Certainly, most of the bird attacks are influenced by, if not essentially stolen from, *The Birds*: the murder of the Neilsens; the extended sequence with Joe and Carmen's family trapped in their car on the beach as birds bombard the vehicle; the attack on Cathy's birthday party which leaves her grandfather and his nurse dead and everyone else seeking refuge inside his house while the birds attempt to invade the home by shattering windows or coming down the chimney. Yet given the heavy-handed allusions to war made by the characters, the depiction of the bird assaults are also comparable to war movies as well.

As the bird attacks increase in intensity and locations, in accumulation and acceleration, Vanessa and Peter are trapped in a small Spanish town isolated by hordes of birds which have successfully cut off the roads and are massing for a final assault. Their frantic conversation with local officials in a tavern plays out like a requisite strategy session seen in a standard war film. A police officer points to a map, which the viewer cannot see within the shot, and explains, "These two areas — here ... and *here*—were already attacked ... this morning ... at dawn." Not only could the clichéd dialogue be derived from any war film, but by stating the attacks occurred "here ... and *here*," the battery of constantly shifting locations in the film becomes a generic site that is now simply "here ... and *here*" under continual assault by the forces of nature. Yet in keeping with the acerbic self-commentary of the film, the dire tone is completely undercut when the mayor explains that they are in a "precarious situation," and Peter retorts, "You mean we're *sitting ducks!*" The shot cuts to Vanessa, her eyes rolling, as she remarks, "That's not funny, Peter!" and Peter responds, absolutely deadpan, "It's not meant to be funny!" In fact, the exchange cannot help but being anything but intentional self-parody in the improbable realm of B-movie horror occupied by *Birds of Prey*.

Realizing the futility of trying to escape the bird attacks, impossible due to the sheer mass and mobility of the birds, Vanessa and Peter convince the besieged locals to centralize power in targeted areas, to mass their own force against the birds by moving bodies into the target zones rather than away from them. With the roads blocked, the only available mode of transportation is a passenger train. The antithesis of the mobile, fluid "lines of flight" of the attacking birds, the train is perhaps the definitive symbol of modernity — the machine on a fixed course determinedly moving from one point to the next unless — or until — it derails (as noted, a train also serves as a metaphor for the Johnsontown social machine literally grinding up bodies in its path in *Guyana*).[19] More specifically, the climactic train attack parodies the World War II saga *Von Ryan's Express* (1965, dir. Mark Robson), in which an American officer (Frank Sinatra) leads a group of mostly British escaped POWs and hijacks a train to escape to unoccupied Europe; they narrowly escape a bombing

5. Lines of Flight, or Death from Above

raid by the Royal Air Force and an attack by *Luftwaffe* fighters pursuing the hijacked train. In *Birds of Prey*, American journalists Vanessa and Peter assume control of a train piloted by Spanish soldiers and whose passengers are mostly British punks — one even sports the Mohawk haircut commonly known as a "kingfisher."[20] The air assaults, needless to say, are provided by the birds.

In this context, another concept central to *A Thousand Plateaus* can be considered: the *war machine,* which is used by Deleuze and Guattari in a far more complex sense than its common connotation as a military-industrial complex. The war machine is simply concerned with mass mobility, mobilization, and movement — the macrohistorical "constellation" which houses the specific microhistorical "stars": nomadic tribes, ancient Empires, and the modern State.[21] However, the State is not simply the constitutional framework of government:

> States are made up not only of people, *but wood, fields, gardens, animals, and commodities....*"[T]he political power of the State is *polis*, police, that is, management of the public ways ... the gates of the city, its levies and duties, are barriers, *filters against the fluidity of the masses, against the penetrating power of migratory packs,*" people, animals, and goods.[22]

In this regard, nature itself can be considered as one particular manifestation of the war machine: migrations, mating seasons, spawning, stampedes, hunting packs, feeding frenzies. In the animal kingdom, aggression, reproduction, territorial acquisition, and survival is impulsive, instinctual, and necessarily related; actions are devoid of moral, romantic, or political justifications. It is an anarchic, continuous process that creates while it destroys; it is not simply a deliberate and systematic course to destroy the enemy (civilized modern warfare). "The difference between the two poles is great, even, and especially, from the point of view of death: the line of flight that creates, *or* turns into a line of destruction, the plane of consistency that constitutes itself, *or* turns into a plan(e) of organization and domination."[23] Above all, in Deleuze and Guattari's formulation, the war machine and the State exist in a fundamentally *antagonistic* relationship: "War machines take shape *against the apparatus that appropriate the machine* and make war their affair and their object: *they bring connections to bear against the great conjunction of the apparatus of capture and domination.*"[24] In this respect, *Birds of Prey* depicts the potentially cataclysmic moment nature as a war machine is placed in direct opposition to a modern civilization: the war machine of "wood, fields, gardens, animals, and commodities" contained within the State, and the potential power "fluidity" and "penetrating power" of nature which rises against the State seeking to appropriate, control, constrain, and exploit it. The attack of the birds is not simply a spontaneous protest or an organized war, but a *revolution*. While the birds are a massive force of destruction in one sense, they also represent a fundamental aspect of the war machine: the mass political movement as creation and transformation through revolution and insurrection — or "feathered mutiny." Deleuze and Guattari contended:

> If guerilla warfare, minority warfare, revolutionary and popular warfare are in conformity with the essence [of the war machine], it is because they take war as an object all the more necessary for being merely "supplementary": *they can make war only on the condition that they simultaneously create something else,* if only new nonorganic social relations.²⁵

While revolutions alter governmental and even societal structures, they only do so on the *micro*historical line occupied by the State and the level of "new nonorganic social relations"—the paradox of most revolutionary movements replacing one inadequate government with another inadequate government. The glaring problem of *Intolerance* from the perspective of *A Thousand Plateaus* is precisely when the microhistorical moment and the overcoded segmented line (the United States *ca.* 1916) permanently reterritorializes the macrohistorical mutant quantum flow (mass movement). In *Birds of Prey*, the "variable map of masses" arises as a definitive disruption, or deterritorialization, of "the self-reproduction of classes" contained in the history of humanity's domination of nature: be it revenge against the Incas who exploited the labor of the great firebirds, or chickens with skewers up their asses roasted for food in Madrid grocery stores.

Rehearsal for the Apocalypse

Describing the end of *Birds of Prey* as "anti-climactic" does not do justice to the film's conclusion; a cynical assessment could suggest that the film reached an adequate running time and Cardona simply ended the movie with the birds suddenly ceasing their attacks. After the assault on the train ends in a stalemate, a brief and sudden epilogue begins with a close-up of Vanessa talking directly to the camera (and the film audience); the shot zooms out to reveal she is on a television set broadcasting a news bulletin. Throughout the epilogue, close-ups of Vanessa speaking to the camera are interspersed with shots of Vanessa on the television itself. Peter somberly listens, standing in the "wings" of the news studio, surrounded by lighting equipment; the news studio and film soundstage become indistinct spaces as the film draws to a close. A shot of Carmen zooms out to show her and her family watching the broadcast in their plush bourgeois home, still in disbelief. This is followed by a slow zoom-in depicting the woman attacked in the opening hang-gliding sequence watching Vanessa's report in stunned silence. The zoom-in ends in a close-up of the woman's face, with butterfly bandages securing a gash in her left cheek: the final, morbid punch-line that a "peck on the cheek" is indeed a sign of predatory violence which results in a permanent scar. Elsewhere, a young woman sets her baby in a stroller and sits down to watch Vanessa's broadcast. Over this montage, Vanessa does not provide a conclusion for the film, but a series of possible conclusions:

5. Lines of Flight, or Death from Above

> In all parts of the world, the birds appear to have returned to their normal behavior. All attacks have ceased, and we seem to be at peace. The nightmare ended the same way it started: suddenly and inexplicably. Perhaps they knew they could never defeat the most cruel [sic] killer of all: man. Or perhaps their message was sent: to care for this fragile sphere we call Earth, to nurture and share the riches with all of God's creatures, if we are to survive. Or maybe it was a rehearsal, some kind of natural master plan, a plan to discard any and all who disrupt nature's perfect harmony: a plan to choose who will survive.

As Vanessa stares at the camera and utters the final, ominous line, the shot cuts to a close-up of the gurgling baby in the stroller as his eyes dart about his surroundings. In this respect, the baby recalls a key image in *Intolerance*: the recurring shots of the metaphysical Great Mother (Lillian Gish) anxiously monitoring an infant in a rocking cradle, a metaphor of the flow of macrohistory under the precarious lines of microhistory. The last shot of *Intolerance* shows the Great Mother now calm, and the infant presumably peacefully asleep in the cradle as it gently sways from side to side: the perpetual crisis of History at last resolved, finally quelled (or, rather, reterritorialized) in the early 20th century with the United States of America. Conversely, the infant at the end of *Birds of Prey* fidgets in the stroller: agitated, alert, curious, and wide-awake.

To make the film both more unsettling and more melodramatic, Cardona follows Vanessa's report with a montage of backwards footage of rain falling on bodies of water accompanied by loud, dissonant, pounding music — as if a generic disco rhythm track had been overdubbed with the buzzing flies heard during the opening massacre scenes in *El Topo*. Not only reminiscent of early surrealist films, the sequence implies that the forces of nature have become even more inexplicable and dangerous — the rain flowing *upwards* from the ground and into the sky in direct violation of the laws of science. This montage ends with a shot of the rain moving in reverse into the sky before freeze-framing on still waters with garbage floating on the surface. The grinding atonal music fades out as a harpsichord-driven jazz-rock closing theme fades in, music one might expect from Eurotrash cinema scores. The closing theme is accompanied by an excerpt from the Bible, which crawls upward over the freeze-frame (the words following the direction of the rain): it is the "Prophecy of Joel," which both warns of the impending wrath of God and offers the promise of His salvation. While the inclusion of Scripture couches the environmentalist message in a moral imperative to end the film (a variation of "Repent sinners — the end is near!"), the conclusion of *Birds of Prey* does not simply imply a brief protest, dire warning, or even a preview to the End of the World. In *Birds of Prey*, the sudden attacks and equally abrupt ceasing of hostilities by the birds suggests the persistent continuum of "accelerations" and "stupors" of macrohistorical forces: the continuous and relentless flow of macrohistory and masses over which the segmented moments of microhistory transpire and transform. If the attack of the birds has indeed only been "a rehearsal," the only question left for humanity is when — and how — the war machine will resurface next.

6

National Oedipus:
Santa sangre (*Holy Blood,* 1988)

The family has become the locus of retention and resonance of all the social determinations ... wherever one turns, one no longer finds anything but the father-mother — this Oedipal filth that sticks to our skins.[1]

— Gilles Deleuze and Félix Guattari,
Anti-Oedipus

"Goodbye to the Holy Mountain":
Jodorowsky after El Topo

Flush with the international success of *El Topo* and his sudden status as the leading counterculture film director, Alejandro Jodorowsky embarked on his next project: *The Holy Mountain* (1972), with Allen Klein providing a budget that could match Jodorowsky's extravagant — or grandiose — visions. Certainly, *The Holy Mountain* is Jodorowsky's most ambitious, self-indulgent, and, yes, pretentious film: a sprawling epic that made *El Topo* seem positively myopic in comparison. Incorporating as many mythological, religious, mystical, philosophical, Modernist, and cinematic references that could be shoved into one film, *The Holy Mountain*, if nothing else, certainly demonstrated Jodorowsky's self-professed goal of becoming "the Cecil B. DeMille of the Underground." Indeed, *The Holy Mountain* became Jodorowsky's attempt to create a new religious tract for the modern world; he proclaimed at the time, "Maybe I am a prophet. I really hope one day there will come Confucius, Mohammed, Buddha, and Christ to see me. And we will sit at a table, taking tea and eating brownies."[2]

If any plot synopsis is at all possible, *The Holy Mountain* begins with a beggar and Christ figure encountering an array of surreal events on the streets of Mexico City: a parade of soldiers in gas masks carrying crucified goat carcasses; an American tourist with a home-movie camera filming his wife being raped by a soldier; Mod prostitutes with a chimpanzee mascot soliciting customers in front of a cathedral; a reenactment of the Spanish conquest of Mexico by the "Great Toad and Chameleon Circus"— reptiles dressed as conquistadors and Aztec warriors blown apart on a cheap set of exploding pyramids. Eventually, the beggar climbs a skyscraper and encounters a figure that may or may not be God (or a composite of various religious conceptions of God). Not surprisingly, "God" is played by Jodorowsky dressed in a kind of psychedelic pilgrim outfit. After an extended cleansing process, including a memorable alchemical steam bath where the beggar is locked in a plastic bubble and his excrement converted into gold, Jodorowsky explains they will be joined by the seven most powerful people in the world. Their mission: to scale the Holy Mountain on Lotus Island and conquer the Nine Immortals.

Another lengthy section follows, and each of these "Seven Accomplices" is introduced: each represents a planet, the correlate in Roman mythology, and the specific aspect of the world under their domain. The man representing Venus controls the production of love; the woman representing Mars controls the production of the world's munitions; the man representing Jupiter controls the production of art; the woman representing Saturn controls the production of toys; the man representing Uranus controls international finance; the man representing Neptune controls the police; and the man representing Pluto controls architecture.[3] These characters also reflect Jodorowsky's gender and sexual politics. Venus, the goddess love and sex, is represented by a man instead of a woman; Mars and Saturn, both male gods in Roman mythology, are the only two women of the Seven Accomplices and are largely responsible for the spread of war in the world. Neptune, the representative of the police, is a sadistic, homosexual gladiator who collects young boys' testicles in jars.

After purifying themselves by burning their money, they set off on their epic journey through Mexican jungles and ruins, replete with the patented Jodorowsky array of surreal imagery, visions, and rituals as they become a metaphysical, collective body rather than individual beings. However, their arrival on Lotus Island proves highly disappointing, to say the least. They discover that all the travelers before them inevitably abandoned the journey to the Holy Mountain to wallow in the decadence of the Pantheon Bar: a gaudy Pop Art discothèque representing Western culture. Undaunted, they continue their quest. After more visions and rituals, they eventually reach the summit and the table of the Nine Immortals, where *The Holy Mountain* ends as either the ultimate postmodern shaggy-dog story or a colossal cop-out: the Nine Immortals are manikins in hooded robes. After a hearty chuckle, Jodorowsky addresses his entourage: "We have not obtained immortality, but we have attained reality. But is this life a reality? Zoom back, camera!" As the camera pulls back to reveal the cast surrounded by the film crew, Jodorowsky concludes, "This is *maya*! Goodbye to the Holy Mountain: real life awaits us." Indeed, the final shot, a long shot of the Holy Mountain in the distance, becomes remarkably similar to an iconic image associated with the Hollywood "dream-machine": the Paramount Pictures logo.

Whereas *El Topo* can be considered Jodorowsky's conversion of counterculture idealism and politics into an epic myth, *The Holy Mountain* can be read as a deft satire of a counterculture becoming an "over-the-counterculture." The most powerful capitalists in the world — the postmodern Illuminati exploiting art, sex, war, and revolution for profit — become epic heroes seeking immortality and omnipotence through spiritual enlightenment. The biographical sketches of the Seven Accomplices play out as a series of avant-garde industrial films, and are rife with irony: Venus explains he only makes love to his female factory workers during office hours, and then they are promoted to secretaries; Mars demonstrates "psychedelic shotguns" marketed to aspiring revolutionaries as if she were a runway model; Jupiter creates an assembly line where people have their naked buttocks covered in paint and then sit on canvases — in effect, modern art becomes mass-produced, multi-colored "crap." When the journeying heroes reach Lotus Island and the Pantheon Bar they encounter a hippie in an Uncle Sam top hat spouting turgid poetry, as well as a man in lederhosen gorging on LSD from a sliver platter while incoherently pondering *The Tibetan Book of the Dead* (one of the canonical counterculture texts, it was championed by Timothy Leary, who may well be the specific object of parody in the scene).

In a wonderful bit of comedy, a Greek demigod with a hiker backpack and boots demonstrates his amazing power to walk through matter (via the magic of old-fashioned jump-cuts) and traverse across Lotus Island in seconds. However, when asked, "How long until you reach the summit?" he issues a hilarious response: "I can only advance horizontally and that's enough: from bottom to top — I can't do. But anyway, I am a champion! I have conquered the Holy Mountain, horizontally! Horizontally, I am a champion!" His "horizontal power" comments on emerging intellectual trends of the 1970s, specifically the philosophical work of Michel Foucault and Gilles Deleuze, the "champions" of philosophy as a process of exploring horizontal connections versus vertical hierarchies of power (the analogy used by Deleuze and Guattari in *A Thousand Plateaus*: tracing the underground roots rather than mapping the visible tree).[4] While this philosophical shift allowed a radical and important rethinking of the complexities of power in modern society, to think political power as a mechanistic collision of variances and velocities (the forces of horizontal power) minimizes the fundamental question of who wields and manipulates power (the forces of vertical power): the ultimate impotence of the Greek god-hiker who continually skirts the parameters but cannot scale the Holy Mountain. Moreover, *The Holy Mountain*'s extremely disappointing cheat ending becomes an indictment of postmodern consciousness and its acceptance, if not outright endorsement, of how signs and images of reality were increasingly becoming more tangible — and more interesting — than reality itself. In short, *The Holy Mountain* demanded a rejection of the *maya* of the "holy mountain" of postmodernism by a rejection of the overblown *maya* of the film itself—an intentional self-parody of Jodorowsky by Jodorowsky—and an embrace of something less flashy and far cruder: the challenge of real life.[5]

Unfortunately, *The Holy Mountain* was not received as a profound philosophical treatise or a clever political satire, but the predictable result of Jodorowsky's artistic excesses and philosophical pretensions fueled by the controversial success of *El Topo*. Despite the often stunning imagery that dominates the first part of the film, *The Holy Mountain* frequently digresses into a pastiche of Christian iconography, Eastern philosophy, the Tarot, Pop Art, Psychedelia, Buñuel, Godard, and, of course, Artaud. At times, it resembles *The Ten Commandments* as directed by the cinematic master of style over substance, Ken Russell. Perhaps inevitably, *The Holy Mountain* failed to meet the expectations of Jodorowsky's fervent supporters, and provided considerable ammunition for his strongest critics. A rough cut of *The Holy Mountain* was hastily completed for its world premiere at the 1973 Cannes Film Festival, where it received an unenthusiastic response. Moreover, Marco Ferrari's *La Grande Bouffe* (*The Great Feast*), a provocative black comedy about the bourgeoisie eating itself to death, became the surprise hit of the festival. Klein, who specifically attended Cannes for the disappointing premiere of *The Holy Mountain*, seized the opportunity and purchased the American rights for *La Grande Bouffe*. Jodorowsky, also dissatisfied with the version screened at Cannes, reedited *The Holy Mountain* and cut 20 minutes, reportedly removing several dialogue-driven scenes (considering the portentous dialogue and ponderous pacing which plagues the latter half of *The Holy Mountain*, one can only surmise what these omitted scenes entailed).

Eventually, Klein only gave *The Holy Mountain* limited release in America, insisting his goal was shielding Jodorowsky from a probable box-office disaster and a certain critical drubbing. At best, *The Holy Mountain* maintained Jodorowsky's cult-film prestige but did little to change the critical perception that he was little more than a counterculture curiosity—or charlatan. Attempting to rekindle Jodorowsky's rapidly fading stardom, Klein suggested a film version of the infamous erotic novel *The Story of O*: a project more overtly controversial but also more immediately accessible—and therefore marketable—than *The Holy Mountain*. Instead, Jodorowsky proposed *Mr. Blood and Miss Bones*: a pirate film he envisioned starring Frank Zappa and intended for an all-ages audience (one can only imagine the results if Jodorowsky helmed, for instance, *Willy Wonka and the Chocolate Factory*).[6] The impasse soon resulted in Klein and Jodorowsky severing their business ties, and Klein, the owner of the rights to *El Topo* and *The Holy Mountain*, has effectively shelved both films since the 1970s.[7]

Following the disappointment of *The Holy Mountain*, Jodorowsky embarked on another ambitious failure by attempting to bring Frank Herbert's science-fiction epic *Dune* to the silver screen, a film adaptation that would have been "space opera" owing as much to Richard Wagner as to Flash Gordon. Over the course of developing the film in the mid–1970s, Pink Floyd agreed to do the soundtrack, and Hollywood icons such as Gloria Swanson and Orson Welles were rumored to be cast (one assumes Welles would have portrayed the obese, bellowing Baron Harkonnen). However, perhaps the greatest casting coup was enlisting Salvador Dalí to play "The Emperor of the Universe."[8] After over two years of preproduction, Jodorowsky's *Dune* was scrapped in 1976, deemed impossible to make and market by Hollywood executives and financiers. Jodorowsky later claimed that numerous designs for *Star Wars* were lifted from his storyboards, thousands of which circulated in Hollywood during his attempts to finance the film. Moreover, the creative team Jodorowsky recruited for *Dune*— Swiss painter H. R. Giger, French cartoonist Jean "Moebius" Girand, English illustrator Christopher Foss, special-effects artist Dan O'Bannon — were all instrumental in making Hollywood's other science-fiction box office bonanza of the 1970s, *Alien*.[9] To add insult to injury, in 1984 Dino De Laurentiis eventually produced his own bloated version of *Dune* directed by David Lynch, an effort that demonstrated Lynch's forte clearly lay in postmodern *film noir* rather than big-budget science-fiction epics. Jodorowsky had the last laugh with *Dune*, as recounted by L. Loud:

> "When I knew David Lynch will do *Dune*," moaned Jodorowsky, "I was ill for a year! Then my children take me to the theater, and I start to see the film.... Suddenly, I start to do this..." As if infused with helium, Jodorowsky begins to rise, an expression of delight breaking across his troubled countenance. Halfway out of his seat, Jodorowsky triumphantly yelled, "FANTASTIC! *DUNE* IS A HORRIBLE PICTURE! If picture was good," he added, dropping back into his seat, normal again, "I think I die of jealousy."[10]

After spending years on the ill-fated *Dune* project, Jodorowsky finally completed a film in 1979: the disastrous *Tusk*. An all-age, heavy-handed allegorical melodrama intertwining the lives of an English girl and an elephant in Colonial India, the project could be cynically described as a postcolonial variation of *The Jungle Book*. Jodorowsky recounted that the film was doomed from the outset, largely due to a producer that provided only $500,000 of a promised five-million-dollar budget. After an abysmally received premiere at the 1980 Flimex Film Festival in Los Angeles, and a subsequent panning in *Variety*, the film was never released in the U.S.[11] Admitting he only finished *Tusk* in order to avoid following *Dune* with another uncompleted project, Jodorowsky was uncharacteristically succinct about the end result: "Don't see *Tusk*. I bury the film."[12]

From Gunslingers to Giallo

Throughout the 1980s, Jodorowsky lived in Paris, concentrating on writing graphic novels, many in collaboration with Moebius.[13] For the most part, Jodorowsky retired from cinema: "At that point I stopped making pictures.... I decided I wouldn't do a film just to make a producer rich."[14] However, in 1988 Jodorowsky was approached by Claudio Argento, producer of brother Dario Argento's seminal *giallo* horror films, including *Profundo rosso* (*Deep Red*, 1975), *Susperia* (1977), and *Tenebre* (*Darkness*, 1982). The proposition was simple: if Jodorowsky was interested in writing and directing a film, Argento would produce it. After providing an initial treatment for *Santa sangre* and receiving a guarantee of creative control and a feasible budget, Jodorowsky returned to Mexico City to film *Santa sangre*, where none other than René Cardona, Jr. became involved in the project as an executive producer.

Jodorowsky loosely based *Santa sangre* on the case of a famous Mexican serial killer, Gojo Cardinas. However, Jodorowsky's own interest did not center on the grisly particulars of his murders, but the aftermath of the crimes:

> He was criminal but he forgot he killed fifteen women, he went to an asylum for ten years. Then he came out a normal person after I met him. I realized redemption was possible. So then I began my picture. He forgot everything; he knew about himself through newspapers and books. He changed and became a lawyer. But that is normal — a criminal who becomes a lawyer.[15]

Much like *El Topo*, *Santa sangre* depicts the personal transformation of its main character, Fenix (Axel Jodorowsky), through a surreal, symbolic, and often harrowing journey. It is also an intensely personal film for Jodorowsky, who described the film as "subtle psychoanalysis" based on his own childhood with a domineering father and a smothering mother ("a castrate woman by my father and she wanted to live her life through me"), his relationships with his own sons, and his own attitudes toward women ("I was also a killer, a psychological killer, a misogynist, destroying women").[16] If *El Topo* was Jodorowsky's Western, *Santa sangre* can be seen as Jodorowsky's version of *giallo*, not at all surprising given the pivotal role of Claudio Argento, who not only produced but received co-writing credit on the screenplay. *Santa sangre* shares the essential characteristics of the *giallo* films: highly-stylized filmmaking revolving around serial murders with strong psychoanalytic undercurrents, including Oedipal fixations, obsessive fetishes, and the blurred distinctions between sex and violence. Using the *giallo* genre as a setting *Santa sangre* allowed Jodorowsky to explore themes of politics, sexuality and violence — in some respects, far more successfully than *El Topo*; in other ways, reiterating the same problematic stances of *El Topo*. Indeed, and like *El Topo*, *Santa sangre* is a thoroughly political film, with its politics cast in terms of allegory and symbolism. While El Topo was the counterculture Odysseus, Fenix's Oedipal psychodrama becomes a thinly-disguised "national allegory" of the political relationship between Mexico and the United States of America.[17]

The Ugly American: Circo del Gringo

Santa sangre begins with a disconcerting shot of Fenix naked, perched on top of a tall tree truck in a large, antiseptic hospital room. The medical personnel bring him a dinner on a restaurant cart — a choice between a cooked steak and a raw fish. Fenix emits a primal shriek and jumps from his perch, snares the raw fish, and begins devouring it. Immediately, one is struck by the depiction of the mental institution, a surreal space between cave dwelling and modern psychiatric ward where Fenix is situated between the Freudian pleasure principle (self-will) and reality principle (the demands and constraints of civilization). The tree trunk also serves as a symbol of the character's Oedipal trauma. When the attendants arrive in his room, Fenix is perched at the v-shaped top of the tree, seeking refuge in a symbolic vagina (far cruder, his obsession with the raw fish also has a vaginal connotation). Moreover, the tree truck with its branches removed suggests the dismembered, armless figures of women — specifically his mother — which become central to *Santa sangre*.

As the attendants begin to dress him, the shot slowly zooms in from a medium shot of Fenix from the waist up to a tight close-up of his face, allowing the viewer to study the large tattoo of a red, white, and blue bird covering his chest — a signifier with two important connotations which become crucial later in the film. One is the mythological Phoenix (Fenix), and the film as a chronicle of Fenix's own psychological and spiritual rebirth. The other is that the tattoo on Fenix's chest is identical to the eagle on the back of the U.S. dollar, and done in the national colors of the U.S. (in this respect, the eagle specifically does *not* represent the eagle on the national flag of Mexico).[18] The close-up of Fenix staring blankly into the distance slowly dissolves to a close-up of an eagle, explicitly establishing the connection between the two to start the lengthy flashback sequence that makes up the first half of the film.

Pérez Prado's mambo number "Caballo negro" ("Black Horse") begins on the soundtrack. Placed in this setting, the driving percussion, dissonant horn blasts, and grunted vocals of Prado's song provide an ominous effect, one that becomes much more pronounced when the same music is later used to accompany the first murder committed by Fenix. The inclusion of the Prado number is also important in that he was a highly popular crossover artist in both Mexico and the U.S.A., underscoring Fenix's filmic journey, in national allegorical terms, as the (traumatized) offspring of Mexico and the U.S.A. The camera adopts the point of view of the eagle as it flies across the city, following the path of a street. It is the first of several allusions in *Santa sangre* to Alfred Hitchcock's *Psycho* (1960), and echoes the famous "bird's-eye" establishing shot of *Psycho* where the camera pans across a cityscape and slowly zooms in through a hotel room window where Marion Crane (Janet Leigh) has just finished an afternoon sexual tryst.[19] In *Santa sangre*, the shot from the point of view of the eagle moves down the street until it reaches a circus tent composed of red and white stripes and large white stars over a blue field, and cuts to the eagle landing on the marquee advertising the *Circo del gringo* ("Circus of the Foreigner," with *gringo* a pejorative word usually reserved for a White American). Like the Great Town in *El Topo*, the *Circo del gringo* is certainly a representation of the United States of America.[20]

With the pervasive presence of the U.S.A. *in* and *over* Mexico established by the *Circo del gringo* and the symbolic presence of the eagle atop the tent, the scene cuts to a brief "beauty pageant" in the streets where Mexican prostitutes meet and greet potential customers with casual but officious handshakes: the convergence of economic and sexual exchange — or, more correctly, exploitation — which becomes central in framing *Santa sangre*'s allegorical depiction of colonialism through sex and power relationships (prostitution, incest, sadism, masochism, rape, murder). This procession of *putas* cuts to a more official parade as the members of the *Circo del gringo* march down the streets, officially announcing that the circus (the U.S.A.) has come to town (Mexico). Amid the waving U.S. flags and circus members representing the gaudiest aspects of Americana — Las Vegas showgirls and clowns in blackface — a much younger Fenix (played by another of Jodorowsky's sons, Adan) is dressed as a Latin lover; he holds an umbrella and rides on the back of an elephant, accompanied by the circus dwarf, Aladin (Jesús Juárez). Here Jodorowsky self-references two of his previous films. One is *El Topo*, with Fenix a prepubescent gigolo rather than an intimidating *charro*; Aladin, rather than El Topo's naked son, recalls the Small Woman, El Topo's soul mate. The other reference is the child-elephant relationship in the ill-fated *Tusk*, his previous film and another allegory of colonialism, which is renounced with a certain malicious satisfaction by Jodorowsky later in *Santa sangre*.

The dominant figure in the *Circo del gringo* is Fenix's father: the abusive, alcoholic, obese knife thrower "Orgo" (Guy Stockwell).[21] Orgo is a monstrous parody of Uncle Sam: long, platinum blonde locks and dyed beard replace the distinguished grey hair; a kitsch, glittery white and silver cowboy outfit with red and blue undergarments replaces Uncle Sam's dapper red, white, and blue tuxedo. Drunkenly staggering into the circus tent, Orgo encounters the Tattooed Lady (Thelma Tixou), literally a "painted woman." Both his assistant and his mistress, she leers at him seductively and removes her robe, revealing her voluptuous tattooed body, clad only in a bikini. The circus clowns rush into the shot and gather around her, comically kneeling at her feet in an act of sexual worship; throughout the film, the clowns function as a sort of Felliniesque Greek chorus, commentating on the scenes as they appear in them though mime and gestures rather than verbal interjections. Orgo and the Tattooed Woman's rehearsal of the knife-throwing act leaves little to the imagination as to the status of their relationship, and specifically the domineering presence of Orgo and his knife, which becomes a blatant phallic symbol. As the Tattooed Woman writhes against the circular target (painted blue with red and white trim), Orgo hurls knives at her. She fondles and stokes one that lands next to her hip, lewdly licks a second that finds its mark next to her face, and when the final knife strikes the target perilously close to her vagina between her legs, she grasps it in both hands and her body shudders, achieving orgasm.

In contrast to the lurid sexual display between Orgo and the Tattooed Lady, this early scene in the circus tent also establishes a close relationship between Fenix and the only other child in the circus, Alma (played in the flashback sequences by Faviola Elenka Tapia): "Alma" is Spanish for "soul" or "spirit." A deaf-mute in mime makeup, Alma is being taught — or trained, like a performing animal — to walk a fiery tightrope under the abusive directions of her adopted mother, the Tattooed Woman. When their parents become preoccupied with practicing their knife-throwing routine (having sex), Fenix produces a rose through some rudimentary slight-of-hand and presents it to Alma, who then confidently traverses the flaming tightrope. This is not to say that Jodorowsky is necessarily implementing the cliché of "childhood innocence" to contrast the sordid relationship of Orgo and the Tattooed Woman, but rather to establish their prepubescent, non-sexual relationship, pivotal in the film's conclusion, as one of the few relationships in *Santa sangre* (along with Fenix and Aladin) which is rooted in love and compassion rather than sex, domination, and exploitation.

Liberation Theology: The Church of Holy Blood

As Alma practices on the tightrope, a shot of Fenix clinking hanging bottles with sticks to supply her musical accompaniment abruptly cuts to a shot of police officers in riot gear behind a fence, pounding on the barrier with truncheons. A woman emphatically argues with the police, branding them blasphemous and sacrilegious: Concha, Fenix's mother (Blanca Guerra). A long tracking shot depicts Fenix, accompanied by the Clown Chorus, as he runs towards the uproar from the *Circo del gringo* tent to a nearby church (the *Circo* tent is seen in the background in the beginning of the shot as the camera tracks Fenix running town the street to the church in a single take, with the circus and church constructed in actual physical proximity on location in an urban setting). A riot has broken out pitting members of a church against police and a landowner boldly standing atop a bulldozer, telling the police to "get them off my land!" Concha defiantly challenges the police to remove them; as the bulldozers begin to plow through the fences, the parishioners respond by waving sticks and throwing rocks — the shot strongly recalling newsreel footage of violent protests and mass evictions. Suddenly, the shot cuts to Concha, arms outstretched as she walks towards the camera, as she proclaims: "We are not afraid of you!" Behind her the congregation gathers, with a "Santa Sangre" billboard visible on the building directly behind and above her; the large sign is a floral arrangement and more akin to a decoration on parade float than the marker of a church (to avoid confusion with the film's title, the church proper will be referred to as "the Church of Holy Blood"). Now armed with various guitars, percussion instruments, and even an accordion, the congregation does not respond with violence, but a musical performance of a popular folk song.

In this sense, the Church of Holy Blood represents a nexus of populist politics and Catholic iconography. All the Church members wear identical red robes with a white symbol on the chest — two intersecting arms that form a sort of double X; in this context, the red on the Mexican national flag is often interpreted as symbolizing the blood of heroes, and white symbolizing purity.[22] However, red is also associated with Communism — the collective society and "people's revolution." Similarly, the intersecting arms which replace the crucifix resemble revolutionary iconography of the 1960s: poster images of clenched fists or clasped hands. These images connecting Catholicism and revolution are particularly important given the context in which *Santa sangre* was made. Héctor Aguilar Camín and Lorenzo Meyer noted, "After the ascent of Pope John Paul II and his visit to Mexico in 1978, a new activist church had begun to emerge in the country.... [A] Mexican church, as the Polish one before, should become a center for organization for a civil society."[23] By the early 1980s, especially in Latin America, a wave of radical thought erupted in the Catholic Church over its role in social activism: Liberation Theology and its emphasis on the plight of the lower classes, in some cases advocating socialist policies and even adopting Marxism alongside Catholic doctrine. However, this school of thought, and political agenda, ran completely antithetical to Pope John Paul II, whose use of the Catholic Church for political activism in Poland was to assist a staunchly *anti*–Communist, pro-democracy (and pro-capitalist) Solidarity Movement directed against the Marxist-Stalinist government of Poland. In 1984, the Vatican under Pope John Paul II officially repudiated Liberation Theology, arguing that Marxism by its very nature was incompatible with Catholic orthodoxy.[24] It is this political conflict between the Catholic orthodoxy and the people's Church of Holy Blood that becomes critical as the scene unfolds.

A long shot of the demonstration situates the police in blue uniforms armed with guns and batons, and the church members in matching red gowns armed with musical instruments and long-stem flowers ("flower power"). A limousine slowly drives into the fray — like Moses "parting the seas" of bodies and dividing them into their respective factions on each side of the film frame. The Monsignor (Sergio Bustamante), who bears a distinct resemblance to Pope John Paul II, emerges from the limo, dressed in *purple* — literally mediating the dispute as Catholicism between police *blue* (the State) and church *red* (the masses). "Peace ... I bring peace," he piously intones. The Monsignor is accompanied by his young aide, dressed in a white suit, and his presence serves two proposes. One is to reaffirm the symbolism of white as virginal, innocent, and pure (also manifest in the "white face" of Alma), and the jeopardy his religious and political "virtue" is placed in once inside the Church of Holy Blood. Second, his white suit provides the necessary compliment to the blue police uniforms and the red gowns of the members of the Church of Holy Blood to manufacture the combination of red, white, and blue: the omnipresent colors of the U.S.A. which permeate *Santa sangre*. Frantically informed by Concha that the police and landowners plan to demolish the building, the Monsignor consoles her and asks to see their church. As they enter the dimly lit temple, saturated in red hues, Concha proudly states: "This is where we worship our beloved saint." However, the Monsignor is utterly baffled when he sees this "beloved saint"— a statue in a display case framed by red neon lights which resembles a combination thrift-store doll, showroom manikin, and the *Venus di Milo*. Leading the Monsignor through the church, Concha explains that their saint was a young girl who was raped, dismembered, and murdered many years ago in the building. Folk art drawings depicting various moments of the murder decorate the walls in a parody of the classical paintings depicting the Stations of the Cross in traditional Catholic Churches— the final station depicting the girl with her arms amputated and left to die in a pool of her own blood. Instead of holy water, a swimming pool in the center of the church is filled with red liquid that Concha claims is the "holy blood" of the girl. She has become a saintly martyr for the people not through the mystery of Immaculate Conception, but the ordeal of Crucifixion as rape and dismemberment of women by men: an essential motif in constructing the national allegory in *Santa sangre*.

Incredulous, the Monsignor glares at Concha: "It's paint! Do you hear me crazy woman, it's paint!" As the two violently argue, nearly coming to blows, the congregation joins in a choir of dissent. Exacerbating the conflict, Concha directs a young woman into the pool in a parody of the baptism ritual. As the Monsignor looks on in disgust, he denounces her actions as "sacrilege" and announces, "The Church will never recognize this heresy!" (Pope John Paul II and the rejection of Liberation Theology). Within the diffuse red lighting of the church, the Monsignor's attire itself seems to become *blue* rather than purple, signifying him as joining the ranks of the oppressors (the State, the police). Defiantly, Concha replies, "We don't care ... this is our saint!" The young girl, now waist deep in the pool, ecstatically begins to shout, "Holy Blood! Holy Blood!" The congregation gathers around the pool and bursts into a reprise of the folk song as the baptism in holy blood becomes another moment of political dissent by the people, now directed against the Catholic orthodoxy itself. Incensed, the Monsignor leads his young aide out of the church, cradling his head and telling him that he doesn't want the display to taint his "pure soul." The "sacrilege" the Monsignor desperately shields him from is Liberation Theology as a popular manifestation of Catholicism: one that embraced passion, action, and the living conditions of the people over vague metaphysics and theology. Storming outside, the Monsignor gives the police and landowner his "blessing." "Go ahead ... destroy this abomination!" As the bulldozers demolish the Church of Holy Blood, it represents the destruction of a populist, even revolutionary expression of Catholicism by the people, aided and abetted by the Catholic hierarchy working in tandem with the landlords and police.

The Holy Family and the Colonial Triangle

Distressed by the defeat and demolition of the Church of Holy Blood, Fenix and his weary mother return to the *Circo del gringo* tent. Orgo and the Tattooed Woman continue to flaunt their sexual relationship as she performs a burlesque strip-tease number while Orgo sits and watches, holding a knife as if he were fondling his penis. This phallic symbolism reaches a point of (possibly unintended) comedy when the Tattooed Woman knells down in front of him and licks the knife, obviously a metaphor for fellatio. Incensed, Concha interrupts them, seizing Orgo's knife-phallus and brandishing it at the cowering Tattooed Woman. Orgo, more inconvenienced than shocked by his symbolic castration, confronts Concha with a mixture of conceit and predatory determination. Roughly grabbing her arm and waving the knife-phallus back and forth in front of her face, Orgo hypnotically seduces Concha; she briefly struggles against Orgo's "charms" before submitting to him, still holding the knife-phallus but unable — or unwilling — to wield its power against him. He turns his back to her and, facing the camera, confidently sheds his jacket and pulls down his blue shirt, revealing his own tattoo of the American eagle across his massive chest; Orgo's deliberately exaggerated, theatrical gesture directs audience attention to its significance as a reference to the United States. When Concha charges after him, the viewer initially suspects she might stab him; instead, she throws her arms around his expansive stomach, the knife dangling in her hands like a flaccid penis. Carrying the limp, submissive Concha on his back, Orgo triumphantly walks off-frame. Fenix and several clowns follow, hoping to voyeuristically witness the inevitable sex act that will occur; however, another clown suddenly runs into the shot and blocks their path, comically but sternly informing the entourage of potential voyeurs (and, by extension, the film viewer) to leave the couple alone, and "no one goes any further"— the only line of dialogue uttered by a member of the Clown Chorus throughout the film.

As the clowns disperse, Fenix surreptitiously finds a vantage point outside the *Circo del gringo* tent to watch Orgo and his mother. Of course, he is aghast when he peers into the *Circo* tent and sees his mother atop Orgo, who is unseen below the bottom edge of the frame. The Oedipal complex is immediately manifest as the horrified Fenix observes his mother having intense, almost animalistic sex with his father; it even appears that Concha and Fenix make eye contact as he watches them. As she and Orgo reach orgasm, Concha's expression is not necessarily one of ecstasy, but pain and surrender. Sexual intercourse is not an act of sexual enjoyment between partners, but the domination of the man over the woman: while Orgo's presence cannot be seen in the shot, his phallic and political power can nonetheless certainly be "felt."[25] Paradoxically, in the context of the film where the violation of women makes them more saintly than their purity, Fenix witnessing his mother's seduction and violation by the father makes her *more* sacred (in effect, turning the "Madonna-whore complex" on its head). Within the national allegory of the film, Fenix is appalled to see Mexico sullied by the United States of America, and equally revolted by the awareness that he is the progeny of that sexual-political relationship: the holy family of "daddy-mommy-me" is also manifest as the colonial relationship "U.S.A.-Mexico-me." The shock of watching his parents having sex immediately cuts to a sequence featuring the circus elephant's sudden death, inexplicably stricken with a mysterious malady as torrents of blood jettison from its trunk.[26] It is both a metaphor of male sexual ejaculation (Orgo's climax) and another self-reference to Jodorowsky's previous and disowned film *Tusk*. The simplistic and sentimental allegory of colonialism in *Tusk*—British girl and Indian elephant—is obsolescent in the brutality of *Santa sangre*. The moment Fenix realizes he is the conception, or product, of the domination of Orgo-father-U.S. over Concha-mother-Mexico—to be vulgar, Mexico being fucked by the United Sates of America—is precisely the moment the elephant, the symbol of the oppressed under colonialism in *Tusk*, is promptly murdered by Jodorowsky with a degree of ruthless and gratuitous satisfaction.

In one of the most surreal moments of the film (which is not to say *Santa sangre* does not have a wealth of surreal moments), the *Circo del gringo* members stage a funeral procession as the mammoth Art Deco coffin of the elephant is slowly paraded through the streets of Mexico City on a flatbed truck.[27] The procession becomes particularly disorientating to the extent that the *Circo* mourners appear as chiaroscuro figures within a color world. Especially noticeable and hideous is Orgo, who leads the procession on a white horse, guzzling liquor, and holding an American flag done in various shades of black and white. Eschewing his gaudy Uncle Sam apparel for an equally kitsch all-black cowboy outfit, he now becomes a monstrous and pathetic parody of El Topo: the brooding, revolutionary *charro* reduced to a bleached-blonde, bloated, wobbling drunkard. Concha wears a black version of her Church of Holy Blood gown, signifying the death of her own church and loss of power: her seduction-domination by Orgo which corresponded to the elephant's death. Fenix alone wears a garment that is not black, but the traditional red gown of the Church of Holy Blood, suggesting that he is momentarily the new symbol of Mexican populism and revolutionary struggle. After winding through the streets of Mexico City, the procession culminates at a garbage dump, where the coffin is balanced on a large ramp angling downward into a pit full of trash. After an obligatory trumpet fanfare by one of the *Circo* musicians, Orgo uses his omnipresent knife to cut the rope holding the coffin in place; one is struck by how many of Orgo's actions in *Santa sangre* entail using — and wielding — his phallic knife. In a long, slow-motion shot, the coffin crashes into the pit. It becomes another savage repudiation of *Tusk*, with Jodorowsky throwing the corpse of his previous film's primary symbol into the garbage, recalling Jodorowsky's concise comment about *Tusk*: "I bury the film." The death and unceremonious entombment of the elephant represents a burial of *Tusk*'s idealistic symbolism. For the people, the elephant is not a dignified metaphor of oppression but something far more utilitarian: the body is a source of much-needed food, and the disheveled masses — all covered in white ash — storm into the pit and joyously dismember the elephant's body.

Fenix is the only character who weeps at the funeral, grieving its death and, by extension, the triumph of colonialism (in contrast, in keeping with the tradition of the New Orleans jazz funeral, the mourners literally dance away from the "elephant's graveyard" as the *Circo* musicians break into Dixieland music). Orgo is particularly disgusted by his son's weeping, and mutters: "Quit crying like a little girl — I'll make you a man." The scene shifts to Orgo bringing Fenix to an abandoned art studio, where he immediately removes Fenix's red Church of Holy Blood robe with his knife, stripping the signifier of Mexican populism, and his mother's dress, from his son with the symbol of phallic, patriarchal power. Naked from the waist up, Fenix is tied to a chair, his arms secured behind him; it renders him *armless* and symbolically feminatized by the loss of his arms, bound behind the chair and out of camera range. Several close-ups of an eagle stencil are provided as Orgo affixes it to Fenix's chest. As noted, the eagle tattoo is unmistakably identical to the eagle on the back of the U.S dollar (the companion symbol on the back of the U.S. dollar, the Eye in the Pyramid, is inscribed on signs throughout the Great Town at the conclusion of *El Topo*). Dipping the knife-phallus in ink, the father tattoos the eagle onto his son's chest, an ordeal Jodorowsky captures primarily through a forty-five second close-up of Fenix as tears stream down his contorted face while Orgo literally carves the symbol of U.S. commerce onto Fenix's body.

Upon finishing the tattoo, or branding, Orgo leads his son to the mirror so the boy can gaze at himself with his newly acquired bloody mark. As Fenix ponders his wound, it suggests Lacan's mirror-stage: "The deflection of the specular *I* into a social *I*... the dialectic that will henceforth link the *I* into socially elaborated situations."[28] As previously suggested regarding Mara's obsession with the mirror in *El Topo*, the mirror-stage becomes a point of narcissism and defining of her own power; for Fenix, it only encompasses alienation. Indeed, the moment Fenix rec-

Dollar signs: Young Fenix (Adan Jodorowsky) tattooed with the eagle on the U.S. dollar bill by his father Orgo (Guy Stockwell).

ognizes himself as a subject is precisely the moment he has *already* been branded with a signifier — the eagle on the U.S. dollar. He is "always-already" the subject produced by the vicious Oedipal-colonial relationship; in the mirror, he can only see his own predetermined status as the offspring of that ferocious relationship. As Louis Althusser suggested:

> Before its birth, a child is ... always-already a subject, appointed as a subject in and by a specific familial ideological configuration which is "expected" once it is conceived ... this familial ideological configuration is, in it uniqueness, highly structured ... implacable and more or less "pathological."[29]

Filled with pride, Orgo stands next to his son and displays his own eagle tattoo in the mirror, producing a doubling effect: Fenix not only sees his own image, but his father's image, both father and son now adorned with a symbol that defines them as the U.S.A. As in *El Topo*, the son's entrance into manhood requires he *become* the father, and to complete Fenix's transition, Orgo dresses him in a replica of his own garish red, white, and blue cowboy outfit and parades him into the streets. Fenix is forced to become a miniature carbon copy of the kitsch version of Uncle Sam. In his new "Son of Orgo" persona, Fenix encounters Alma outside the studio, still in mime makeup and her funeral attire — a black tutu and a sort of kitsch Aztec headdress. She places her hands on her chest and mimes a fluttering bird, a poignant gesture intended to liberate Fenix's mind — and spirit (*alma*) — from the insignia brutally placed on his body: the mark of the Father, the mark of the United States of America.

Circo del Giallo

While the depiction of the *Circo del gringo* owes greatly to Fellini (*La strada*, *I clowns*), the *Circo*'s final performance and its horrific finale is inspired by the circuses depicted in Tod Browning's classic horror films (*The Unknown* and especially *Freaks*), coupled with the stylized, sexually-charged violence of *giallo* films. The Tattooed Woman works the crowd, whoring autographed pictures of her against the knife-thrower's target. Fenix, announced as "the Boy Magician," enters the circus ring accompanied by Alma, dressed identically to her funeral attire but with a noticeable change in color: with the exception of the yellow trim on her outfit she is dressed in the *Circo* colors of red (the body stocking), white (the mime makeup) and blue (the lace skirt). Alma crouches in a glass case which is covered in a sliver sheet; after Fenix's obligatory magician hand-waving gestures, the sheet is removed and Concha appears in her place, dressed in a gold costume suggesting a cross between a pixie and a Las Vegas showgirl. The circus acrobat, Concha performs a routine suspended in mid-air, hanging by her hair. One is struck by the prevalence of yellow on the circus tent roof—a color not absent in the earlier scenes in the *Circo* tent, but previously overwhelmed by the domination of red, white, and blue. The marked appearance and emphasis of yellow in these sequences becomes crucial in signifying the coming collapse of the *Circo del gringo* empire.

Concha notices Orgo and the Tattooed Woman brazenly flirting before exiting the circus ring and into the adjacent dressing room. She becomes enraged, and loudly interrupts her performance, demanding to be lowered, suggesting she is no longer "hung up" on Orgo. Whether to protect her son or prevent him from interfering in the impending violence, Concha locks Fenix in Orgo's dressing room trailer. It is painted red, white, and blue, and embossed with the words "El Gran Orgo" and the eagle that serves as the defining tattoo of both Orgo (father) and Fenix (son). As Concha prowls the *Circo* grounds searching for Orgo and the Tattooed Woman, alternations of flashing red and *green* lights drench the shots. The correlation is to the symbolic meaning of the colors on the Mexican national flag: red as the blood of heroes; green as hope and/or the struggle for independence. While *Santa sangre* is constantly saturated with the color red, the moment of Concha's revolt against Orgo is one of the few moments the color green significantly appears in the film. The lime-green robe and dominant green hues of the Tattooed Woman's body art suggests that hope in modern Mexico only exists in a vulgar, prostituted form of woman (with Concha—red and white—being the "holy" symbol of the Mexico people); independence is only to serve as the mistress of Orgo (the U.S.A). Another green-saturated moment comes during the elephant's funeral, with the bright green foliage of trees and bushes in and around the garbage dump suggesting at that moment that there is hope for the people simply because they are going to have food for that day.[30]

With Orgo and the Tattooed Woman about to have sexual intercourse in the dressing room (saturated in yellow hues), Concha takes a bottle of acid from a locker and exacts her revenge. Her first act of castrating Orgo is removing his blonde wig, revealing that he is prematurely bald. Again, the reference is the Biblical story of Samson, which is frequently used as a symbolic motif in Jodorowsky's films, specifically the removal of the fascist Colonel's toupee in *El Topo*.[31] The other aspect of this action is that the removal of the blonde wig strips Orgo of the color yellow: the color that now defines Concha and her dissent (in this way, a parody of the traditional symbolism of yellow as cowardice). As the Colonel's symbolic castration is followed by El Topo severing his penis with a knife, Concha also performs a direct method of physical castration: she pours the acid on Orgo's crotch. While certainly an act of violence motivated by her sexual jealousy, Concha's attack on Orgo also represents the moment of rebellion and liberation of the woman against the man—the literal destruction of the penis and source of phallic power. Moreover, within the national allegory of the film, the assault represents Mexico seeking its independence from and retribution against its domination by the United Sates.

6. *National Oedipus*

Achieving sainthood: Concha (Blanca Guerra) prepares to be murdered.

Enraged, Orgo drags Concha from the dressing room through the curtain separating the circus ring — a U.S. flag billowing in the foreground of the shot — and shoves her against the red, white, and blue knife-throwing target, her arms outstretched in the Crucifixion pose (as noted, another common trope in Jodorowsky's films). Rather than expressing any fear, let alone regret, Concha reacts with triumphant and even ecstatic laughter. In an overhead, slow-motion shot, Orgo swings the knives upward and amputates Concha's arms at the shoulders. She becomes the murdered "beloved saint," dismembered by Orgo: Mexico rendered armless and powerless, brutally crippled by an emasculated United States that can no longer seduce her, rape her, or, simply put, fuck her over. Orgo then lurches outside, myriad lights flashing on his face as he looks off-frame; the shot cuts to a long shot of the red, white, and blue circus tent (now punctuated with *yellow* lights) and the brightly lit "CIRCO GRINGO" sign: the gaudy trappings of Orgo's empire, with Orgo its naked and neutered king. As his final gesture of lost phallic mastery, he disgustedly draws the knife against his throat (again, recalling *El Topo* when the Colonel also kills himself after his castration). The scene cuts to Fenix watching in horror through the trailer window, and then to Alma watching Orgo's suicide with equal terror. These reaction shots cut back to Orgo lying dead. Behind him a disinterested group of homeless city dwellers huddle around a bonfire; stray dogs sniff the corpse and lap up the pools of blood. Like the dead elephant and the chickens seen pecking at one of Concha's detached arms immediately after her murder, the bodily symbols in *Santa sangre* are rendered into food once their thematic utility is exhausted.

Almost indifferently, the Tattooed Woman quickly escorts Alma to her van. A close-up of Alma, crying and staring out the rear window as it drives away, cuts to a Fenix frantically pounding on the trailer window, unable to escape its confines. The castration-as-revolution is not a cathartic, political-psychological moment of liberation (as in *El Topo*), but instead imprisons Fenix, the product of the Oedipal-colonial order, in perpetual trauma (with the trailer resembling a kind of anamorphic brain): the abuse of his tyrannical Father (the U.S.A.), the murder of his martyred mother (Mexico), and, above all, the loss of his "spirit"—Alma.[32]

The Red, White, and Blue Light District

The scene abruptly returns to the asylum, where the much older Fenix is lead through the ward by attendants. The lengthy flashback both provides the narrative backstory to explain Fenix's current metal anguish and constructs the allegorical conflict that will be played out for the remainder of the film: Fenix's struggle for liberation from the trauma of the Oedipal-colonial configuration. Deciding a night away from the asylum might be therapeutic for Fenix, the doctors send him and four mentally retarded boys to the city to see an adventure film about Robinson Crusoe. As they meet and greet a man in a comical, if slightly grotesque, Robinson Crusoe costume outside the theater, their chaperone from the asylum describes Crusoe as "one of life's great castaways." Crusoe's saga of being marooned in the world references Fenix and his own indeterminate isolation as a "castaway" within the Oedipal-colonial triangle.[33] Also, as evidenced by the tiger in the Dalí-influenced movie poster, there is a sly self-reference: the film is *Robinson Crusoe* (1968, U.S. title: *Robinson Crusoe and the Tiger*), which was directed by *Santa sangre*'s executive producer, René Cardona, Jr. However, the quaint evening at the movies is detoured by a sleazy pimp (Teo Jodorowsky), who corrals Fenix and the boys while dismissively pointing at the posters advertising René Cardona, Jr. films: "This kind of stuff will make you sick ... I'll take you somewhere else that is much more fun than the movies." His proposition is underscored by another, far cruder in-joke: as the Pimp takes the money from the boys, producing a packet of cocaine and, later, the opportunity to gangbang a plump prostitute, he stands in front of lobby cards for René Cardona, Jr.'s all-ages adventure film *Viaje fantástico en globo* (1974)—*Fantastic Trip in a Balloon*![34]

6. National Oedipus

The fall of the *Circo del gringo:* Orgo's unceremonious death in *Santa sangre*.

As the Pimp leads his new entourage down the street lined with prostitutes (some obviously men dressed in drag), Fenix remains unresponsive while the boys excitedly dance to the music of Pérez Prado provided by the pimp's portable stereo. These seedy sections of Mexico City in *Santa sangre* are frequently stagy and purposely artificial; they resemble tacky, even campy musicals rather than a horror film. One brief, hilarious confrontation between the Pimp and a rival parodies the studied dance-rumbles in *West Side Story*. The obvious artificiality also suggests that these settings are indeed "fantasies," and specifically fantasies that are reified, kitsch images and stereotypes taken from Hollywood as well as Mexican film and popular culture (hence, the acerbic irony of the Pimp's comment that "this kind of stuff will make you sick.... I'll take you somewhere else that is much more fun than the movies"). In this regard, Fenix's perspective and the camera's perspective become intertwined in a free indirect subjective. Subjective thoughts are depicted as actual events (on-screen productions of Fenix's mind), and actual events are framed from the perspective of a character's point of view (events seen through Fenix's troubled psyche, or his "sick world-view"). Moreover, patterns of red, white, and blue color combinations are obsessively used in many of the shots and sequences through juxtapositions of scenery and lighting. While the *Circo del gringo* may have collapsed, Mexico City continually remains under the domain of the *Cine del gringo*: first, by the Hollywood images and references that serve as the basis of Fenix's very thoughts; second, by the overdetermined cinematic representation of Mexico City as a tawdry space of prostitution and poverty continually bathed in the national colors of the United States.

The trip to the city has an unexpected effect on Fenix. While the mentally retarded boys wander off for their "fantastic voyage" with the heavyset prostitute, Fenix stands alone in the street in his catatonic haze before he recognizes a disturbing figure of the past: the Tattooed Woman as she lewdly dances with various men in the streets. A visible emotion finally appears on Fenix's face — rage. Yet the next morning at the asylum, Fenix literally performs cartwheels for the doctors and orderlies to express his exhilaration over his trip to the city. They are delighted with Fenix's apparent breakthrough, but Fenix's new vigor and release from catatonia has a far different motivation — it has given him the resolve to escape from the asylum and begin his retribution. Attaching a rope to his legs, he climbs to the top of the limbless tree that serves as his perch and leaps to the window. Staring outside, he sees his armless mother Concha standing stoically in the street, wearing a red sweater and pink dress. In effect, Concha is a living version of the iconic "beloved saint" of the Church of Holy Blood — the *Venus di Milo* as *chica moderna*. He repels down the walls of the asylum on the rope, the escape becoming a metaphor of both birth and Oedipal attachment. Still connected to the mother (branchless tree trunk) by the umbilical cord (rope) as he leaves the womb (the exit from the asylum through the window), Fenix joins Concha as they walk down the street and disappear into the fog — a symbol of Fenix's own clouded mind.

The scene returns to another sordid night on the ersatz streets of Mexico City, the set bathed in red hues, literally suggesting the space is the "red light" district. Juxtaposed with the saturation of red lighting is a constant flow of white and blue colors on the screen (walls, clothing). Even more so than the previous night's street scenes, the tawdry and artificial Mexico City where prostitution is the norm is a space almost entirely defined by the national colors of the U.S. Three soldiers stumble into a tenement building, where they are greeted by the Tattooed Woman, who leads them into her shabby apartment (red bed, white floors, blue walls) decorated in Mexican bric-a-brac. Two of the men wear green uniforms; if the green of the Tattooed Woman's body art suggests that "hope" in Mexico exists in a debased form of the woman, the soldiers suggest it also exists as a manifestation of the brute force of the State. One initially suspects the Tattooed Woman has now become a prostitute (or officially become a prostitute). In fact, she has become a madam, and leads the largest, most brutish of the soldiers through a lace curtain into Alma's dingy bedroom, captured in a striking overhead shot flooded in red light, except-

6. National Oedipus

ing the blue light shining on Alma in her bed and the white curtain. "She's a deaf-mute," the Tattooed Woman cajoles, "You can do whatever you want to her."

The already unnerving moment becomes even more perverse when the sexually aroused soldier begins cradling Alma like an infant. Horrified, Alma fends off the assault by rendering the soldier unconscious with a bottle, escaping into the streets in a white nightshirt. In this case, white can be read as signifying purity and virginity; if the danger to the purity of the Monsignor's young aide is the threat of Liberation Theology to Catholic orthodoxy, for Alma white represents a struggle to maintain purity in a world of sexual-economic exploitation. However, like the Monsignor's aide whose white suit also completes the combination of red (Church of Holy Blood) and blue (the police) into red, white, and blue, Alma's white nightshirt, within the red and blue hues that dominate the city scenes, similarly serves to complete the triptych of the national colors of the U.S.A.—colors which do not merely dominate *Santa sangre*, but overdetermines the presence of the U.S. in Mexico throughout the film.[35] She next encounters a businessman (blue suit, white collar, red tie), which is even more surreal and disturbing than her encounter with the soldiers. Silently, he stares at Alma, then tears off his own ear and attempts to stuff it into her mouth. Certainly, the reference is to Van Gogh's famous gesture of unrequited love, as well as self-reference to a tender scene in *The Holy Mountain* when an old man gives his glass eye to an underage prostitute. It is also a symbolic representation of Alma's own deafness and muteness, unable to speak out against the abuse she is subjected to as an object of prostitution. Fleeing this new, strange assailant, Alma runs into an intersection where she is almost hit by passing cars: the first scene of these city sequences bearing any hint of urban realism. However, when she does find refuge, it is on another symbol of Americana: the roof of a Kenworth semi-truck (painted, of course, red, white, and blue).

This scene cuts to a shot of an expressionistic shadow moving against the wall of a building; the shot not only suggests horror film conventions, but the letters on the neon sign are all red and blue, except one "n," which is white, an inclusion done simply to complete the constant motifs of red, white, and blue color combinations in the city shots. A lengthy point-of-view shot follows as the camera enters the building as the drunken solders leave, and maneuvers through a maze of tenement hallways, accompanied by a reprise of Pérez Prado's "Caballo negro." The dizzying shot echoes the overhead, point-of-view "bird's eye" shot that began the long flashback sequence comprising the first part of the film, and Prado's driving mambo number becomes even more menacing as it becomes a strangely appropriate accompaniment for murder. With the camera still assuming the point of view of the unseen figure, a hand with long, red fingernails enters the frame to push open the door, and the Tattooed Woman stares in horror at the camera. As she recoils onto the bed, the shot cuts to a close-up of a gleaming knife flying through the air: the flight of the eagle (the U.S.) now becomes the flight of the knife (the phallus). This shot "cuts" to the knife striking the Tattooed Woman in the sternum, blood pouring from her mouth. It is much more reminiscent of the graphic, stylized murders of the *giallo* genre than Hitchcock, specifically Jodorowsky's parody of *Psycho*'s legendary shower scene, in which the sheer violence is generated by editing: the relentless "cutting" of the shots segmenting and dismembering Marion's body on the screen, matched by shrieking, atonal violins. As Jodorowsky noted, the influence of *giallo* and the use of Prado were consciously incorporated to explicitly distance *Santa Sangre* from Hitchcock and *Psycho*: "I laugh to myself about the 'great' crimes of Hitchcock — they are poor crimes, they are nothing to me! Television crimes! *I want a bad taste crime*, a violent crime with the Mexican dancing music and more blood, more! A fantastic crime!"[36]

The Lady-Killer and the Lady Killer

Following the murder of the Tattooed Woman, the scene shifts to a burlesque theater where photos and posters advertise performances by "Concha and her Magic Hands." The stylized black and white photos — close-ups of hands — are reminiscent of the work of Man Ray. One of the posters near the ticket office parodies Botticelli's painting *The Birth of Venus*, with Concha in a blue evening dress replacing the nude Venus floating on the water while standing on a clamshell (*concha* is Spanish for "shell" — and also used as a slang term for the vagina). The scene cuts to Concha on stage in the dress seen in the poster. Barely visible, Fenix stands directly behind her in a mime's black body suit, his arms extending from her shoulders to provide her arms and "magic hands." As a line of Mariachi musicians at the rear of the stage provides the musical accompaniment, Concha quotes passages from the book of Genesis as if she were telling a fairy-tale to children, while Fenix illustrates the descriptions with hand gestures.[37] As Concha lists the various animals created by God, Fenix mimes their various actions, including fluttering birds (his gesture almost identical to the one Alma responded with when first seeing his eagle tattoo). With the introduction of evil to the Garden of Eden, Fenix's hands portray the slithering Serpent waving in front of Concha's face; he then cups his hands near his mother's mouth as Concha mimes eating the Apple. Finally, Fenix interlocks his fingers and slaps his palms together as Concha wails, "Sin: Universal Sin!" Copulation, as "Universal Sin," manifests itself in *Santa Sangre* in two respects. One is the incestuous relationship between Concha and Fenix, the violation of the most essential and "universal" of social taboos, where literally "two become one" in the physical and mental union of mother and son. The second is the degree sex and sin becomes inseparable via relationships defined by exploitation and domination throughout *Santa sangre*: the mother and son, the husband and wife, the married man and mistress, the john and the prostitute. In this context, the immorality of sex and sin in *Santa sangre* must be understood in relationship to Liberation Theology: a sin is not a specific, inherently evil act (sex); a sin is *any* action that negatively affects another, and a civil society at large.

With the depiction of Universal Sin completing the performance, a row of showgirls dart on stage while Concha shimmies off-stage, with Fenix in tow behind her, literally attached to his mother. Irritable, she impolitely orders Fenix to disconnect himself from her and then storms off to the dressing room. While Fenix stands backstage, he is approached by Rubi (Gloria Contreras). As a stagehand injects her with narcotics, Rubi places Fenix's hands on her breast and brashly suggests they could make "a great act — *between your hands and my body*" (emphasis added). It is a macabre and darkly ironic foreshadowing of the act they will soon perform, and ultimately what — or *who*— comes between Fenix's hands and Rubi's body. The scene suddenly cuts to a shot from the perspective of the audience in the balcony, and the curtain opens to reveal Rubi, like the patron saint of the Church of Holy Blood, as a schoolgirl; moreover, her navy blue sailor's costume, white scarf, red hair and lipstick again defines sexual exploitation in the color scheme of red, white, and blue. Amid the cartoon-like classroom backdrop, she sits at a desk, legs spread in a classic pin-up position; behind her stands an older man in a lavender suit and handlebar moustache, presumably the teacher.[38] As a mushy pop song begins, he starts to lip-synch as Rubi performs the customary bump-and-grind maneuvers for the audience. As she walks onto the runway, an overhead shot depicts the men in the audience swarming around her, arms reaching upward: a parody of Marilyn Monroe's "Diamonds Are a Girl's Best Friend" number in *Gentlemen Prefer Blondes* (1953). No longer spectators, the "male members" of the audience begin tearing off all of Rubi's clothes, save her G-string. The removal of Rubi's clothes concludes the striptease number, with the added dimension that the men in the paying audience, and not Rubi herself, have been given the task — or privilege — of stripping the woman. In his essay "Striptease" (ca. 1957), Roland Barthes noted that the power of the striptease is in the act of removing clothing — the tease rather than the strip — and "woman is desexualized at the moment when she is stripped naked."[39] If the sexual component of the striptease is manifest in the act of shedding clothes and not the naked body, Rubi's number is staged so the *men* are no longer passive voyeurs, but active participants in removing her clothing and determining her status: the woman stripped, and desexualized, by men.

Intrigued by Rubi's proposition, and aroused by her performance, Fenix asks her to meet him at the burlesque theater after hours. When she arrives for her date, Fenix emerges from the back of the theater. He is dressed as his father Orgo, resplendent in the gaudy, sequined red, white and blue cowboy outfit as he swaggers towards the stage. Initially stunned, Rubi quickly and completely submits to Fenix: "I'll do anything you want." Fenix explains they will perform a knife-throwing act, and to better facilitate the performance, he will "hypnotize" her. As Orgo did with Concha before seducing her, Fenix waves the knife-phallus back and forth in front of Rubi's face, and she succumbs to his hypnotic-sexual control (his motions also recall his miming of the Serpent's seduction of Eve during the "Creation of the World" performance). A recreation of the knife-throwing act between Orgo and the Tattooed Woman ensues, with Jodorowsky inserting shots from the previous sequence, juxtaposing footage of the Tattooed Woman with Rubi similarly reacting with sexual excitement to the knives precariously hurled at her. However, as Fenix is about to throw the last knife between Rubi's legs to consummate and climax the act, Concha interrupts them, and she orchestrates the final outcome of Fenix and Rubi's encounter: "You know what to do.... This girl has defiled you with her lust." Fenix's knife hand shakes violently, as he attempts to maintain control of his limb and pleads with his mother not to force him to do what she demands. "I'm not asking you: I'm *ordering* you! *My* hands and *my* parts to kill her! KILL HER!" As Concha maneuvers in front of Fenix, his arms becoming her arms while she literally comes between Fenix's hands and Rubi's body, the knife is hurled into Rubi's heart.

The grisly climax of the knife-throwing routine complete, Concha orders Fenix to dispose of the body, and they are going "home," a command Concha punctuates with a suggestive kiss on Fenix's neck. However, Rubi's burial is played out as surreal black comedy. Aladin drags out a mammoth rabbit costume with which to wrap Rubi's body; it references *El Topo* and the rabbit as a symbol of fertility, which is killed by the "disease" carried by the man: the influence of a devious, powerful, seductive woman (Concha). The scene cuts to a cemetery, the set design highly influenced by James Whale's graveyards in *Frankenstein* and *Bride of Frankenstein*. Accompanied by loud, overwrought church music, Fenix slathers Rubi's corpse in white paint, an attempt to purify the woman he (or, more correctly, his mother) murdered. As Fenix begins to fill the grave with dirt, a strange phenomenon occurs: white light begins to shine from the grave, and the shot abruptly jump-cuts to a slow-motion shot of a swan hovering over the grave, wings flapping wildly. The ascension of Rubi's soul into Heaven is symbolized through surreal, dark humor akin to Buñuel.

As suggested previously, most of the images in *Santa sangre* are on-screen projections derived from Fenix's troubled mind, or objective events filtered through Fenix's subjective state of madness, his "sick world-view." Moreover, many of Fenix's perceptions are informed by Hollywood cinema: his very thoughts are recycled by-products of old movies. Throughout *Santa sangre*, numerous classic Hollywood films, horror films, and even Santo films are referenced, most obviously James Whale's *The Invisible Man* (1932). However, another classic horror film from the 1930s invites comparison to *Santa sangre*: Karl Freund's *Mad Love* (1935). In *Mad Love*, a famous concert pianist looses his hands in an accident and undergoes a radical surgical procedure whereby a new set of hands are transplanted: those of a recently executed murderer whose violent impulses foments a compulsion to kill.

However, in *Santa sangre*, the malevolent force that takes possession of Fenix's hands is specifically *the mother*. While Fenix can adopt the "lady-killing" persona and powers of his father (early in the film, Fenix makes a point of telling Aladin his father is from America but can never return because "he killed a woman"), his mother thoroughly controls him within the Oedipal framework, leading to the inevitable comparison of *Santa sangre* with *Psycho*, with Fenix a Norman Bates by way of Fellini. While Norman Bates dresses as his mother and adopts her persona to kill the object of lust, Fenix and Concha become physically and mentally intertwined to eliminate all obstacles in their consuming Oedipal relationship. In this respect, one of the more fascinating moments of the film is the interaction between Axel Jodorowsky and Blanca Guerra, whose acting relationship is at once highly theatrical and yet uncannily symbiotic—or, at the very least, quite intimate. As Alejandro Jodorowsky recounted:

> Every shot needs different angles, different positions to disguise [her arms]. But it works — Blanca and Axel were a good couple, because she held my son's sex in her hands all the time — that's why they're doing so well. I approved the technique — it's not so moral, but it's like that! The incest thing worked well like that!"[40]

Look, Ma — No Hands!

Rubi's burial scene shifts to a long zoom-in to Fenix thrashing about in bed in white, silk pajamas with frilly cuffs. His arms are stretched in the air, emphasizing his long fingernails and red nail polish, suggesting emasculation and even feminization under the tyranny of the mother (the "mama's-boy"). Subjective shots of his nightmare are intercut into the scene: exactly recreating a shot in the flashback, the older Fenix watches the elephant die in the den of the family home, followed by shots of Fenix himself, naked and kneeling, with blood prodigiously pouring from *his* nose. The elephant, the symbol of the oppressed by colonialism in *Tusk* who dies when Orgo (the U.S.) and Concha (Mexico) have sex, is now specifically connected to Fenix, the offspring of their sexual and political relationship. Moreover, blood and male ejaculate is equated: Fenix's delayed climax to Rubi's murder coordinated by his mother; his own Oedipal desire which is literally "overflowing." As he fitfully rolls over, he drapes his arm over Concha, dressed in a similar white silk nightgown, the two sleeping next to each other as if they were a married couple rather than mother and son. Greatly annoyed, she snarls, "Wake up! You can't atone for your sins with nightmares!" The moment his mother awakens, Fenix subsumes his own identity in the overriding presence of Concha; he literally becomes an extension of the maternal figure. As they lay in bed she yawns, and Fenix's hand — now Concha's surrogate hands — automatically rises to cover her mouth, and he emits a sympathy yawn. Shortly after getting out of bed, Concha elegantly stands in her fancy nightgown, a surreal convergence of the *Venus di Milo* and Gloria Swanson in *Sunset Boulevard* (1950). She remains motionless until Fenix can maneuver behind her, simply so he can provide the exaggerated hand gestures as she delivers her lines in a highly melodramatic manner.

While the couple eats breakfast together (literally), Concha points out a film poster of Whale's *The Invisible Man* on the wall. The colors of the poster are enhanced by the fact that much of the décor of the mansion is in shades of black, white, and grey; not surprisingly, *The Invisible Man* poster depicts the title character in a red robe, sporting white bandages, and set against a blue background. Orgo, the hideous parody of the cowboy and Uncle Sam, is replaced by a new symbol of the U.S.: Fenix as the doomed "invisible man" taken from an iconic Hollywood horror film.[41] Concha contemptuously comments on the poster, her derision augmented by overstated gestures (provided by Fenix): "Without me, you're *nothing*.... No one sees you, no one notices you, just like your *stupid* hero!" In this respect, a key shift in the latter part of *Santa sangre* is Concha becoming the film's "monster" in lieu of Orgo: a figure of cruel domination and emasculation, combining the role of the absent castrating father and the object of forbidden desire, the mother. The new status of Concha as a brutal tyrant as well as a beloved saint reflects the extent to which the Oedipal psychodrama and the national allegory become inseparable. Until his death, Orgo is the cruel, dominant and dominating figure of the film: a character seducing, controlling, exploiting, and even torturing those under his domain — the oppressor as a kitsch embodiment of the Ugly American. In the latter part of the film, Concha assumes the role of Fenix's master: the symbol of a Mexico rendered powerless, the mother(land) savagely and literally crippled and dismembered by the father(land), which Fenix clings to with complete devotion and unrequited desire. In turn, Concha demands Fenix serve her with complete subservience: a menacing and malevolent figure, a symbol of the results of colonialism devoid of sentimentality and pathos, the antithesis of the dead elephant (*Tusk*) cast into the garbage dump. In short, Fenix becomes the national allegory of a Mexico born from the economic and cultural domination of the U.S., and cast in the Oedipal structures of the "pathological" holy family: a disgusting and despotic father; a maimed and domineering mother; the son perpetually subjected to the tyranny of both parents as the traumatized product of his father(land) and mother(country). In this extent, and like *El Topo*, *Santa sangre* also plays out through "Master-Slave" dialectical conflicts. Initially, the Master-Slave dialectic is constructed between Orgo and his sexual domination of women (Concha, the Tattooed Woman). The dialectical resolution of the Slave's liberation from the Master is achieved when Concha castrates Orgo, while she is murdered and mutilated: an act of rapturous defiance and a revolutionary action that elevates her to sainthood. This event constructs a new Master-Salve dialectic: the Master now

Concha and the Slave now Fenix ("the invisible man" in the image of the father yet existing entirely to serve the mother — the master who assumes the slave is nothing without her, when in actuality the master is nothing without the slave).

While the relationship of Orgo, Concha and Fenix has been addressed in terms of the Oedipal holy family as a national allegory for colonialism, there is a third element that defines these relationships: the order of *sadism* versus the order of *masochism*. In *Coldness and Cruelty*, Gilles Deleuze suggests the literature of Sade and Masoch, and the two sexual practices named after the respective authors—sadism and masochism — must be viewed as distinct and independent procedures. Sadism and masochism are not inherently connected and cannot be conflated into "sadomasochism," but are two different expressions of sexual power and servitude entirely — each with its own rituals, dynamics, and ends. Deleuze argued:

> In [sadism] the fantasy acquires maximum aggressive power, systemization, and capacity for intervention in the real world: the idea is projected with extraordinary violence. The masochistic use of fantasy is totally different: it consists of neutralizing the real and containing the ideal within the fantasy.[42]

In sadism, power must be constantly actualized and continually demonstrated as material evidence of and on the body: sex acts, bodily functions, beatings, rape, even murder. In contrast, as Deleuze contends, "*Waiting and suspense* are the essential characteristics of the masochistic experience."[43] Power in masochism is kept at the virtual, in a state of suspension — performance, fetish, bondage — which are manifest in the motifs of "physical suspension" in Masoch's *Venus in Furs*.[44] Moreover, sadism and masochism revolve around parental and patriarchal premises, but of a completely different, antithetical nature. According to Deleuze's formulation, "In the case of sadism, the father is placed above the laws; he becomes a higher principle with the mother as his essential victim. In the case of masochism, the totality of the law is invested upon the mother, who expels the father from the symbolic realm."[45]

In *Santa sangre*, the *Circo del gringo*, which exalted the father (Orgo) and negated the mother (Concha), is a thoroughly sadistic order. However, the collapse of the sadistic order follows with the construction of a masochistic order. Elements of sadism are certainly contained within the relationship of Concha and Fenix, specifically his serial murders and Concha's depiction as the stereotypical controlling, punishing "sadistic Oedipal mother" fantasy (the mother of Norman Bates in *Psycho*).[46] The world of Concha and Fenix is private, hermetic, and, as revealed in the film's conclusion, an elaborate illusion Fenix constructed around his long-dead mother: "Neutralizing the real and containing the ideal within the fantasy." It becomes a world composed of fetishes and symbols in which the mother assumes complete idealization and the father expelled: the Mother as the Law (or, so to speak,

Concha in Furs). Fenix does not merely acquiesce to her authority; he literally exists in a state of "bondage" to Concha, physically and mentally connected to her in a completely subservient relationship. Fenix becomes doubly entrapped within the Oedipal-colonial order of *Santa sangre* through two different psycho-sexual power dynamics: the sadistic rule of the father–U.S.A. amid the frenzy of the *Circo del gringo,* and the masochistic devotion to the Mother-Mexico within the isolation of the home.

Concha announces the next activity for the morning: piano practice. As well as a parodic reference to *Mad Love,* the black comedy is derived from the cliché of the reluctant boy who must take "piano lessons" not only per the dictates of his mother, but through his mother. After a few seconds of playing, Concha impatiently berates Fenix for his lack of grace and style, and announces the next selection will be for the "patron saint." A shrine has been constructed in the alcove similar to the one in the Church of Holy Blood: the statue of the armless schoolgirl surrounded by religious curios, bathed in red light — another stunning contrast to the otherwise black, white, and gray interiors of the mansion. The duo begins a rousing music-hall version of the folk-song the church members sang in defiance of the landowner, police, and the Catholic hierarchy earlier in the film. As Concha belts out the song, Fenix hammers out the accompaniment on the piano keys. The camera slowly zooms in to his contorted face as pounding kettledrums and loud white noise begins to overwhelm the piano and singing. A delirious barrage of images follow: chickens pecking at a bloody, dismembered arm on the grand piano; Fenix, very much resembling Christ, pelted by a torrent of live chickens; an insert of an earlier shot with a bulldozer demolishing the Church of Holy Blood cutting to Fenix collapsing under the onslaught of chickens. The montage constructs the metaphorical relationship between Fenix, Christian iconography, the destruction of the people's church, and the death and dismemberment of his own patron saint: his mother/mother-country. The shot cuts back to Fenix — or, more correctly, Concha — slamming both hands against the piano keys in frustration. She screams: "Stop it! It's always roosters or swans! You never see anything else in your ridiculous hallucinations!" While the line is a highly ironic self-reference to the visions themselves, it also suggests that Concha's maternal bond, and control, over Fenix is so complete she also sees the on-screen, subjective, tormented "ridiculous hallucinations" of her son: even the interaction between Fenix's inner thoughts and the camera must be filtered, mediated, and critiqued by the mother. A third musical selection is attempted, a lounge-style romantic ballad (in a touch of surreal comedy, Aladin, dressed in a black fakir's costume, delicately places a large candelabra on the piano). Mother and son sing and play in unison, ending their rendition with a sensual kiss on the lips, none-too-subtly implying the incestuous component of the relationship.

Following his obligatory piano practice, Fenix watches *The Invisible Man* on a small television; he is dressed identically to the title character and mimics his gestures. Another large *Invisible Man* movie poster adorns the walls, and the room itself is a laboratory modeled on Whale's film. Aladin, supplying more surreal comic relief, is dressed in a suit and a doctor's surgical mask, a parody of the classic horror film assistant to the mad scientist. Reenacting a scene from *The Invisible Man*, Fenix drinks his experimental potion. After throwing himself about in agony, he unravels the bandages around his head while the TV shows the famous scene when Claude Rains reveals his invisibility to the shocked townspeople. Yet Fenix has not become invisible, and he gazes in the mirror with great disappointment, recalling the scene in the mirror after the eagle tattoo is carved into his chest. Again, Fenix only experiences the alienation inherent in the mirror-stage, the realization that he is trapped in a role "always-already" assigned to him and not the image-ideal he longs to become: not only a figure that cannot be controlled, but cannot even be seen — a figure who is no longer a "social *I*" and no longer even a "specular *I*." While Concha considers Fenix "a nothing" who cannot function without her, the bane of his existence is that he cannot be "nothing," he cannot fade into thin air to escape her domination: the Slave (son) who has yet to realize that he can function as a thing-in-itself, not merely as an "appendage" of the Master (mother). As Fenix storms out of the laboratory in frustration, Concha, standing at the top of the stairs in her red Church of Holy Blood robe, is quick to point out the futility of his experiment — and escape attempt — and harshly reminds him of his place: "So, you failed again! Come here! Come here! COME!" To compound the insult of his failure, Fenix must become Concha's hands for a task associated with feminine domestic duties: knitting new stockings for the shrine statue. As Concha intently concentrates and mutters, "Knit one, pearl two," Fenix stares blankly, resigned and humiliated. To this extent, *Santa Sangre* also reiterates the problematic representation of women that underscored *El Topo*: powerful and evil forces who not only seek to dominate but thoroughly emasculate the main male character.

The Man-Woman in the Silver Mask

Still pursing his efforts to become invisible, Fenix walks to the nearby pharmacy for the necessary ingredients. The clerk at the store clearly expresses her romantic interest in Fenix and suggests a dinner date for that evening, to which Fenix absent-mindedly agrees. However, as he is about to leave, Fenix notices an advertising float in the street for an upcoming wrestling match featuring the world's strongest woman, *La Santa* ("the Saint," gender feminine). A new, iconic statue appears to him: a large *papier-mâché* figure of a woman in a *lucha libre* mask and tights. The startling reaction shot depicts Fenix in a wrestling match of his own: a mammoth python now emerged from his pants and coiled around his torso (the Freudian symbolism itself being self-evident). It is also the first shot of the film clearly specified as a subjective image; in her reaction shot, the baffled clerk only sees Fenix wrestling an invisible object in the air: his penis (which, perhaps, has been made invisible courtesy of Concha).

La Santa is obviously a parody of the legendary *El Santo, el Enmascarado de Plata* (*the Saint, the Silver-Masked Man*). Undoubtedly the most famous *luchador* in the history of Mexican pro wrestling, Santo starred in over fifty *lucha libre* films from the late 1950s to the early 1980s, and remains one of the most important figures in Mexican popular culture. In this respect, the parody of Santo as La Santa in *Santa sangre* becomes import for two reasons. One is the gender-skewing and transformation of the epitome of Mexican masculinity, the *luchador* (and specifically Santo), into a hermaphrodite.[47] Another is the political significance of the Santo mythos in Mexican popular culture. In all of his films, Santo is not even the cliché of the two-dimensional character, but a one-dimensional character: a national allegory affirming the myths of Mexican democracy, justice, and progress whose duty is saving Mexican society from forces impeding those goals.[48] As Orgo is a monstrous parody of the United States in the form of its pop-culture icons (Uncle Sam, the cowboy), La Santa becomes a perverse parody of the cultural and political myths of pre–Tlatelolco Mexico embodied by Santo.

After plying La Santa with an abundance of liquor, the two retire to a small theater in the basement of the mansion, where Fenix plans to entertain La Santa with a magic act. Fenix opens with the customary "Ladies and Gents..."—a hilarious line in that La Santa is the only person in the audience, and both a "lady" and a "gent." After announcing he will "change the mummy in the sarcophagus onstage into 100 flying doves," the act goes horribly awry when Fenix opens the Mummy's coffin to reveal the Mommy: Concha, dressed as another Hollywood iconic image, Elizabeth Taylor in *Cleopatra* (1963). The small theater transforms from magic show into *Grande Guignol* as Concha spits out her orders for Fenix to kill La Santa, commanding her son to eliminate another object—and rival—of sexual attraction. Unable to control his hands, Fenix literally jumps into action and attacks La Santa, clawing his/her face with his fingernails. A broad parody of action-film sequences ensues, mixing stylized *giallo* violence, Peckinpah-style slow-motion, martial arts films, and the stagy fight scenes of *lucha libre* films where *luchadores* and monsters battled in catacombs as if they were in the wrestling ring. Fenix is soon defeated, and La Santa attempts to exit the dank, underground theater in revulsion. Livid, Concha hisses: "Use the sword!" Fenix obeys and eviscerates the brawny *luchador(a)* with an appropriately larger phallic weapon than the one employed on Rubi. La Santa, the parody of El Santo, symbol and national allegory of Mexican democracy and justice for a previous generation of Mexican filmgoers, is brutally dispatched by a new national allegory: Fenix, the troubled and traumatized offspring of the relationship between the U.S. (the pitiless, abusive father Orgo) and Mexico (the crippled, domineering mother Concha).

Sanity: Redemption and "Liberation"

While the grisly events with La Santa transpire, Alma is reintroduced into the film. Drifting through the city after the murder of the Tattooed Woman, she wanders past the burlesque theater and learns the address of the mansion where Fenix and Concha have relocated. As she investigates the estate, the mansion becomes a virtual mélange of horror film scenery: the *giallo* setting of the main room with the red-lit shrine becomes a disorientating hallway owing to *The Cabinet of Dr. Caligari*, which, in turn, leads to a dreary, disheveled bedroom derived from classic haunted house movies (*Psycho*; Whale's *The Old Dark House* from 1932). After discovering a mysterious object in the bed (which is unseen by the audience in order to maintain the suspense leading to the revelation of the object in the finale), Alma proceeds to a make-up table where she begins to apply white face paint — returning to her existence as the circus mime. Again, this is explicitly not to say that this gesture is an attempt to recoup "lost innocence," and from the very outset of the film, Alma and Fenix "always-already" live under the colors of the *Circo del gringo*. Rather, it is Alma's symbolic attempt to return to the time before the trauma of the Oedipal-colonial psychodrama was originally and horrifically manifest: a final effort to redeem Fenix.

A montage is formed of Alma's reflection in the mirror as she applies the white mime makeup and Fenix caressing the whitewashed face of La Santa's corpse in the graveyard, his futile effort to bring purity to another victim of his violence (or the violence performed under the directives of his mother). Another surreal hallucination quickly overwhelms him. Bodies begin to rise from the graves, naked women covered in white paint clad only in wedding veils (also symbols of virginity); one dead bride leads a white horse covered in tattoos resembling those of the Tattooed Woman through the scene.

Jodorowsky stated the sequence was both homage to and parody of the archetypal zombie film, George Romero's *Night of the Living Dead* (1968): "I made some echoes, but I played with them. In *Night of the Living Dead*, they are terrible people coming back from the dead, and here they are beautiful women. *It is anti-terror.*"[49] The scene also suggests Italian horror cinema — not only the zombie films of Lucio Fulci, but Mario Bava's *Il rosso segno della follia* (*The Red Mark of Madness*, 1970; U.S. title: *Hatchet for a Honeymoon*), a *giallo* film about a serial killer whose victims are young brides. As he falls to his knees, covering his head and begging for forgiveness from his victims, the disturbed logic of Fenix has reached an unbearable and untenable crisis that must not only be understood in the framework of the Oedipal complex (the sadistic Oedipal mother of *Psycho*), but the perspective of national allegory: the controlling, vengeful mother as a figure of the nation literally crippled by colonialism, and the Oedipal obsession of a perverse nationalism. Bloodshed and serial murder, the staple of the *giallo* world of sex and violence, becomes Fenix's misguided mission to keep Mexico (the woman, specifically the mother-image) "pure," and prevent it from being violated and dominated by the Orgos of the world (the U.S.A.) and producing more Orgos — one being Fenix himself. In the untenable contradictions of Fenix's trauma and "sick world-view," the murder and purification of women is tantamount to the misguided creation of political heroes through "holy blood."

The scene shifts back to the mansion as Fenix careens through the rooms; the camera physically rocks back and forth to the point of producing as sense of motion sickness for the viewer, accompanied by over-amplified crashing sounds as he knocks over furniture and objects begin to fall from the walls. The mansion — Fenix's mad, masochistic fantasy-order — begins to fall apart with his increasing mental anguish.[50] He stumbles into the shrine, where the statue now is a wax figure of his mother in the girl's school clothes. Fenix is only calmed when he notices Alma sitting in the room, patiently waiting for him, now dressed identically to the costume she wore for the elephant's funeral. He implores: "You come ... to take me away?" They embrace and kiss — only to be interrupted by a demented Concha. Still adorned in the Church of Holy Blood robes, she hysterically proclaims, "You will never take my son away from me!" In a highly melodramatic battle for the control of Fenix's mind between Concha and Alma, Fenix madly lurches between the two before his mother assumes mastery. Seizing a pair of knives from the shrine, mother and son begin to pursue Alma, facing the camera as it tilts sideways in an exaggeration of horror film clichés, seemingly stalking the film audience as well as the victim, the audience assuming the point of view of the victim.[51] However, the ill-timed arrival of the pharmacy woman for her dinner date with Fenix interrupts the macabre ritual of murder; Fenix throws a knife at her but misses, sending the terrified woman screaming into the street for the police. Now standing behind his mother, once more physically as well as mentally attached to her, even subsumed by her (the domination of his mind *and* body), Fenix is reduced to serving as her arms for her malicious intentions — destroying any object that could sever their national–Oedipal connection. Concha (and, by extension, Fenix) pursues Alma, who backs away but otherwise offers no resistance. As the tumultuous music builds, Alma stands in place, arms outstretched (the Crucifixion posture), allowing the opportunity for Concha-Fenix to deliver a lethal thrust with the knife. Instead, Fenix plunges the blade into Concha's stomach — or his mother's womb. As Concha staggers away from the two and stands beside the shrine of the original patron saint, she laughs deviously before she disappears — or becomes invisible: "You'll *never* be free of me!"

The moment his mother disappears abruptly cuts to a flashback montage,

Mama's boy: Fenix (Axel Jodorowsky) and his mother Concha (Blanca Guerra) united in the conclusion of *Santa sangre*.

filmed as a news report with a jiggling hand-held camera; another news camera can be seen in a number of these shots as well. A catatonic young Fenix is carried away from the trailer by various circus clowns while the armless corpse of his mother is hauled away on a sheet-covered stretcher. "My mother is dead," the older Fenix states with a mixture of relief, resignation, and sorrow (a realization that his *mother country* is dead as well). As ghosts of the Clown Chorus appear (or, more correctly, on-screen manifestations of Fenix's memories), Alma leads Fenix to the bedroom. The sheet is pulled away, revealing a life-sized ventriloquist doll of Concha laying in the bed — the most overtly parodic reference to *Psycho* and the climactic moment when Norman Bates' mother is also revealed to be an inanimate body: the mother's decayed corpse brought to life through Norman mimicking her screeching voice (ironically, the wooden, lifeless doll recalls Gloria Swanson in *Sunset Boulevard* as strongly as Concha's hilariously melodramatic parodies). An inserted shot reveals that the mother and son musical duets were simply Fenix singing and moving his arms, miming playing piano while holding the Concha dummy in front of him. Unlike López Moctezuma's *Alucarda*, where the subjective and objective continually converge but are never differentiated, *Santa sangre* clarifies that much of the film, especially the second half, has been a series of surreal events filtered through the main character's insanity. As powerful and poignant as the conclusion is, it also manufactures a degree of dramatic, or, perhaps more correctly, "poetic" weakness. The final revelation, or concession to the viewer, that the character's madness and the narrative were in fact merged to produce the film's surrealism, to explicitly differentiate the objective events with Fenix's "sick world-view," dilutes the poetic power of the free indirect subjective in favor of supplying narrative cohesion and resolution.

With the assistance of the clowns, Fenix flings the dummy off the balcony of the staircase to indeed demonstrate her obsolescence, then demolishes the shrine and throws the statue of the patron saint next to the ventriloquist doll.[52] Using a candle from the shrine, Alma sets the dummies aflame, providing a funeral pyre for the rebirth of Fenix (Phoenix). As the clowns dance round the flames, Alma removes one of two remaining physical signifiers of parental domination from Fenix's body — the long, red fingernails needed to convert his hands into his mother's hands — and in the process, restores Fenix's masculinity from the clutches of his mother. The clowns applaud the act of liberation and disappear, followed by Fenix's comic sidekick and spiritual companion Aladin in a tearful farewell. As Fenix stands next to the pyre, Alma then repeats the same gesture she performed when Fenix was initially scarred with the tattoo of the American eagle and forced to adorn the hideous, kitsch-cowboy attire of Orgo in their youth: she places her hands on his chest and mimes a fluttering bird as she raises her arms in the air. The rebirth of the mythological Phoenix becomes the final gesture of liberation. While Fenix cannot remove the physical scar inflicted by Orgo, he can be freed psychologically and

6. National Oedipus

spiritually from the yoke of his father (the U.S.A.) as well as his mother (Mexico) through recovering his own lost spirit: Alma.[53]

Fenix and Alma exit the mansion, now filled with smoke from the funeral pyre; in this sense, Fenix leaves the fog he literally entered when he escaped from the asylum and first joined his armless mother on the city streets. Nevertheless, it can also be assumed that Alma does not exist as well, but is an onscreen projection of Fenix's still-troubled imagination. They are greeted by a *new* set of flashing red and blue lights: police sirens. A mechanical, disembodied voice from a megaphone provides the classic and clichéd line: "Put your hands up!" At Alma's urging, Fenix raises his hands, his act of surrender to the police paradoxically his first act of free will: he can now raise his hands under his own volition. "My hands!" he ecstatically repeats as a mantra, holding them aloft. The final shot slowly zooms out to depict Fenix, hands stretched over his head, surrounded by police pointing pistols at him, their fedoras and trench coats anachronistic throwbacks to *film noir* and Hollywood gangster movies. The shot ends in freeze-frame, and an excerpt from Psalm 143 appears:

> I stretch out my hands to thee:
> My soul thirsts to thee like a parched land...
> Teach me the way I should go
> For to thee I lift up my soul.

The overtly religious citation, and with it Fenix's spiritual rebirth — his redemption — through the inclusion of Psalm 143, is as much a political statement as a religious affirmation, especially in the context of contemporary Liberation Theology. With *El Topo*, individual enlightenment is a prerequisite for an unrealized social liberation, the "fully illuminated personality" that ultimately cannot bring enlightenment to a world of non-illuminated personalities. In *Santa sangre,* the redemption and salvation of the soul is inherently tied to social liberation of the masses. Fenix reaches his "hands to thee" to sate his thirsting soul: a "parched land." The hands (which replace the cross as the iconic symbol of faith on the Church of Holy Blood robes), the land (the eviction of the Church of Holy Blood by the landowners, aided by the Catholic Church and the State), and the people (the downtrodden covered in white ashes observing the elephant's funeral and then performing communion with the body for their daily sustenance) become inseparable in Liberation Theology. In this moment of both religious and political awakening, and with his hands finally free, Fenix attains self-determination over his own action and destiny, an act within the national allegory of *Santa sangre* representing his liberation from his traumatic and traumatizing conception by a dominating United States of America and a dominated Mexico; the rape and murder of Mexico by the U.S.A.; and his suffocating, devotional care for the mutilated ghost of Mexico.

Nonetheless, Fenix's redemption and liberation which ostensibly concludes

Santa sangre is highly problematic. Certainly, the conflation of Christianity with Marx (as opposed to *El Topo*'s Nietzsche), an issue rooted in Liberation Theology itself, reiterates the essential problem of *El Topo*'s mystification of contemporary politics into a moral and spiritual struggle. Moreover, like *El Topo,* the end reflects the idea that there is one Master who cannot, and perhaps *should* not, be conquered: the Father (El Topo's son's refusal to kill El Topo—"How can I kill my Master?"). Fenix's liberation from the Oedipal order becomes very tenuous. While *Santa sangre* calls for usurping the tyranny of the Oedipal holy family, the inherent problems of Fenix's liberation ultimately makes *Santa sangre* incompatible with the most famous and damning critiques of Freud and the Oedipal order, Deleuze and Guattari's *Anti-Oedipus*, despite their surface similarity. For Deleuze and Guattari, social liberation is predicated on the evolution of the Oedipal repressed man to an Anti-Oedipal schizoid man (with "schizoid" explicitly not used in the punitive, psychiatric sense) in a social order where the production of desire is unencumbered by the restrictions and neuroses of the "Oedipal nursery."[54] However, as Herbert Marcuse observed:

> The overthrow of the king-father is a *crime, but so is his restoration—and both are necessary for the progress of civilization.* The crime against the reality principle is redeemed by a crime against the pleasure principle: redemption thus cancels itself.... There is guilt over a deed that has not been accomplished: liberation.[55]

Indeed, Fenix's true "crime" has been the overthrow of the Oedipal order itself, but this crime must also be punished by another "crime" by society: the restoration of the father in the form of the church — and also the State. As Marcuse noted, "Liberation is therefore followed by a 'better' domination: '*The development of the paternal domination into an increasingly powerful state system.*'"[56] Indeed, the ending of *Santa sangre* reflects Marcuse's ambivalence, even pessimism, with the prospects of liberation and redemption, rather than any utopian aspirations. From a Freudian perspective, Fenix has left the world of the pleasure principle, the realm of self-will, and entered the reality principle, the regime of civilization. His freedom to "put up his hands" is a literal surrender to God, the Law, the State, to new fathers. Indeed, in the final freeze-frame, a *blue* police siren appears in the lower left corner of the frame, a *red* light shines on a wall in the upper right, and *both* Fenix and a police officer are clad in *white*— Fenix (the national allegory) in his bloodstained formal shirt, and the policeman (the law) wearing an off-white trench coat. Even in the moment of his "liberation," Fenix remains marked — or "always-already" marked — by red, white, and blue. In this respect, the color green — hope and independence — is completely absent from the shot. Fenix might never be free of his mother Concha, and he also may never be free from the *Circo del gringo* and his despotic father, El Gran Orgo. In *Santa sangre*, Fenix's liberation is opposed to the Anti-Oedipus. His is the transformation from the *repressed man* to the *redeemed man*, and his liberation from "the Oedipal nursery" precisely occurs through his accepting "a 'better' domination" — putting his hands up in surrender to the Fathers of Church and State — and thus ultimately achieving a *cancelled* social liberation through personal redemption.

Conclusion

The Tlatelolco massacre, with its traumatic effect on the Mexican national psyche and its shattering of the dream and vision of Mexican modernity, was one of many historical moments of political crisis in 1968: a year that defined a modern world in chaos. The turmoil of the late 1960s gave way to the political ennui and doldrums of the 1970s, which, in turn, yielded to the conservatism in the 1980s as a political and cultural antidote to the bedlam and desperation of the previous two decades. Yet the legacy of 1968 and its aftermath can be seen in the films of Alejandro Jodorowsky, Juan López Moctezuma, and René Cardona, Jr.; and the films focused on in this project can be seen as more than pessimistic reactions to a historical era defined by dissent, genocide, massacres, revolutions, and war. Rather, the key dilemma in these films is the historical movement of humanity towards the goal of utopia — and its inherent potential for disaster.

In his analysis of Disneyland, Louis Marin described the massive theme park as a "degenerate utopia": the "conversion of ideology into myth" where historical and ideological contradictions are rectified by idealistic, simplified, utopian spaces such as Frontierland, Tomorrowland, and Main Street, U.S.A.[1] Moreover, utopia is not simply a specific location (space); it is also a discourse and an idea(l) of the future: a text (novel, poem, film, painting, manifesto, theme park) that posits an alternative to "the nightmare of history." While Thomas More's *Utopia* presented a perfect society already realized, most utopian literature posit perfected societies of the future: Edward Bellamy's *Looking Backward*, H. G. Wells' *The Shape of Things to Come*. Most famous are the dystopian visions of the future presented in George Orwell's *1984* and Aldous Huxley's *Brave New World*. Yet the binary of "utopia" versus "dystopia" suggests there are two distinct paths for modernity: *either* perfection *or* disaster. The possibility exists that *all* utopias are degenerate utopias with inherent and potentially catastrophic defects as they seek to resolve the nightmare of history; it is only a question of how evident the flaws become, and how dramatically they will materialize. A given dystopia is not a perversion of modernity's quest towards utopia into an anti-utopia, but one of many possibilities which could easily result in modernity's drive towards rational progress and its conversion from ideology into myth: spaces and futures that do not attain social perfection but imprison their inhabitants in the modern world's contradictions, uncertainties, and horrific failings. Huxley's *Brave New World* becomes a degenerate utopia where modern comfort and security is a suffocating future of numbing — and numbed — pleasant blandness; Orwell's *1984*, a degenerative utopia of post–World War II political life defined by totalitarian governments, simplistic rhetoric, unlimited surveillance, and continuous warfare. Even the great, ostensibly utopian works can be read as degenerate utopias. Mulford Q. Sibley noted that More's *Utopia* "advocated a kind of patriarchal, nondemocratic communism to integrate the isolated individual into an ideal community."[2] Wells' *The Shape of Things to Come* is essentially a positivist version of *Brave New World*: an ideal autocratic society based on scientific order and progress.[3]

The films addressed in this discussion present "degenerate utopias" as well. In the wake of 1968, with the nightmare of history being realized on a worldwide scale, modern reason and progress seemed to be reverting unavoidably towards the irrational and the barbaric. For Jodorowsky, López Moctezuma, and Cardona, a fundamental concern became depicting this regression of modernity by the dramatic and often disturbing construction of shocking, surreal, sickening new worlds careening towards inexorable, inexplicable and unreasonable destruction — or self-destruction: *El Topo*'s endless cycles of cruelty and domination in a stark, surreal Western frontier; *Mansion of Madness*' ridiculous and harrowing version of the modern world as the *reductio ad absurdum* within asylum walls; *Alucarda*'s apocalyptic collision of modernity and tradition in the confined and confining convent; *Guyana*'s regression of the Johnsontown social-machine into savagery and self-annihilation; *Birds of Prey*'s seething force of History becoming a brutal, devastating, global, material war machine; and *Santa sangre*'s national allegory of colonialism as a surreal, sadistic-masochistic Oedipal order of kitsch and horror. These films, and their respective degenerate utopias, do not suggest a way out of the nightmare of history. If anything, history can only be a recurring nightmare.

Filmography

Only primary crew and cast members, figures involved in several productions, or notable individuals are listed. Customarily, Mexican films are dated by the year they began principal production, not the year of their release; the dates supplied are in keeping with this practice. In that these films have appeared in a variety of versions under various titles, alternate release titles have been supplied, and the specific home video version screened and discussed in this project has been noted. My thanks to David Wilt, whose research and whose book *The Mexican Filmography, 1916–2001* I have relied on greatly.

El Topo (The Mole, 1969)

Executive Producer: Roberto Viskin; Associate Producer: Juan López Moctezuma; Director: Alejandro Jodorowsky; Story and Screenplay: Alejandro Jodorowsky; Director of Photography: Rafael Cordiki; Editor: Federico Landeros; Music: Alejandro Jodorowsky, Nacho Méndez (arrangements, orchestration); Production Designer: Alejandro Jodorowsky; Set Designer: Alejandro Jodorowsky; Cast: Alejandro Jodorowsky (El Topo), Jacqueline Luis (the Small Woman), Mara Lorenzio (Mara), Brontis Jodorowsky (El Topo's son — child), Robert John (El Topo's son — adult), Paula Romo (The Woman in Black), David Silva (the Colonel), Hectór Martinez "El Borrado" (First Master), Juan José Gurrola (Second Master), Berta Lomeli (Universal Mother), Victor Fasado (Third Master), Agustín Isunza (Fourth Master), José Antonio Alacraz (the Sheriff), Felipe Díaz Garza (the Deputy), Juilán de Meriche (the Priest), Alfonso Arau (bandit).

Note: Shot in Spanish and filmed in Mexico. The rights to *El Topo* were purchased by Allen Klein in June of 1971. Following the dissolution of his relationship with Jodorowsky in the mid-1970s, Klein withdrew *El Topo* and *The Holy Mountain* from circulation. *El Topo* is only currently available on home video in the U.S. in various imported and/or unauthorized versions. In 2004, it was announced that Jodorowsky and Klein's ABKCO Films reached an agreement on U.S. re-release of the original and restored versions of both *El Topo* and *The Holy Mountain*. In December of 2006, ABKCO began limited theatrical releases of *El Topo* and *The Holy Mountain* in select cities scheduled through early 2007 (*www.abkcofilms.com*). DVD release is expected in 2007; at the time of this writing (January 2007), this has not occurred.

Version discussed: DVD reissue by SPO Entertainment (date unknown; redubbed and edited Japanese import). Jodorowsky's scene-by scene discussion of the film in *El Topo — A Book of the Film* was used in reference, and as the final arbitrator, in regard to some inconsistencies in the dubbed dialogue.

La mansión de la locura (The Mansion of Madness, 1971)

Producer: Roberto Viskin; Director: Juan López Moctezuma; Story: Edgar Allan Poe, "The System of Doctor Tarr and Professor Fether"; Screenplay: Carlos Illescas, Juan López Moctezuma, Gabriel Weiss (additional material); Director of Photography: Rafael Cordiki; Editor: Federico Landeros; Music: Nacho Méndez; Production Designer: Gabriel Weiss; Art Director: Gabriel Weiss; Wardrobe Supervisor: Leonora Carrington; Cast: Claudio Brook (Raúl Fragonard/"Dr Maillard"), Arthur Hansel (Gastón Leblanc), Ellen Sherman (Eugénie), Martin LaSalle (Julién Couvier), Mónica Serna (Julién's cousin), David Silva (the Priest), Susan Kamini (priestess), Max Kerlow (Dr. Maillard), Jorge Berkin (Henri).

Note: Shot in English and filmed in Mexico. Originally released in the U.S. in an edited version as *Edgar Allan Poe — Dr. Tarr's Torture Dungeon*.

Version discussed: restored DVD reissue by Mondo Macabro (2004). Also available in unrestored version (*Dr. Tarr's Torture Dungeon*) on Brentwood Home Video as part of a 10-DVD budget package called *Curse of the Dead* (2004).

Alucarda, la hija de las tinieblas (Alucarda, Daughter of Darkness, 1975)

Executive Producer: Eduardo Moreno; Producers: Eduardo Moreno, Max Guefen; Director: Juan López Moctezuma; Screenplay: Juan López Moctezuma, Yolanda López Moctezuma, Alexis T. Arroyo; Director of Photography: Xavier Cruz; Editor: Max Sánchez; Music: Tony Guefen; Art Director: Kleomenes Stamatiades; Cast: Tina Romero (dual-role: Alucarda/Alucarda's Mother), Susan Kamini (Justine), Claudio Brook (dual-role: the Gypsy/Dr. Oszek), David Silva (Father Lázaro), Tina French (Sister Angélica), Lily Garza (Daniela Oszek).

Note: U.S.-Mexican coproduction shot in English and filmed in Mexico. Released in the U.S. as *Sisters of Satan*, *Mark of the Devil 3*, and *Innocents from Hell* (home video title). Version discussed: restored DVD reissue by Mondo Macabro (2003).

Guyana, el crimen del siglo (Guyana, Crime of the Century, 1979)

Producer: René Cardona, Jr.; Associate Producer: Alfonso López Negrete; Director: René Cardona, Jr.; Story and Screenplay: Carlos Valedmar, René Cardona, Jr.; Director of Photography: Leopoldo Villaseñor; Editor: Earl Watson; Music: Alfredo Díaz Ordaz, Jimmie Haskell; Assistant Director: Roberto Schlosser; Dialogue Supervisor: David Silvan; Cast: Stuart Whitman (Jim Johnson), Gene Barry (Lee O'Brien), Bradford Dillman (Dr. Gary Shaw), Jennifer

Ashley (Anna Kazan), Joseph Cotten (Richard Gable), John Ireland (Dave Cole), Yvonne De Carlo (Susan Ames), Tony Young (Ron Harvey), Nadiuska (Leslie Stevens).

Note: Mexican-Spanish-Panamanian coproduction. Shot in English. Originally released in the U.S. in 1979 through Universal Studios in an edited version as *Guyana, Cult of the Damned*.

Version discussed: DVD reissue of *Guyana, Crime of the Century* by VCI Entertainment (2004)

Ataque de los pájaros (Attack of the Birds, 1986)

Executive Producers: Francisco "Pancho" Medina, Gary Green, Producer: René Cardona, Jr.; Associate Producer: Angelo Iacono; Director: René Cardona, Jr.; Story and Screenplay: René Cardona, Jr., David Silvan (English translation), Roberto Schlosser, Eric Wenston (additional dialogue); Director of Photography: Leopoldo Villaseñor; Second Unit Director: René Cardona III; First Assistant Director: Roberto Schlosser; Editor: Jesús Paredes; Music: Stelvio Cipriani; Cast: Christopher Atkins (Peter), Michelle Johnson (Vanessa Cartwright), Sonia Infante (Carmen), Salvador Pineda (Joe), Gabrielle Tinti (Rod), Aldo Sambrell (Arthur Neilsen), Nene Morales (Sharon), Manuel Pereyro (Bob [the elderly hunter]), Carol Connery (Susan), Carol James (Nurse), May Heatherly (Olivia Neilsen), Kunio Kobayasy (Dr. Murayama), Eva Cooper (Cathy).

Note: U.S.-Mexican-Puerto Rican-Peruvian-Spanish-Italian (!) coproduction. Probably shot without sound and dubbed in appropriate languages for various international markets in post-production. For the U.S. version, some of the ancillary characters appear to have been dubbed by different actors. Shot on location(s). Released in the U.S. as *Beaks: The Movie*, *Birds of Prey*, and *Evil Birds* (home video title).

Version discussed: DVD reissue of *Birds of Prey* by Brentwood Home Video included on a 10-DVD budget package called *Night Chills* (2004).

Santa sangre (Holy Blood, 1988)

Executive Producers: René Cardona, Jr., Angelo Iacono; Producer: Claudio Argento; Director: Alejandro Jodorowsky; Story: Alejandro Jodorowsky, Roberto Leoni (screen adaptation); Screenplay: Alejandro Jodorowsky, Claudio Argento, Roberto Leoni; Director of Photography: Daniele Nannuzzi; Editor: Mauro Bonanni; Music: Simon Boswell; Production Designer: Alejandro Luna; Costume Designer: Tolita Figueroa; Cast: Axel Jodorowsky (Fenix), Adan Jodorowsky (Young Fenix), Blanca Guerra (Concha), Guy Stockwell (Orgo), Thelma Tixou (the Tattooed Woman), Sabrina Dennison (Alma), Faviola Elenka Tapia (Young Alma), Jesús Juárez (Aladin), Sergio Bustamante (the Monsignor), Gloria Contreras (Rubi), S. Rodríguez (La Santa ["the Saint"]), Teo Jodorowsky (the Pimp).

Note: Italian-Mexican coproduction shot in English and filmed in Mexico. International title: *Santa Sangre*.

Version discussed: Republic Home Video VHS (1998), uncut version (NC-17).

Chapter Notes

Introduction

1. Héctor Aguilar Camín and Lorenzo Meyer, *In the Shadow of the Mexican Revolution: Contemporary Mexican History, 1910–1989*, trans. Luis Alberto Fierro (Austin: University of Texas Press, 1993), 201. Emphasis added.

2. For further elaboration on the political, social, and cultural discourses and implications of mexploitation films, see my own *Mexploitation Cinema: A Critical History of Mexican Vampire, Wrestler, Apeman and Similar Films, 1957–1977* (Jefferson, NC: McFarland, 2005), especially 166–9.

Chapter 1

1. Alejandro Jodorowsky, *El Topo—A Book of the Film* (New York: Douglas, 1971), 97.

2. The biographical accounts of Jodorowsky's life are drawn from his recollections in *El Topo—A Book of the Film*, 136–9. Another source—which also provides some of the necessary qualifiers on Jodorowsky's sometimes stream-of-consciousness accounts—is J. Hoberman and Jonathan Rosenbaum, *Midnight Movies* (New York: Da Capo, 1991). I gratefully acknowledge the reliance on Hoberman and Rosenbaum's work in my own discussion on Jodorowsky.

3. Recounted in an interview with *Penthouse* (June 1973).

4. As quoted in Hoberman and Rosenbaum, 88.

5. See *El Topo—A Book of the Film*, 138; it is unclear in Jodorowsky's account whether he made his version of *The Transposed Heads* while in Paris working with Marceau in the 1950s or during his Panic Movement activities in the 1960s. Hoberman and Rosenbaum situate the film's origin as the 1950s; see *Midnight Movies*, 88.

6. See *Midnight Movies*, 89–90.

7. As quoted in Hoberman and Rosenbaum, 89.

8. Antonin Artaud, "The Theater of Cruelty (First Manifesto)," in *Selected Writings*, ed. Susan Sontag, trans. Helen Weaver (Berkeley: University of California Press, 1988), 242.

9. *Midnight Movies*, 90.

10. As quoted in L. Loud, "The Virgin Mary Is a Chicken," *American Film*, March 1990: 80. Also archived at the highly-recommended "The Symbol Grows: Alejandro Jodorowsky" website: *www.hotweird.com/jodorowsky/chicken.html*. Accessed 10/1/2005.

11. Jodorowsky, *El Topo—A Book of the Film*, 137.

12. See Eric Zolov, *Refried Elvis: The Rise of the Mexican Counterculture* (Berkeley: University of California Press, 1999), 117, 135. *1, 2, 3, 4, 5 a Go-Go!* was created and originally produced by Alfonso Arau, who appears as one of the three bandits in *El Topo*. In America, Arau is best known for directing *Como agua para chocolate* (*Like Water for Chocolate*, 1991). *Zona Rosa* was a neighborhood in Mexico City that became a hub for counterculture activity, akin to New York's Greenwich Village or San Francisco's Haight-Asbury districts. The eponymous publication was a combination of cultural critique and self-glorification (see Zolov, 135).

13. *Refried Elvis*, 108–9.

14. When *Fando y Lis* was eventually released in America, most of the critical discussion focused on the film being a pedestrian imitation, if not an outright copy, of Fellini's *Satyricon* (1969). Jodorowsky himself conceded the similarities to *Satyricon*, but insisted he made *Fando y Lis* years before seeing Fellini's film. He also attributed the critical panning to the American distributor, Cannon Productions:

"They edited the film with the taste of the *New York Times* critic in mind, and they killed it" (*El Topo — A Book of the Film*, 139). This critic, of course, was Vincent Canby, who panned *El Topo*. See also Hoberman and Rosenbaum, 93.

15. Jodorowsky, *El Topo — A Book of the Film*, 140–1.

16. *El Topo* was not banned in Mexico; however, it was severely edited by censor boards when it premiered in May 1971. The Mexican government also refused to sponsor it as an entry at the 1971 Cannes Film Festival.

17. Lennon attended the 1971 Cannes Film Festival to exhibit his experimental films made with Yoko Ono. Jodorowsky's partner in the Panic Movement, Fernando Arrabal, had ventured into cinema, and his surrealist film about the Spanish Civil War, *Viva la muerte* (*Long Live Death*), was shown at Cannes. It greatly impressed Lennon, who discussed the possibility of Klein buying the American rights for *Viva la muerte*. After seeing *El Topo*, Lennon had Klein pursue Jodorowsky instead. See Hoberman and Rosenbaum, 95.

18. As quoted in Hoberman and Rosenbaum, 102.

19. However, Jodorowsky pointed to Buster Keaton as a primary influence on *El Topo* and the emphasis on precisely staged action within the shot verses camera and editing manipulations (a strategy which also owed to Jodorowsky's own considerable experience in theater). See *El Topo — A Book of the Film*, 128, 131.

20. *El Topo — A Book of the Film*, 105–6.

21. The review was also included in Vincent Canby, *Film 71–72 — An Anthology* (New York: Simon and Schuster, 1972). Also archived at "The Symbol Grows: Alejandro Jodorowsky" website: *www.hotweird.com/jodorowsky/canby/html*. Canby's review produced a backlash from the *El Topo* faithful, and the *Times* eventually printed a sort of retraction — a subsequent laudatory review of *El Topo* by art critic Peter Schjeldahl (see Hoberman and Rosenbaum, 95).

22. *Uncovering the Sixties: The Life and Times of the Underground Press* (New York: Pantheon, 1985), 155. See also Marc James Estern, *A History of the Underground Comics* (Berkeley: Ronin Publishing, 1993), especially Chapters 5 and 6. Estern defends Wilson as more than vicious male chauvinism, but a Sadean representation of sex and violence in a world of perpetual decay.

23. See Estern, Chapters 5 and 6; Peck, Chapter 13.

24. As quoted in Hoberman and Rosenbaum, 97. Emphasis added.

25. As quoted in Hoberman and Rosenbaum,

101. Kael's criticisms of *El Topo* primarily reside in its male chauvinism rather than its sex or violence. In her first review for *The New Yorker* in 1967, she defended Arthur Penn's *Bonnie and Clyde*; she later championed Bertolucci's *Last Tango in Paris* (1972). Indeed, Kael's critics have pointedly commented on her own "taste for violence and erotic cruelty" (Hoberman and Rosenbaum, 37).

26. As quoted in Donald M. Lowe, *History of Bourgeois Perception* (Chicago: University of Chicago Press, 1983), 132.

27. *Midnight Movies*, 90. During the peak of *El Topo*'s popularity in the spring of 1971, the Elgin ran *Blood of a Poet* as the evening feature prior to *El Topo*'s midnight screening.

28. *History of Bourgeois Perception*, 132. Emphasis added. However, Artuad detested *both* Cocteau and Buñuel for what he claimed was their the inability to use the dream-state beyond its arbitrary, fragmented images, their failure to manufacture a "poetry of the unconscious ... profound, analogical poetry ... the only true and possible poetry with metaphysical tendencies, of which films like *Blood of a Poet* resolutely turn their back. As well as *L'Age d'Or*, as well as every Surrealist poem ever written" ("Letter to Jean Paulhan [Jan. 1932]," in *Selected Writings*, 281). Ultimately, Artaud abandoned any hope for cinema altogether by the early 1930s, branding it as a medium which could only replicate existing modes of consciousness rather than destroy them: a "stratified and frozen conquest of reality ... a poetry of contingency, a poetry of what might be ... it is not to cinema we must look to restore the Myths of man" ("The Premature Old Age of Cinema," in *Selected Writings*, 314).

29. *El Topo — A Book of the Film*, 97. Emphasis added.

30. See Lee Clark Mitchell, *Westerns: Making the Man in Fiction and Film* (Chicago: University of Chicago Press, 1996), especially Chapter 8.

31. *Westerns*, 224. Emphasis added.

32. "Beauty of a Western," in *Cahiers du cinéma — the 1950s: Neo-Realism, Hollywood, New Wave*, ed. Jim Hiller (Cambridge: Harvard University Press, 1985), 167.

33. In this respect, I draw from Gilles Deleuze, *Cinema 1: The Movement-Image*, trans. Hugh Tomlinson and Barbara Habberjam (Minneapolis: University of Minnesota, 1986), Chapter 8. Deleuze posited a realm of cinematic naturalism which constructs surreal "originary worlds" midway between animal instinct and civilized conduct (Deleuze cites Erich Von Stroheim and Buñuel; I would also suggest Russ Meyer, Sam Peckinpah, José Mojica Marins' "Coffin Joe" films, and the *giallo* genre). While in many ways *El Topo* takes place in an "orig-

inary world," my hesitation with applying Deleuze's "naturalism" to *El Topo* is that in Deleuze's formulation any morality in the originary world is purely immanent, formed out of the cycles of creation and destruction. Despite its surface transgressions, *El Topo* is ultimately steeped in transcendent bourgeois morality, particularly in relationship to sex and gender.

34. Jodorowsky wore black silk underwear with a green circle over the anus under the outfit as a reminder, "so I wouldn't act like John Wayne" (*El Topo—A Book of the Film*, 106).

35. Dennis Hopper, co-star and director of *Easy Rider*, was another of *El Topo*'s more vocal admirers; Hopper's project after *Easy Rider*, *The Last Movie* (1971), was an anti–Western clearly influenced by *El Topo*. Jodorowsky later claimed he helped Hopper edit *The Last Movie*; see "Wrapped in Salamander Cloth, He Played House," *Forced Exposure* 17. Also archived at "The Symbol Grows: Alejandro Jodorowsky" website: www.hotweird.com/jodorowsky/forced.html. Date accessed: 10/1/05.

36. See Anne Rubenstein, "Bodies, Cities, Cinema: Pedro Infante's Death as Political Spectacle," in *Fragments of a Golden Age: The Politics of Culture in Mexico Since 1940*, eds. Gilbert Joseph, Anne Rubenstein, and Eric Zolov (Durham: Duke University Press, 2001), especially 225–6. In regard to Santo and the countermacho mythos, see *Mexploitation Cinema*, 32–3.

37. William L. O'Neill, *Coming Apart: An Informal History of the 1960s* (New York: Times Books, 1971), 298.

38. *Coming Apart*, 196. Perhaps the strangest example of the Left's fascination with revolutionary *machismo* was the short-lived infatuation with Hell's Angels (see O'Neill, 272–4).

39. Mitchell notes that the Oedipal order and its conflicts are key to three key Westerns of the early 1950s: *High Noon* (1952), *Shane* (1953), and *Hondo* (1953). In *High Noon*, the Oedipal father-son order is manifest in the relationship between sheriff Will Kane (Gary Cooper) and his deputy Harvey Pell (Lloyd Bridges); see *Westerns*, 180, 200–1.

40. Due to the legal entanglements surrounding *El Topo* and its availability in America, the version of *El Topo* screened for this discussion is an imported version which underwent several alterations (SPO Entertainment [Japan], release date unknown). Several sequences were edited and there are a number of inconsistencies in the English-dubbed dialogue versus Jodorowsky's scene by scene breakdown of the film included in *El Topo—A Book of the Film*, 7–93. In these cases, I have elected to reference additional portions of scenes which appear in Jodorowsky's discussion of the film. I have also cited dialogue as it appears in *El Topo—A Book of the Film* versus the redubbed version; in some case where the dubbing is markedly different, it will be noted separately. This opening scene was one of the more severely edited, and I refer to Jodorowsky's description in *El Topo—A Book of the Film*, 11.

41. Sigmund Freud, *Civilization and Its Discontents*, ed. and trans. James Strachey (New York: W.W. Norton, 1961), 79. Emphasis added.

42. The bandit sucking on the high-heel shoes was an homage to Buñuel; see *El Topo—A Book of the Film*, 131.

43. This interpretation of Pasolini's application of Sade to Fascism owes greatly to Max Horkheimer and Theodor W. Adorno's reading of *Justine* in *Dialectic of Enlightenment*, trans. John Cumming (New York: Continuum, 1998), 81–119. See also Richard Leppert's useful comments on Horkheimer and Adorno's reading of Sade in Theodor W. Adorno, *Essays on Music*, ed. Richard Leppert, trans. Susan H. Gillespie (Berkeley: University of California Press, 2002), 30.

44. Silva was arguably the most famous actor in the Mexican film industry to appear in *El Topo*; Julián de Meriche (the Priest), Augustín Isunza (the Fourth Master), and Alfonso Arau (billed as "Bandit #1") were also well-know actors in Mexico. Otherwise, Jodorowsky recruited the cast from Mexican theater, pop music, or non-professionals. Paula Romo (the Woman in Black) was an airline stewardess he discovered by chance dancing at a night club; after filming *El Topo*, she returned to the airline industry.

45. An homage to Sergio Leone; see *El Topo—A Book of the Film*, 131.

46. *Uncovering the Sixties*, 155. One particularly popular underground comics of the era was Spain Rodriguez's *Trashman*, a superhero–urban guerilla. In this context, another influential book during the counterculture era was Frantz Fanon's *The Wretched of the Earth* (New York: Grove Press, 1963). Opposing the non-violent resistance of Gandhi, Fanon argued the violence of Third World revolution was a necessary catharsis of the national psyche for the long-oppressed masses. In this respect, the issue of bourgeois morality, as with Nietzsche, became an obstacle rather than path to liberation.

47. *Bulfinch's Mythology* lists Pan as the god of forests, flocks, and shepherds; other sources defined Pan more broadly as the god of nature, fertility, even fornication. The Panic Movement was named after the Greek God Pan.

48. See also *El Topo—A Book of the Film*, 144–5.

49. An homage to Godard's *Pierrot le fou*; see *El Topo—A Book of the Film*, 131.

50. *El Topo—A Book of the Film*, 102. Emphasis added. Jodorowsky also claimed the phallic stone was modeled on his own penis.

51. In the redubbed version of *El Topo* screened for this discussion, Mara's emphasized line is: "*How can I believe you love me unless you prove it?* The alteration is important in that in the screenplay Mara demands the murder of the Four Masters because she will not love El Topo until he is the Master of the desert and fulfills her own lust for domination. In the redubbed dialogue, the murders are motivated by Mara's insecurity and demanding evidence of El Topo's love for her.

52. The introduction of the quest to defeat the Four Masters also suggests the incorporation of another genre into *El Topo*: Asian martial arts films. Jodorowsky was influenced by Kurosawa but was not at all familiar with the martial arts films from China at the time he made *El Topo*, much to his regret: he called discovering the genre after *El Topo*'s completion "the most important experience of my life as a film director" (*El Topo—A Book of the Film*, 101). Nonetheless, one is struck by the affinity between *El Topo* to the martial arts genre as the quest to defeat the Four Masters unfolds, and if Jodorowsky was not influenced by the genre, it is hardly surprising he reacted with such enthusiasm to martial arts films.

53. Jodorowsky: "I designed their costume from one I saw in the *Encyclopedia of Film*: a John Wayne costume. It was one costume, which I cut into two parts.... Two cripples make one John Wayne" (*El Topo—A Book of the Film*, 99).

54. *Dialectic of Enlightenment*, 59.

55. See *Dialectic of Enlightenment*, 32–36, 57–60. See also Frederic Jameson, *Late Marxism: Adorno, or, the Persistence of the Dialectic* (New York: Verso, 1996), 123–54.

56. Hollywood has also adopted this romantic cultural attitude in such films as *Little Big Man* (1970, dir. Arthur Penn), *A Man Called Horse* (1970, dir. Eliot Silverstein) and especially *Dances with Wolves* (1990, dir. Kevin Costner): films in which the white man learns the ways and wisdom of Native American society and returns to modern life a better person, while the culture he learned from is subsequently destroyed.

57. See *El Topo—A Book of the Film*, 108.

58. This information is taken from Jodorowsky's screenplay; see *El Topo—A Book of the Film*, 42. Given the brevity and high angle of the shot, it is impossible to ascertain what these objects are, let alone their symbolic importance as presented in the film.

59. *El Topo—A Book of the Film*, 112.

60. *El Topo—A Book of the Film*, 113.

61. A possible reference is Gary Cooper tossing his sheriff's badge into the dirt at the conclusion of *High Noon*.

62. Emphasis added. This is the line that appears in Jodorowsky's screenplay and discussion in *El Topo—A Book of the Film*, 49. In the version screened for this analysis, the Fourth Master's final statement is repeating, "Means nothing." The significance of stating "You lost" is that the cycle of El Topo's winning the duels and losing himself in the process is completed and explicitly pointed out by the final Master.

63. See *El Topo—A Book of the Film*, 108.

64. For a discussion of the sexism and feminist response to the underground comics, see Estern, Chapter 5; Peck, Chapter 13, which details the rampant sexism in the counterculture and specifically the Underground press of the 1960s (many of which featured underground comics authors to supply the requisite newspaper cartoons and comic strips). Also recommended is Sara Evans, *Personal Politics: The Roots of Women's Liberation in the Civil Rights Movement and the New Left* (New York: Vintage, 1980).

65. As quoted in Legs McNeil and Gillian McCain, *Please Kill Me: The Uncensored Oral History of Punk* (New York: Penguin, 1996), 47.

66. As quoted in Peck, 213. Peck noted that Morgan's essay itself was only published after the women on the *Rat*'s staff demanded the right to edit their own issue of *Rat* after a particularly offensive "Sex and Porn" issue. Afterwards, *Rat* women sought to retain editorial control; the resulting battle split the paper into two factions and was a key event in beginning the feminist revolt in the counterculture (see Peck, 212–7).

67. See Jacques Lacan, "The Mirror Stage as Formative of the Function of the I as Revealed in Psychoanalytic Experience," in *Écrits*, trans. Alan Sheridan (New York: W.W. Norton, 1977), 1–7.

68. There is a very similar scene of a couple having sex in the desert in Russ Meyer's *Cherry, Harry, and Racquel!* (1969), and in this respect, the work of Russ Meyer is highly comparable to *El Topo*. In Meyer's films deserts are the primary zones of male action and struggles, epitomized by *Faster, Pussycat! Kill! Kill!* (1966): Varla (Tura Santana), the sexist woman and the toughest guy in the film, murders the teen heartthrob Tommy in the desert during a vicious fistfight. In contrast, forests and water become the space of female sexual domination, such as in *Vixen* (1968), where most of the title character's predatory sexual conquests take place outdoors in lush settings (fields, forests, streams). For further elaboration on this motif in Russ Meyer's films, see my own *Lips Hips Tits Power: The Films of Russ Meyer* (London: Creation Books, 2004).

69. See G.W.F. Hegel, *Phenomenology of Spirit*, trans. A.V. Miller (New York: Oxford University Press, 1977), 111–9.

70. See Friedrich Nietzsche, *Beyond Good and Evil*, trans. Walter Kaufman (New York: Vintage, 1989), 204–8 (Sect. 260). Kaufman's commentary adds a crucial qualifier to the (mis)readings of this concept as an endorsement of mastery and the precursor to Fascism. Rather, the apparent approval of master morality is simply rooted in Nietzsche's disgust with salve morality as a mindset that becomes a apology and justification for subservience (206). Thus, the contempt for slave morality is rooted in Nietzsche's "antipathy to domination" and not simply a quest for domination — which is not to say that the struggle in *El Topo* cannot be read in the context of Nietzsche's own misogynistic tendencies.

71. Friedrich Nietzsche, *The Portable Nietzsche*, ed. and trans. Walter Kaufman (New York: The Viking Press, 1954), 179 ("On Women," *Thus Spoke Zarathustra*). See also *Midnight Movies*, 83.

72. *El Topo — The Book of the Film*, 101. Emphasis added.

73. See Laura Mulvey, "Visual Pleasure and Narrative Cinema," in *Film Theory and Criticism: Introductory Readings*, 4th ed., ed. Gerald Mast, Marshall Cohen, and Leo Braudy (New York: Oxford University Press, 1992), 753.

74. Wilhelm Reich, *The Mass Psychology of Fascism*, ed. Mary Higgens and Chester M. Rafael, MD, trans. Vincent R. Carfagno (New York: The Noonday Press, 1970), 105. Jodorowsky speaks glowingly of Reich, although, not surprisingly, he tends towards the common simplifications of Reich and the emphasis on the orgasm as a point of personal and political liberation (*El Topo — A Book of the Film*, 144–5). In *El Topo*, the glaring issue is that Mara's orgasm is inflicted on her by El Topo as an act of punishment, which in turn becomes Mara's sexual "enlightenment."

75. *The Portable Nietzsche*, 249.

76. *El Topo — A Book of the Film*, 132. Emphasis added.

77. The town is never named in *El Topo*, and this is taken from El Topo's exclamation, "So this is the great town!" (*El Topo — A Book of the Film*, 58). In the version of *El Topo* screened for this analysis, it is referred to as "the Big Town."

78. See *El Topo — A Book of the Film*, 132.

79. See Hoberman and Rosenbaum, 99–100.

80. Jodorowsky, *El Topo — A Book of the Film*, 160. This element of *El Topo* was specifically influenced by Jung's *Metamorphosis of the Soul* (see 160).

81. See *The Antichrist*, sect. 20, in *The Portable Nietzsche*, 587. Emphasis original. Nietzsche's discussion favoring Buddhism over Christianity can be found in *The Antichrist*, sect. 20–24 (in *The Portable Nietzsche*, 586–92).

82. *Midnight Movies*, 86. Jodorowsky claimed the set was not built but found; it was built for an American Western shot in Mexico, *The Law of Tombstone*, and left abandoned after production finished — a true "ghost town" (see *El Topo — A Book of the Film*, 122).

83. *El Topo — A Book of the Film*, 59–60. In this respect, the Deputy is the precursor to Orgo in *Santa sangre*; Díaz Garza bears an uncanny physical resemblance to American actor Guy Stockwell, who portrayed Orgo.

84. There is a similar scene in *Salò* as well, when the fascist torturers conduct a perverse beauty pageant where the men and women are covered with sheets and bent over so only their buttocks are visible, allowing them to determine who has the "most beautiful ass." In *Salò*, the body is reduced to the utility of an anus that can be raped; *El Topo* codes the violation strictly in terms of homosexuality and authoritarianism.

85. Horkheimer and Adorno, 47–8. Emphasis added. To clarify, the word "true" does not refer to non-fiction, but "true" in the sense that *The Odyssey* is the prototype novel, and the epic poem later subsumed in modernity by the novel proper.

86. *El Topo — A Book of the Film*, 58. Jodorowsky's own view is that El Topo at this point is "androgynous."

87. *El Topo — A Book of the Film*, 124–5. Emphasis added.

88. *El Topo — A Book of the Film*, 166.

89. *Dialectic of Enlightenment*, 44. Emphasis added. Again, this is *not* to say that Nietzsche is free of problematical stances in his own right (his misogyny, his infatuation with national character) or that he had no influence on Fascist ideology. Rather, Nietzsche's contribution to Fascism was the product of selective and simplistic interpretations, and outright misinterpretations, of his philosophy. It might be said holding Nietzsche responsible for Nazi Germany is akin to holding Marx responsible for the Stalinism or Christ responsible for the Spanish Inquisition.

90. Nietzsche as quoted in *Dialectic of Enlightenment*, 44.

91. *The Antichrist*, sect. 48, in *The Portable Nietzsche*, 628–9. Emphasis original.

92. From the perspective of Jungian psychology, Mara represents *logos* (cognition) and the Small Woman *eros* (connectivity). The equation becomes logos-as-evil and eros-as-good, and hardly "beyond good and evil."

93. *Dialectic of Enlightenment*, 57.

94. As quoted in O'Neill, 255. Emphasis added. For an overview of the role of mysticism in the

counterculture, see O'Neill, 254–8. See also Hoberman and Rosenbaum, 99.

95. Artaud's final break from Surrealism stemmed from Breton's embrace of Marxism and making membership in Communist Party mandatory for all Surrealists. For Artaud, any revolution in bourgeois society had to occur at the level of individual cognition rather than social conditions: "a revolution that did not evolve within the hopeless limitations of matter ... [but] a new way of guiding one's thoughts, a new way of relating to appearances" ("In Total Darkness, or, the Surrealist Bluff" in *Selected Writings*, 142).

96. Michel Foucault, *Madness and Civilization: A History of Insanity in the Age of Reason*, trans. Richard Howard (New York: Vintage, 1999), 108–9. Emphasis original.

97. *El Topo—A Book of the Film*, 135. Emphasis added.

98. As quoted in *Penthouse*. Emphasis added.

99. In the final shot of *El Topo*, a huge swarm of bees begin to gather on El Topo's grave, suggesting the formation of an eventual honeycomb, much like the one El Topo removed from the First Master's grave. In death, El Topo has achieved the level of enlightenment of the First Master.

100. As quoted in "Wrapped in Salamander Cloth...."

101. Herbert Marcuse, "A Note on Dialectic," in *The Essential Frankfurt School Reader*, ed. Andrew Arato and Eike Gebhardt (New York: Continuum, 1994), 450. Emphasis added.

102. See Hoberman and Rosenbaum, 99; Peck, 227–9. The Maoist Weathermen, who organized the Days of Rage, hailed Manson and pronounced 1970 as "the Year of the Fork"—in reference to the fork imbedded in Leo LaBianca's corpse. *Tuesday's Child*, a Los Angeles underground paper, parodied *Time* magazine by putting Manson on the cover of one issue, proclaiming him "Man of the Year." Conversely, *Rolling Stone*, certainly the most mainstream and conservative paper of the underground press, dubbed Manson "The Most Dangerous Man Alive." Other counterculture luminaries, such as Ed Sanders, still clinging to the hippie dream in the wake of its growing contradictions, blamed the death of the entire counterculture movement on Manson in his book *The Family*.

103. *Midnight Movies*, 99–100. Emphasis added.

104. *Midnight Movies*, 99.

105. As quoted in Hoberman and Rosenbaum, 94, 96.

106. As quoted in an interview with Jarrod LaBine in *Fad* no. 36 (1996). Also archived at "The Symbol Grows: Jodorowsky" website: *www.hotweird.com/fadinterview.html*. Accessed 10/1/2005.

107. As quoted in Hoberman and Rosenbaum, 97.

108. Horkheimer and Adorno, 44.

109. *Dialectic of Enlightenment*, 45–7. Emphasis added.

110. *Dialectic of Enlightenment*, 45. Emphasis added.

111. *Essays on Music*, 26.

112. Nevertheless, Jodorowsky does make a problematic statement in *El Topo—A Book of the Film*: "Speaking of Hitler ... and Mussolini. The most beautiful speeches I know are Mussolini's. I'm against fascism, but I can recognize beauty" (168). At issue is the question of if aesthetics and ideology can be, or should be, separated in discussing fascism; specifically, the troubling case of Leni Riefenstahl's *Triumph of the Will*, a brilliantly made film that celebrates one of the most horrific moments on modern history—the rise of Nazi Germany.

Chapter 2

1. As quoted in an interview with J.P. Bouyxou and Gilbert Verschooten published in *Cine Girl* (1977). The text interview is included on the highly-recommended Mondo Macabro DVD reissues of *Mansion of Madness* and *Alucarda*.

2. As quoted in an on-camera interview with Pete Tombs included on the Mondo Macabro DVD reissues of *Mansion of Madness* and *Alucarda*.

3. *Midnight Movies*, 92. Emphasis added.

4. While López Moctezuma's work in the early 1970s was crucial in the evolution of Mexican horror films, his film career after *Alucarda* was sporadic and largely unsuccessful. After *Alucarda*, López Moctezuma did not release another film for eight years, serving as director-for-hire on *Matar a un extraño* (*To Kill a Stranger*, 1983). Much like the previous decade's *Mary Mary Bloody Mary* (1974), *To Kill a Stranger* was a Mexican-American co-production, a violent mystery-thriller starring Mexican singer-actress Angélica María (her then-husband, Raúl Vale, produced the film) and American B-movie stalwarts Donald Pleasance, Dean Stockwell, and Aldo Ray. *To Kill a Stranger* went largely unnoticed, and two other films were made but never released theatrically: *Bienvenido Maria* (*Welcome Maria*, 1986), a melodrama about an illegal Mexican immigrant and her son searching for her husband in the U.S.; and *El alimento del miedo* (*The Food of Fear*, 1993), a horror crime film (based loosely on a true event) concerning children being abducted, killed, and their bodies used for filling in taco meat(!). Beset with health problems in his final years, López Moctezuma died in 1995 at the age of

Notes — Chapter 2

62. The biographical material on López Moctezuma owes greatly to David Wilt's "Juan López Moctezuma" webpage: *www.wam,umd.edu/~dwilt/lopexmoc.htm*. Last accessed: 12/10/05.

5. As quoted in Bouyxou and Verschooten.

6. As quoted in interview with Pete Tombs.

7. Walter Benjamin, "On Some Motifs in Baudelaire," in *Illuminations*, ed. Hannah Arendt, trans. Harry Zohn (New York: Schocken Books: 1969), 171. Emphasis added. Conversely, in "The Second Manifesto of Surrealism" (1930), Andre Breton did not hail Poe's literature as an antithesis of "social realism," but castigated the social implications of Poe's mystery formula: "Poe ... in the police magazines, is properly presented as the *master of scientific policemen* ... is it not a shame ... to bestow upon the world a police *method*? Let us, in passing, spit on Edgar Poe" (117). See André Breton, *Manifestos of Surrealism*, trans. Richard Seaver and Helen R. Lane (Ann Arbor: University of Michigan, 1972).

8. See Tzvetan Todorov, *The Poetics of Prose*, trans. Richard Howard (Ithaca, NY: Cornell University Press, 1977). In response to literary critic Jean Cohen, Todorov argues Cohen studies "not phenomena but difference. The one task of poetics, he tells us, is a study of how poetry differs from prose.... [I]n order to define poetry, it is not enough to say that it differs from prose, for the two have a common portion which is literature. Of 'poetic language,' Cohen retains only the adjective forgetting there is also a substantive" (34–5). As Todorov suggests, rather than simply isolating poetics from prose, a more important aspect is the intersection of poetics and prose within the space of literature.

9. Edgar Allan Poe, "The System of Doctor Tarr and Professor Fether," in *Complete Tales and Poems* (Edison, NJ: Castle Books, 2002), 269.

10. The references to Sergei Eisenstein are intended. In discussing his theory of montage, Eisenstein wrote, "Montage arises from the *collision* of independent shots ... this popularized description of what happens as a *blending* has its share of responsibility for the popular misconception of the nature of montage." *Film Form: Essays in Film Theory*, ed. and trans. Jay Leyda (San Diego: Harcourt Brace, 1949), 49. The shock of intellectual montage is produced by this collision, the meanings constructed through the formal violence of impacting images.

11. Specifically, one can also recall the wonderful and infamous opening sequence of the Inquisition tribunal in *The Brainiac* which does not propel the plot through action but a protracted, convoluted, at times incomprehensible series of pronouncements that explain, or attempt to explain, the plot to the viewer. A similar strategy is employed in *Santo vs. the Vampire Women* while the specific peculiarity of their dialogue may stem from dubbing, plot expositions of this type were a common narrative strategy in mexploitation films when the first of the resurrected vampire women provides a long, introductory monologue to explain the major plot points.

12. See "*Santo y Blue Demon vs. Drácula y el Hombre Lobo*," available at his highly-recommended "Films of El Santo" website: *www.wam.umd.edu/~dwilt/santo.html*. Last accessed 12/10/05.

13. In this respect, López Moctezuma is highly comparable to Jean Rollin and his *Vampire* film cycle from 1968 to 71. Rollin's amazing work incorporated diverse influences ranging from F.W. Murnau, Hammer Studios, and Jean-Luc Godard, similarly stressing the poetic power of the specific shot over narrative teleology.

14. The cultural battle between America and Europe is a staple of American literature, such as Henry James' *The American* and, of course, the work of Mark Twain, exemplified by "A Connecticut Yankee in King Arthur's Court."

15. See *Mexploitation Cinema*, especially Chapter Two.

16. "The System of Dr. Tarr and Professor Fether," 268.

17. *Madness and Civilization:* 227. Emphasis added.

18. In his debut film, *La invención del Cronos* (*The Invention of Cronos*, 1992; U.S. title: *Cronos*), Guillermo del Toro cast Brook in a key supporting role in what was Brook's final film — a show of respect to both Brook and López Moctezuma's work.

19. The sheer strangeness of *Simón* is also attributable to the fact that the film was only half-completed before the financing collapsed, leaving Buñuel with an unfinished forty-five minute film; he concluded the incomplete film with a short sequence in a nightclub and stock footage of an A-Bomb explosion as the final shot of the film.

20. *Madness and Civilization*, 99–101. First emphasis added.

21. *Madness and Civilization*, 115.

22. *Madness and Civilization*, 37. Emphasis added.

23. See *Madness and Civilization*, 108–116.

24. *Madness and Civilization*, 64.

25. Matei Calinescu, *Five Faces of Modernity: Modernism, Avant-Garde, Decadence, Kitsch, Postmodernism* (Durham: Duke University Press, 1987), 66.

26. "A Note on Dialectic," in *The Essential Frankfurt School Reader*, 450.

27. *Madness and Civilization*, 264. Emphasis added. See also 74–8.

28. *Madness and Civilization* is not the title of Foucault's original work, which was published in 1965 as *Histoire de la Folie* (*History of Insanity*)— perhaps an even more appropriate comparison to *Mansion of Madness*, given its depiction of the course of world history as continual horror and madness.

29. Of course, Huxley was no stranger to hallucinogenic drugs, having written extensively about his own experiences with LSD in *The Doors of Perception*. However, Huxley was also well aware of their potential for both liberation and repression, as *Brave New World* clearly indicates. As William O'Neill noted, the psychedelic revolution canonized by Leary ultimately served as a counterrevolutionary force: "To 'turn on and drop out' did not weaken the state ... it drained off potentially subversive energies" (*Coming Apart*, 240).

30. According to IMDb, the character's name is "Blanche," a name derived from the French verb *blanchir*—"to whiten." However, the character's name is never given in the film itself.

31. In its opening credit, *Bedlam* cites the art work of William Hogarth (*The Rake's Progress*) as the film's source material.

32. One can draw a comparison to Gilles Deleuze and Félix Guattari, *A Thousand Plateaus: Capitalism and Schizophrenia*, trans. Brain Massumi (Minneapolis: University of Minnesota Press, 1987). In *A Thousand Plateaus*, Deleuze and Guattari introduce the concept of "the rhizome"—the philosophical method of exploring the hidden, myriad linkages rather than the visible structure—their analogy of studying the invisible roots verses the visible tree (see "Introduction–Rhizome," 3–25). Indeed, the line uttered during Eugénie's dance, "Inaction rots and gnaws at the roots of the tree," could have easily appeared in *A Thousand Plateau*'s discussion of the rhizome, given the emphasis on velocity and mobility that characterizes Deleuze and Guattari's work. However, the ramifications of these roots are far different: in Deleuze and Guattari, they offer thought limitless pathways; in *Mansion of Madness*, they trap thought in an unconquerable labyrinth.

33. See Louis Althusser, "Ideology and Ideological State Apparatuses (Notes Towards an Investigation)," in *Lenin and Philosophy and Other Essays*, trans. Ben Brewster (New York: Monthly Review Press, 1971), 176–7. By arguing that individuals are "always-already subjects," Althusser merges Marx and Lacan, arguing the subject is overdetermined from the moment of birth into preordained expectations, obligations, and roles in capitalism's ideological superstructure and the Symbolic Order of signs, images, and language. The subject is not a "blank slate" who determines his or her own destiny, but an "already-written slate" thrown into the realm of language and ideology.

Chapter 3

1. López Moctezuma recounted that Carradine was in very poor health during the filming of *Mary Mary*, necessitating a stand-in be used in virtually all of his scenes except for the close-ups. As a result, Carradine actually appeared in the film for only a scant few minutes (see Bouyxou and Verschooten). David Wilt wryly noted that this strategy unfortunately created an effect not unlike Bela Lugosi's "role" in *Plan Nine from Outer Space*; see his "Juan López Moctezuma" website.

2. A brilliant discussion of the slasher film is Carol J. Clover, *Men, Women, and Chainsaws: Gender in the Modern Horror Film* (Princeton, NJ: Princeton University Press, 1992), especially Chapter 1. Clover argued the slasher film's obsession is with studying gender constructs as much as sex.

3. Georges Bataille, *Erotism: Death and Sensuality*, trans. Mary Dalwood (San Francisco: City Lights, 1986), 18.

4. As quoted in Bouyxou and Verschooten.

5. As quoted in Bouyxou and Verschooten.

6. *Alucarda* was not the only—or first—Mexican entry into the nunsploitation genre. In 1973, *Satánico pandemonium* (*Satanic Pandemonium*, dir. Gilberto Martínez Solares) was made, a sort of classic mexploitation-meets-*The Devils* hybrid about a nun's possession by a demon (who closely resembles a vampire); she commits murders, leads the convent into debauchery, and dies after being stabbed. However, the film ends on a moralistic note: the whole film has been the hallucinations of the nun dying of the Plague–she has cloistered herself in the convent to prevent infecting the other nuns. Like René Cardona, Jr., Gilberto Martínez Solares was a mainstream director who worked for decades in the Mexican film industry in numerous genres, such as comedy, adventure, and *lucha libre* film.

7. *Madness and Civilization*, 257.

8. Perhaps not coincidentally, the vast majority of nunsploitation films were made in Italy, home of the Vatican.

9. Pier Paolo Pasolini, "The Cinema of Poetry," in *Movies and Methods, Vol. I*, ed. Bill Nichols (Berkeley: University of California Press, 1976), 542–58. Pasolini's essay is itself highly difficult, in part due to the inherent complexity of the theory, his own enig-

matic writing style, and the problems of translation: Pasolini's original Italian was translated into French and published in *Cahiers du cinéma*; the French translation was later translated into English.

10. A recommended discussion of Pasolini's "Cinema of Poetry" and the theory of "free indirect subjectivity," including its more problematic aspects, can be found in Naomi Greene, *Pier Paolo Pasolini: Cinema as Heresy* (Princeton, NJ: Princeton University Press, 1990), 110–126.

11. "The Cinema of Poetry," 553. Emphasis original.

12. Again, as with *Mansion of Madness*' collision of poetics and prose, Pasolini's and López Moctezuma's "free indirect subjective" reflects a collision versus a blending of points of view, manifesting a similar violence in film form, much like Eisenstein's concept of montage as a collision versus a blending of shots.

13. "The Cinema of Poetry," 552. Emphasis added.

14. Tina Romero and Susana Kamini are obviously much older than fifteen; Romero was twenty and Kamini presumably around the same age (Kamini's age could not be accurately verified). While the age discrepancy is incongruent in one respect, it also heightens the surrealism; the flipside of Michelle Johnson playing veteran journalist "Vanessa Cartwright" in *Birds of Prey*.

15. As quoted in Bouyxou and Verschooten.

16. In his critique of *Mansion of Madness*, David Wilt noted this distinction between activity within "indoor" versus "outdoor" spaces; see his "Juan López Moctezuma" website.

17. *Cinema 2: The Time Image*, trans. Hugh Tomlinson and Robert Galeta (Minneapolis: University of Minnesota Press, 1989), 167. Emphasis original.

18. *Madness and Civilization*, 184. Emphasis added.

19. "[Artaud] believes in the cinema as long as he considers cinema is essentially suited to reveal this powerlessness to think at the heart of thought. If we consider Artaud's actual scripts, the vampire in *32*, the madman in *La révolte du boucher* [*Revolt of the Butcher*], and especially the suicide case in *Dix-huit seconds* [*18 Seconds*], the hero 'has become incapable of achieving his thoughts,' 'he is reduced to only seeing a parade of images within him, an excess of contradictory images.'" (Deleuze, *Cinema 2*, 166).

20. The naked witch appears to be the same actress who portrayed the gypsy woman. She is not specifically cited in the credits, nor do current databases provide the name of the actress in relation to the character(s) played.

21. *Madness and Civilization*, 194. Emphasis added. It should be noted that "passions" in Foucault's use of the term refers to all that is primal and forbidden in the psyche, not simply sexual urges.

22. *Madness and Civilization*, 196. Emphasis added.

23. In this sense, a direct comparison can be drawn to another Pasolini film, *Teorema* (*Theorem*, 1968). The film chronicles the arrival of a mysterious stranger who may or may not be God into the lives of a bourgeois family and his seduction of every individual in the household. After his departure and the devastating impact his absence has on the family, the family's young maid retreats to a country village, and spends several days in meditation before a miracle occurs: she begins levitating over the town. It is unspecified whether the miracle is an objective event or an onscreen depiction of her subjective state, and ultimately what becomes important is the poetic, evocative power of the shot itself.

24. See *Mexploitation Cinema*, Chapter Three, for a discussion of *El barón del terror* in this regard.

25. Michel Foucault argued that confession was, and still is, an essential tactic in the multiple "discourses of sexuality" in Western society. However, in modernity, and while in many ways unchanged, the domain of the confession has moved from the priest to the psychiatrist. See Michel Foucault, *The History of Sexuality, Vol. 1: An Introduction*, trans. Robert Hurley (New York: Vintage, 1990), especially 58–67.

26. Russell based *The Devils* on Aldous Huxley's novel *The Devils of Loudun*, a fictionalized account of historical events at a French convent in Loudun during the Inquisition in the 17th century. Huxley's novel focused on the political machinations of the Inquisition and its impact on the convent, versus Russell's emphasis on sexual repressions and tensions.

27. The first credit to appear: "Photographed by Xavier Cruz"— the film immediately singling out the cameraman for well-deserved credit.

28. Beyond the use of slow-motion in *Alucarda*'s apocalyptic finale, Sam Peckinpah is most comparable. In his neglected masterpiece, *Bring Me the Head of Alfredo Garcia* (1974), a gun battle—or, more correctly, a massacre—ends the film and cuts to a smoking submachine gun pointed directly at the audience. "Directed by Sam Peckinpah" appears in the corner of the screen to match the image of a gun pointed at the audience.

Chapter 4

1. "The Last Testament of Jim Jones: Jonestown, Guyana, 18 November 1978," in *Secret and*

Suppressed: Banned Ideas and Hidden History, ed. Jim Keith (Portland: Feral House, 1993), 126.

2. For a detailed discussion of these themes in *Night of the Bloody Apes*, see *Mexploitation Cinema*, Chapter 6.

3. Cardona also worked as the second unit director on Don Siegel's Western, *Two Mules for Sister Sara* (1970).

4. *Crackpot: The Obsessions of John Waters* (New York: Vintage, 1986), 126. Of these titles, *Hostages* was the only one made, and was the U.S. title of *Traficantes de pánico* (*Traffickers in Panic*, 1979). Unfortunately(?), it was not about the Iranian hostage crisis but a crime-action film.

5. Proving or disproving the validity of such theory is outside this discussion. Nevertheless, John Judge, "The Black Hole of Guyana: The Untold Story on the Jonestown Massacre," in *Secret and Suppressed*, 127–65, is recommended as much for its meticulous research — sometimes absent in conspiracy theory — as well as raising provocative evidence to ties between Jones and the U.S. Government, in particular Jones' avowed arch-enemies, the CIA.

6. However, Jones' own "liberal" credentials are themselves tenuous. Establishing the first People's Temple at Ukiah, California, in 1965, Jones was active in Nixon's presidential campaigns and closely affiliated with right-wing organizations, including the John Birch Society (See Judge, 135). His transition to "socialism" coincided with his move from rural Ukiah to San Francisco's Mission district in the 1970s.

7. The testament has since appeared in a variety of official and unofficial transcripts. The recording itself (the authenticity of which is questioned by some) has appeared in a variety of edited forms on various underground cassettes and even a record album in the 1980s.

8. *Secret and Suppressed*, 128.

9. See Bill Landis and Michelle Clifford, *Sleazoid Express: A Mind-Twisting Tour Through the Grindhouse Cinema of Times Square!* (New York: Fireside, 2002), 262–3.

10. *I Hated Hated Hated This Movie* (New York: Andrews McMeel Publishing, 2000), 147–8.

11. With the exception of Jim Jones and Leo Ryan, all characters in *Guyana Tragedy* are given pseudonyms as well.

12. See Judge, 145.

13. See Friedrich Nietzsche, *Untimely Meditations*, ed. Daniel Breazeale, trans. R. J. Hollingdale (Cambridge, UK: Cambridge University Press, 1997). In his opposition to the dangers of history as a cycle of repetition and limitation, Nietzsche posits one "antidote" as the "unhistorical." "With the word 'the unhistorical' I designate the art and power of *forgetting* and of enclosing oneself in a bounded *horizon*." ("On the Uses and Disadvantages of History for Life," *Untimely Meditations*, 120; emphasis original.) *Guyana* implies a stance towards the "unhistorical" inscribed in the final image: the freeze-frame of the sunrise/sunset just above "the horizon," signifying History suspended and frozen in a cycle of remembering and repeating disaster.

14. *Guyana, Crime of the Century*'s end credits attribute the music to Jimmie Haskell and Alfredo Díaz Ordaz (the music was redone for Universal's release of *Guyana, Cult of the Dammed* and, in part, composed by mainstream American bandleader Nelson Riddle!). Haskell was a prolific composer for numerous American B-movies. A long-time aspiring musician in Mexico since the 1960s, Díaz Ordaz achieved eventual success in the music industry through his personal and professional relationship with pop music and *telenovela* star Thalia from the late 1980s until his death in 1995. However, Díaz Ordaz's greatest claim to fame was being the son of Gustavo Díaz Ordaz: president of Mexico at the time of the Tlatelolco massacre and often considered one of the key instigators of the events of October 2, 1968. Thus, one of the "composers" of *Guyana*'s music, used to continuously underscore the drive towards mass destruction, is "Diaz Ordaz" — also one of the "composers" of the disaster of Mexican modernity, Tlatelolco.

15. In this respect, Ebert lambasted Cardona for failing to "probe for reasons, motivations ... [or] the personalities of the cult members" (*I Hated.... This Movie*, 147).

16. See Judge, 139; see also 143–6.

17. In letters and interviews, Jim Jones' followers frequently referred to him as "Dad."

18. Landis and Clifford note that the torture scenes of children in *Guyana* were unsettlingly similar to the pedophile films playing in the nearby adult bookstores during *Guyana*'s Time Square grindhouse run (*Sleazoid Express*, 264).

19. *Dialectic of Enlightenment*, 253. Emphasis added.

20. Judge dismisses this theory as "disinformation" designed to obscure the connection of the CIA and right-wing groups (see page 145). If this plan was "disinformation," it was circulated and believed in Jonestown itself. In transcripts of the testament, as well as in the audio recording itself, Jones himself makes several references to Russia, and there are conversations between him and Temple members as to why "it's too for Russia... The next time, you'll get to go to Russia."

21. Michel Foucault, *Discipline and Punish: The*

Birth of the Prison, trans. Alan Sheridan (New York: Vintage, 1995), 58.

22. *Civilization and Its Discontents*, 77. Emphasis added.

23. Herbert Marcuse, *Eros and Civilization: A Philosophical Inquiry into Freud* (Boston: Beacon Press, 1966), 81. Emphasis original.

24. *Eros and Civilization*, 44.

25. To this extent, Gilles Deleuze's delineation of the aesthetics of sadism and masochism, as outlined in my discussion of *Santa Sangre*, are also manifest in political praxis in *Guyana*. The organized spectacles of torture and punishment are expressions of community sadism; the constant rehearsals of the White Night, where mass self-destruction is continually performed at the level of "dramatic suspense," are the ultimate exhibition of community masochism. In *Guyana*, there is an important reversal in this aesthetic of masochism, in that the Father — James Johnson — retains the dominant symbolic role (versus the Mother). The sadistic order is maintained not only by organized displays of public brutality, but, above all, by the dramatic suspense of the masochistic ritual as a rehearsal for genocide. This becomes the especially horrifying possibility of *Salò* as well: the convergence of (sadistic) systematic power with the aesthetic of (masochistic) dramatic suspense — domination and exploitation as endless theatrical performance.

26. Giorgio Agamben, *Homo Sacer: Sovereign Power and Bare Life*, trans. Daniel Heller-Roazen (Stanford: University of Stanford Press, 1998), 125. In some respects, Freud's *Civilization and Its Discontents* (sections IV–VI) bears a similarity to Hobbes as well: that the aggressive and destructive nature of humanity will lead to disorder and eventual ruin, and thus must be curtailed. However, Freud would not subscribe to Hobbes' solution: complete submission to an all-powerful authority — an overriding and castrating Superego for the body-politic.

27. *A Thousand Plateaus*, 230. Emphasis original. In this regard, despite Deleuze and Guattari's explicit distancing of their own work from Freud and Marcuse, there is a certain affinity in their work regarding the inherently self-destructive nature of the repressive, fascist State: be it the consolidation of the Death Instinct or a totalized line of destruction.

28. *I Hated.... This Movie*, 147. Rather, Ebert's description would be appropriate for Powers Boothe's characterization of Jones in *Guyana Tragedy*.

29. See Gilles Deleuze and Félix Guattari, *Anti-Oedipus: Capitalism and Schizophrenia*, trans. Robert Hurley, Mark Seem, and Helen R. Lane (Minneapolis: University of Minnesota Press, 1983), Chapter 3, "Savages, Barbarians, Civilized Men," especially 261. It should be stressed that Deleuze and Guattari are not endorsing modern capitalism, but analyzing *why* capitalism has proven resilient as the dominant mode of production in Western life (224); they particularly fault Marxism for underestimating the dynamics and multiplicities of the coding and decoding process into a simple binary — and the verticality — of class struggle (254–9). Thus, the function of Oedipus in Western Culture is thoroughly economic and political; the Oedipal order provides a necessarily *overcoding* force in capitalist society to prevent the coding and decoding of desire from achieving full fruition, and potentially revolutionary dynamics.

30. See "Panopticism" in *Discipline and Punish*, especially 216–7. This aspect of Foucault's theory is also the most debated, and criticisms have ranged from the contentions that Foucault greatly minimizes the role spectacle still plays in modern society to the possibility surveillance itself is simply a form of spectacle. Guy Debord's *The Society of the Spectacle* is perhaps the most famous challenge.

31. *Anti-Oedipus*, 212. Emphasis original. While Freud's "libidinal binds" and Deleuze and Guattari's "flows of desire" are here admittedly being conflated, it should be stressed that Deleuze and Guattari explicitly distance themselves from Freud to the extent they contend the complexities and variances in the flowing and coding of desire cannot be reduced to a simple binary of "instincts for life" and "instincts for destruction."

32. Jim Jones' longtime aide Timothy Stoen and his wife Grace left the People's Temple in 1978 and demanded the return of their son from Guyana; Jones refused. During the resulting legal battle, Stoen, who worked in the San Francisco District Attorney's office and helped Jones establish political connections in the city, contacted Leo Ryan. See Judge, 137–8.

33. In this regard, I borrow greatly from Maurice Blanchot, *The Writing of the Disaster*, trans. Ann Smock (Lincoln: University of Nebraska Press, 1995). Itself an appropriately difficult and highly fragmented treatise, in it Blanchot contends that the disaster can be discussed and remembered, but never explained or comprehended.

34. Richard Dwyer has become something of a lightning rod in Guyana conspiracy theory. He was reportedly at the airfield at the time of the ambush and at Jonestown immediately prior to the White Night. Some claim that Jones ordering "Get Dwyer out of here!" can be heard on the testament tape. See Judge, 144.

35. According to Judge, 90 percent of Jon-

estown victims were women, and 80 percent were African-American (see "The Back Hole of Guyana," 133).

36. The Hope-Crosby reference I take from George R. Reis, "*Guyana, Crime of the Century (Cult of the Damned),*" achieved at: *www.drive-in.com/reviews/e-h/guyanacrimeofthecentury7980.htm*. Date accessed: 6/26/05.

37. These troops were reportedly dispatched by the Guyanese army, possibly at the request of the U.S. Embassy. See Judge, 132.

38. Layton's role in the airport ambush in *Guyana* is consistent with the eyewitness and journalistic accounts of the attack; see Judge, 132–3. The airfield attack is depicted far differently in *Guyana Tragedy*. Larry Layton (renamed "Larry King") leads the group of gunman on the tractor, with the approval of Jones (*Guyana* never specifies these gunmen at the airport were even sent by Johnson: it is assumed by the audience). Layton was the only person officially charged with the murders of Ryan and the others. The airfield ambush in *Guyana Tragedy* suggests the film, consciously or not, adopted the version presented by the U.S. Justice Department, contrary to most other reports.

39. Ryan's secretary, Jackie Speiers, was wounded but did survive the attack. After the initial ambush, the gunmen inspected the scene only to confirm that Ryan and the journalists were dead — by shooting them in the head. After the departure of the gunmen, the soldiers finally assumed control of the situation (see Judge, 132–3).

40. Bill Nichols, *Ideology and the Image* (Bloomington: Indiana University Press, 1981), 186.

41. *Eros and Civilization*, 25.

42. The deaths of Jim Jones and Maria Katsaris were officially ruled suicides by self-inflicted gunshot wounds by the FBI, contrary to most other accounts. Earlier in *Guyana*, Susan Ames is murdered by unidentified attackers in her home shortly after the airfield massacre and the commencement of the White Night. Sharon Amos and her children were also killed in their home the day of the mass suicides by unknown assailants.

43. *The Writing of the Disaster*, 73.

Chapter 5

1. However, *Frogs* does arguably imply the events on Crockett's estate are not an isolated incident. Near the end of the film, the survivors are picked up on the road by a woman and her son. The woman remarks that the roads are surprisingly deserted for a holiday weekend, and the boy proudly displays his new pet — a frog: "They were all over the place at camp. Did you ever see a monster this size?" Nevertheless, the film returns back to the Crockett mansion for the comeuppance of Crockett by a horde of frogs, suggesting the revenge is complete in the final shot of the film: a shot of the mansion exterior as all the lights suddenly go out.

2. While Atkins and Johnson are arguably the most well-known cast members, Sambrell was internationally famous as a character actor in Spaghetti Westerns; in *Birds of Prey,* he only appears in two scenes: the news interview and his death. Gabriele Tinti, another Italian actor known for his appearances in a number of *Emmanuelle* films, receives prominent billing but only appears in a cameo: another news interview segment in which he and his wife briefly recount a bird attack which happened years prior. His character's name is "Rod" — a reference to Rod Taylor, star of *The Birds.*

3. Bertolt Brecht, *Brecht on Theater: The Development of an Aesthetic*, ed. and trans. John Willet (New York: Hill and Wang, 1964), 126.

4. As well as his frequent strategy of "making the camera visible," and his own use of Brechtian estrangement effects on the film audience, Godard frequently made films about making films: *Mépris* (*Contempt*, 1964) and *Passion* (1982).

5. Kenneth Anger recounted that the on-screen brutality was quite real: for an entire week of shooting, Hedren's feet were bound to the floor while live, agitated birds were attached to her dress and thrown at her from off-camera. She finally suffered an emotional breakdown, causing filming to be halted for a week. See *Hollywood Babylon II* (New York: Plume, 1984), 165–6. Even more perversely, the name of Hedren's character, Melanie, was taken from Hedren's infant daughter, actress Melanie Griffith.

6. These signs do figure prominently in UFO lore of the era as evidence of extraterrestrial life having visited Earth in the form of ancient astronauts (*Chariots of the Gods*). While Cardona does not pursue this angle in *Birds of Prey*, another vogue in paranormal phenomena of the times — the Bermuda Triangle — is prominently featured in his film *El triángulo diabólico de las Berumdas* (*The Diabolical Bermuda Triangle*, 1977; U.S. title: *The Bermuda Triangle*), another *Lifeboat*-influenced story of a small group marooned in the middle of the Bermuda Triangle and the mysterious events they experience.

7. See Raymond Bellour, *The Analysis of Film*, ed. Constance Penley (Bloomington: Indiana University Press, 2000), 66–7.

8. *Men, Women, and Chainsaws*, 167. Emphasis added.

9. However, Michael Powell's *Peeping Tom* (1960) addresses many of the themes of *Psycho* far more concretely and disturbingly, with its story of a killer whose weapon is a (phallic) spear that extends from his camera, allowing him to film women at the precise moment he murders them. Elliot Stein succinctly noted that *Peeping Tom* "equates watching movies with fucking and killing" (as quoted in Clover, 177).

10. In *Night of the Bloody Apes* (the U.S. version of *El horripilante bestia humana*), one of the more infamous shots is a close-up of the ape-man crushing a man's skull with his bare hands, causing one of his victim's eyes to pop out of its socket. While this scene in *Bloody Apes* was in all probability added by American director Jerald Intrator, who re-edited and filmed several additional gore scenes, the shot is remarkably consistent with *Birds of Prey* and its own assault on the eye.

11. See also Bellour, 50–56, for his detailed reading of this sequence.

12. See Clover, 31.

13. *Playback* is a particularly vicious psychological-erotic thriller that variously recalls *Dressed to Kill*, *9½ Weeks*, *I Spit on Your Grave*, and Arrabal's plays. *Playback* also starred Sonia Infante (Carmen in *Birds of Prey*). A well-known actress in Mexican cinema and the niece of Mexican screen icon Pedro Infante, she began her film career with supporting roles in Cardona's *Luchadoras* films *Doctor of Doom* and *Las lobas del ring* (*She-Wolves of the Ring*, 1964).

14. See *Mexploitation Cinema*, Chapter Four.

15. Slavoj Žežik, *The Sublime Object of Ideology* (New York: Verso, 1989), 192. *Jouissance*, a term essential to Lacan, is specifically different than "pleasure," specifically in the sense of Freud's "pleasure principle." Alan Sheridan suggests, "'Pleasure' obeys the laws of homeostasis that Freud evokes ... through discharge, the psyche seeks the lowest possible tension. '*Jouissance*' transgresses this law and, in that respect, is *beyond* the pleasure principle" ("Translator's Note," in Lacan, *Écrits*, xi. Emphasis original).

16. *A Thousand Plateaus*, 221. Emphasis added.

17. *A Thousand Plateaus*, 221.

18. Deleuze and Guattari, *A Thousand Plateaus*, 221. Emphasis added.

19. One of the most chilling symbols of the train as modernity running amok is the end of Émile Zola's novel *La Bête humaine* (*The Human Beast*), in which a driverless train careens through the mountains transporting drunken soldiers to the front lines of a war.

20. One of the Spanish soldiers is played by René Cardona III, who was also *Birds of Prey*'s special-effects supervisor and second unit director.

21. See *A Thousand Plateaus*, 423.

22. *A Thousand Plateaus*, 385–6. Emphasis added. The quote cited by Deleuze and Guattari is Paul Virillo. In contemporary U.S. politics, this can be framed around the issue of immigration, specifically from Mexico. The "war machine" is simply the movement of mass, the migration of bodies across space. The State responds by attempts to control this migration: designating legal versus illegal immigration, quotas, border security, and deportations — controlling the "fluidity of the masses."

23. Deleuze and Guattari, *A Thousand Plateaus*, 423. Emphasis original. Given Deleuze and Guattari's overall hostility to binary thinking, one is struck by the "either-or" aspect of the war machine as a "line of flight [and] plane of consistency" that creates *or* a "line of destruction [and] plan(e) of organization and domination" that destroys.

24. *A Thousand Plateaus*, 423. In this sense, the military-industrial complex is not the war machine, but the reterritorized, microhistorical manifestation of the war machine appropriated in the confines, and for the purposes, of the modern State.

25. *A Thousand Plateaus*, 423. Emphasis original.

Chapter 6

1. *Anti-Oedipus*, 269.

2. As quoted in Hoberman and Rosenbaum, 102.

3. The beggar not only represents Christ but Mercury, the messenger of the gods (Jodorowsky and the Seven Accomplices). Shortly before the journey ends, Jodorowsky sends the beggar away, telling him he should now "go and change the world." By process of elimination, Jodorowsky represents Earth — and God.

4. See Deleuze and Guattari, *A Thousand Plateaus*, especially 3–25, 294–5.

5. The most famous postmodern text is this regard is Jean Baudrillard's *Simulacra and Simulations*. In fairness to Baudrillard, his argument that postmodern society is one where the images of reality become more real that reality is not necessarily a ringing endorsement of postmodern society, but rather that the transition from an industrial age to an information age — from museums and factories to mass media and computers — has made this emphasis on simulated reality's triumph over real conditions of existence inevitable and unavoidable. However, his acceptance and fascination with this fundamental

shift has prompted numerous criticisms that he minimizes, ignores, or even justifies the potentially dangerous political ramifications of this phenomenon. Fredric Jameson, *Postmodernism, or, the Cultural Logic of Late Capitalism* (Durham: Duke University Press, 1990), remains the most illuminating critique of the pitfalls of postmodernism.

6. Jodorowsky alluded to this pirate film project as early as 1970; see *El Topo — A Book of the Film*, 133.

7. This account of *The Holy Mountain* owes greatly to Hoberman and Rosenbaum, 107–8.

8. A fascinating and quite hilarious account of the failed making of *Dune* written by Jodorowsky, "The Movie You Will Never See," is available at "The Symbol Grows: Alejandro Jodorowsky" website: *www.hotweird.com/jodorowsky/dunestory.html*.

9. According to Hoberman and Rosenbaum, Ridley Scott attempted to make a film version of *Dune* after Jodorowsky's project fell through; it was similarly abandoned as financially unfeasible (see *Midnight Movies*, 248). The creative unit Jodorowsky assembled for *Dune* was retained to make *Alien*.

10. As quoted in "The Virgin Mary Is a Chicken."

11. See Hoberman and Rosenbaum, 108.

12. As quoted in *Fad* 36.

13. Arguably their most famous collaboration is *The Incal* series of graphic novels. Two *Incal* stories were serialized in *Heavy Metal*: "The Incal Light" (February–August 1982) and "The Third Incal" (February–June 1984). Jodorowsky and Moebius later sued Luc Besson for copyright infringement, claiming his film *The Fifth Element* (1997) was plagiarized from an *Incal* story, "The Fifth Essence." The suit was dismissed, largely because Moebius worked on *The Fifth Element* as a production designer.

14. As quoted in "Wrapped in Salamander Cloth...."

15. As quoted in *Fad* 36.

16. As quoted in "Wrapped in Salamander Cloth...."

17. The term "national allegory" in this specific sense is taken from Fredric Jameson, "Third World Literature in the Era of Multinational Capitalism," *Social Text* 5: 3 (1986): "Third world texts, even those which are seemingly private and invested with a properly libidinal dynamic — necessarily project a political dimension in the form of national allegory: *the story of the private individual destiny is always an allegory of the embattled situation of the public third-world culture and society*" (69, emphasis original).

18. While an unintended irony, the eagle also references the perched bald eagle on the mountain-top that serves as the film's very first image in the American home video version screened for this discussion — the Republic Pictures logo.

19. Bellour notes the fact that the character's name "Crane" is referential to the film's opening, elaborate "crane shot." See *The Analysis of Film*, 254; see also 250–1.

20. In this respect, Jodorowsky offers a far different depiction of the political implications of the "carnival" as a point of popular resistance derived from Mikhail Bakhtin's work (*Rabelais and His World*). In Elissa J. Rashkin, *Women Filmmakers in Mexico: The Country of Which We Dream* (Austin: University of Texas Press, 2001), Rashkin suggested Dana Rothberg's *Angel del fuego* (*Angel of Fire*, 1991) depicts "a rundown circus and an evangelical puppet show ... as the setting of spatial and social marginality" (192). In *Santa sangre*, the circus is a space of colonial oppression and revolution.

21. According to Jodorowsky, his long-time associate Dennis Hopper was the original choice for the role of Orgo, and one can certainly imagine Hopper as Orgo, especially given his comeback performance as the vile, psychotic sadist Frank Booth in David Lynch's *Blue Velvet* (1986). Jodorowsky offered Hopper $50,000 for a week of filming. Hopper declined, and with some bitterness, Jodorowsky noted that Hopper instead directed *Colors* (1988), "A film about how cops are beautiful." See "Wrapped in Salamander Cloth...."

22. Interpretations of the specific symbolic meaning of the colors on the Mexican flag vary. However, general interpretations are consistent: green as representing hope and/or the struggle for independence; white as representing purity, and sometimes specifically Catholicism; red as representing the blood of heroes, *unión* with Europe, or, more generally, unity. The play on the symbolism ascribed to the colors of the Mexican national flag — red, white, and green — and, of course, their collision throughout the film with the colors of the U.S. national flag — red, white, and blue — is as pivotal in understanding *Santa sangre*'s textual ruptures and violence as much as the film's primary tactic: the free indirect subjective between Fenix's madness and the camera.

23. *In the Shadow of the Mexican Revolution*, 262–3.

24. The official proclamation, "Instruction on 'Theology of Liberation,'" was primarily authored by Pope Benedict XVI (Cardinal Ratzinger), successor of Pope John Paul II.

25. This is comparable to Andrea Dworkin's highly controversial thesis in *Intercourse* (New York: The Free Press, 1987). While Dworkin's book is

hampered by simplistic arguments and questionable rhetorical strategies, her contention that the act of sexual intercourse in a patriarchal order is inherently political and permeated with power is nonetheless compelling.

26. This sequence was heavily edited in the original American release of *Santa sangre*, much to Jodorowsky's displeasure. See "Wrapped in Salamander Cloth...."

27. The scene is possibly an homage to René Clair's surrealist short film *Entr'acte* (*Intermission*, 1926), which ends with an equally bizarre funeral procession in the streets of Paris.

28. Lacan, "The Mirror Stage..." in *Ecrits,* 5.

29. *Lenin and Philosophy and Other Essays*, 176.

30. However, it bears mention that the uniforms of the *Circo* marching band are green with yellow trim, a symbol of the *Circo*'s "built-in" collapse.

31. As noted in Chapter One, El Topo's head is shaved to complete his enlightenment in the cave. Similarly, *The Holy Mountain* begins with Jodorowsky shaving two women's heads, and during the final quest to find and overthrow the Immortals, the nine seekers all ritualistically shave their heads as part of their collective spiritual transformation.

32. In this respect, *Santa sangre* is markedly different to Fanon's *Wretched of the Earth*, which argued that the violence of Third World revolutions is an act of political catharsis as well as insurrection.

33. Returning to the Homeric element of *El Topo*, Robinson Crusoe is specifically mentioned by Horkheimer and Adorno in comparison to Odysseus as another "adventure hero" who embodies capitalist principles (see *Dialectic of Enlightenment*, 61–2). Certainly, Jodorowsky is far more concerned with these figures as lost souls seeking enlightenment and redemption than their potential ideological ramifications.

34. Interviews with Jodorowsky regarding *Santa sangre* also refer to the controversial scene where the boys snort the cocaine on-screen (obviously, not actual cocaine).

35. It should be noted that the Pimp in the earlier scenes wears a white, sleeveless t-shirt — a style of shirt that has gained a recent, pejorative description in American pop culture as a "wife-beater" t-shirt. In this case, the white shirt certainly does not signify purity, but allows the Pimp, in the pervasive red and blue hues of the city, to also manufacture the constant red, white, and blue color combinations in the city shots.

36. As quoted in "Wrapped in Salamander Cloth...." Emphasis added.

37. In the end credits, Jodorowsky's mentor, Marcel Marceau, is specifically cited as the inspiration for "The Creation of the World."

38. The sequence could also be an homage to Ionesco's *La Leçon* (*The Lesson*), his brilliant absurdist play about an older teacher and his young female student.

39. *Mythologies*, trans. Annette Lavers (New York: Hill and Wang, 1972), 84.

40. As quoted in "Wrapped in Salamander Cloth...."

41. In another sense, the invisible man on the poster in his red, white, and blue trappings could represent the ghost of Orgo.

42. Gilles Deleuze, *Masochism: Coldness and Cruelty* (New York: Zone Books, 1989), 73. It bears mention that *Coldness and Cruelty* tends to be avoided or even dismissed by Deleuze-influenced thinkers, not only for its reliance on Deleuze and Guattari's eventual arch-enemy Freud, but the highly rigorous binary logic in diametrically opposing sadism and masochism.

43. *Coldness and Cruelty*, 71. Emphasis added. See also Gaylyn Studlar, "Masochism and the Perverse Pleasures of Cinema," in *Film Theory and Criticism*, 4th ed., op. cit.: "[I]n the masochistic aesthetic, dramatic suspense replaced Sadean accelerating repetition of action" (775).

44. See *Coldness and Cruelty*, 71–72.

45. *Coldness and Cruelty*, 90. As Deleuze also contended, "The paternal and patriarchal theme undoubtedly dominates in sadism ... sadism is in every sense the active negation of the mother and an exaltation of the father who is beyond all laws" (59–60).

46. See *Coldness and Cruelty*, 67. Deleuze suggests the other dominant mother fantasy, "the uterine mother," is expressed in the form of the prostitute: a key figure in *Santa sangre* as well.

47. In this sense, Deleuze suggests that sadism is obsessed with androgyny and masochism the hermaphrodite. Sadism seeks to obliterate gender, and hence the primacy of the anus in sadism — the point that anyone (man or woman) can be made the subject of phallic power (again, a key and often overlooked aspect of the equation of fascism and sodomy in Pasolini's *Salò*). Masochism merges the prestige of phallic power onto the image of the mother — a figure of both genders, rather than genderless. See *Coldness and Cruelty*, 67–8.

48. See *Mexploitation Cinema*, Ch. 4.

49. As quoted in "Wrapped in Salamander Cloth..." Emphasis added.

50. An allusion to Poe's "The Fall of the House of Usher," in which a man's madness and guilt over burying his sister alive culminates in the sister's resurrection — or escape from the tomb — and the

physical collapse of the house itself. Like López Moctezuma's *Alucarda*, in Poe's tale the supernatural events and the character's madness become indistinguishable.

51. In this respect, Jodorowsky reverses a controversial and much-criticized film tactic of 1980s American slasher films: the point-of-view shot from the perspective of the killer (usually a man) pursuing the victim (usually a woman), ostensibly suggesting that the audience is encouraged to vicariously enjoy the act of killing from the perspective of the murderer. While not to justify the overall misogyny of many slasher films, this argument is problematic in that it is a highly arbitrary criterion. John Carpenter's *Halloween* (1978), the film that pioneered the "first-person-killer" perspective, was widely hailed by critics, including Roger Ebert, who later spearheaded attacks on misogyny and sadism in the slasher films manifest in their frequent use of the killer's point-of-view shot in his essay, "Why American Movie Audiences Aren't Safe Anymore," *American Film*, vol. 6, no. 5 (March 1981): 54–6. See also Clover, especially Chapter 4, which offers insightful discussion on the limitations and reductive interpretations of the effectiveness of the killer's point-of-view shot.

52. Besides Fellini, the comparison is to the silent film *He Who Gets Slapped* (1924, dir. Victor Sjörström), which ends with the death of the main character, an esteemed scientist whose public humiliation in academia prompts him to become a clown in the circus. Throughout the film, a clown periodically appears spinning a globe, not unlike the Great Mother observing the rocking cradle in *Intolerance*, and he serves as a form of Greek Chorus. In the remarkable final shot of the film, the circus clowns are superimposed on a spinning globe and throw the professor-clown's dead body off the face of the Earth.

53. Raymond Bellour, in a close reading of *Psycho*, suggests key points comparable to *Santa sangre*. The subtitle inscribed the locale of *Psycho* is "Phoenix" (Phoenix, Arizona). Throughout *Psycho*, Bates is surrounded by signifiers equating birds, women, and the lack of a phallus: Marion "Crane"; the dead birds that fill the Bates Motel as Norman's taxidermy experiments; above all, his castrate and castrating mother who subsumes Bates' identity, and who might be described as a classic "old crow." The rebirth or resurrection of the Phoenix, the great mythic bird, in *Psycho* represents Norman Bates' continual castration in the form of his dead and resurrected mother manifest by Norman, who is not a woman—"nor-man." See *The Analysis of Film*, 254.

54. For Deleuze and Guattari, the Oedipus complex represents the most effective vestige of recoding and overcoding the production of desire in capitalism. The Anti-Oedipus represents the possibility of freeing the production of desire from limited representation (the unconscious as theatrical psychodrama) to an order of unlimited production (the unconscious as churning factory), allowing capitalism to radically evolve and "breakdown" through unlimited decoding of flows of desire. See *Anti-Oedipus*, especially 134–5; 262–71; and 296 in this regard. In positing post–Oedipal capitalism, Deleuze and Guattari tend to veer towards anarchism rather than Marxism in their political viewpoint.

55. *Eros and Civilization*, 68. Emphasis added.

56. *Eros and Civilization*, 68. Emphasis added. The emphasized quote Marcuse cites is from Otto Rank, *The Trauma of Birth* (1929).

Conclusion

1. See Louis Marin, "Disneyland: A Degenerate Utopia," *Glyph* 1 (1977): 50–66. Marin's critique of Disneyland is comparable to Louis Althusser's concept of overdetermination; see Louis Althusser, *For Marx*, trans. Ben Brewster (New York: Verso, 1996), 89–128. The contradictions of capitalism manifest in the ideological superstructure (art, culture, religion, school) work to continually conceal and yet inherently reveal these contradictions. Representations such as Disneyland, or, for instance, a typical episode of *The Lawrence Welk Show* (as well as the socialist realism of the Soviet Union and Communist China), attempt to rectify ideological contradictions, and, in their overt simplicity, make these contradictions all the more apparent.

2. Mulford Q. Sibley, *Political Ideas and Ideologies: A History of Political Thought* (New York: Harper and Row, 1970), 361.

3. The science-fiction genre, by its very premise of "speculative fiction" set in the future, has presented numerous degenerate utopias: Fritz Lang's film *Metropolis*, J. G. Ballard's novel *High-Rise*, and John Brunner's novels *Stand on Zanzibar* and *The Sheep Look Up* are immediate examples. The Jodorowsky-Moebius graphic-novel series *Incal* also depicts a degenerate utopia of the far future.

Bibliography

Adorno, Theodor W. *Essays on Music*. Edited by Richard Leppert. Translated by Susan H. Gillespie. Berkeley: University of California Press, 2002.
Agamben, Giorgio. *Homo Sacer: Sovereign Power and Bare Life*. Translated by Daniel Heller-Roazen. Stanford: University of Stanford Press, 1998.
Aguilar Camín, Héctor, and Lorenzo Meyer. *In the Shadow of the Mexican Revolution: Contemporary Mexican History, 1910–1989*. Translated by Luis Alberto Fierro. Austin: University of Texas Press, 1993.
Althusser, Louis. *For Marx*. Translated by Ben Brewster. New York: Verso, 1996.
_____. *Lenin and Philosophy and Other Essays*. Translated by Ben Brewster. New York: Monthly Review Press, 1971.
Anger, Kenneth. *Hollywood Babylon II*. New York: Plume, 1984.
Artaud, Antonin. *Selected Writings*. Edited by Susan Sontag. Translated by Helen Weaver. Berkeley: University of California Press, 1988.
Barthes, Roland. *Mythologies*. Translated by Annette Lavers. New York: Hill and Wang, 1972.
Bataille, Georges. *Erotism: Death and Sensuality*. Translated by Mary Dalwood. San Francisco: City Lights, 1986.
Bazin, André. "Beauty of a Western." In *Cahiers du cinéma — the 1950s: Neo-Realism, Hollywood, New Wave*, 165–167. Edited by Jim Hiller. Cambridge: Harvard University Press, 1985.
Bellour, Raymond. *The Analysis of Film*. Edited by Constance Penley. Bloomington: Indiana University Press, 2000.
Benjamin, Walter. *Illuminations*. Edited by Hannah Arendt. Translated by Harry Zohn. New York: Schocken Books, 1969.
Blanchot, Maurice. *The Writing of the Disaster*. Translated by Ann Smock. Lincoln: University of Nebraska Press, 1995.
Brecht, Bertolt. *Brecht on Theater: The Development of an Aesthetic*. Edited and translated by John Willet. New York: Hill and Wang, 1964.
Breton, André. *Manifestos of Surrealism*. Translated by Richard Seaver and Helen R. Lane. Ann Arbor: University of Michigan Press, 1972.
Calinescu, Matei. *Five Faces of Modernity: Modernism, Avant-Garde, Decadence, Kitsch, Postmodernism*. Durham: Duke University Press, 1987.
Canby, Vincent. "Is El Topo a Con?" *Film 71–72 — An Anthology*. New York: Simon and Schuster, 1972. Also archived at *www.hotweird.com/jodorowsky/canby/html*.
Clover, Carol J. *Men, Women, and Chainsaws: Gender in the Modern Horror Film*. Princeton: Princeton University Press, 1992.
Deleuze, Gilles. *Cinema 1: The Movement-Image*. Translated by Hugh Tomlinson and Barbara Habberjam. Minneapolis: University of Minnesota Press, 1986.
_____. *Cinema 2: The Time-Image*. Translated by Hugh Tomlinson and Robert Galeta. Minneapolis: University of Minnesota Press, 1989.

_____. *Masochism: Coldness and Cruelty.* New York: Zone Books, 1989.

_____, and Félix Guattari, *Anti-Oedipus: Capitalism and Schizophrenia.* Translated by Robert Hurley, Mark Seem, and Helen R. Lane. Minneapolis: University of Minnesota Press, 1983.

_____ and _____. *A Thousand Plateaus: Capitalism and Schizophrenia.* Translated by Brian Massumi. Minneapolis: University of Minnesota Press, 1987.

Del Toro, Guillermo. Interview with Pete Tombs. Included on the DVD editions of *Mansion of Madness* and *Alucarda* (Mondo Macabro).

Dworkin, Andrea. *Intercourse.* New York: The Free Press, 1987.

Ebert, Roger. *I Hated Hated Hated This Movie.* New York: Andrews McMeel Publishing, 2000.

Eisenstein, Sergei. *Film Form: Essays in Film Theory.* Edited and Translated by Jay Leyda. San Diego: Harcourt Brace, 1949.

Estern, Marc James. *A History of The Underground Comics.* Berkeley: Ronin Publishing, 1993.

Evans, Sara. *Personal Politics: The Roots of Women's Liberation in the Civil Rights Movement and the New Left.* New York: Vintage, 1980.

Fanon, Frantz. *The Wretched of the Earth.* New York: Grove Press, 1963.

Foucault, Michel. *Discipline and Punish: The Birth of the Prison.* Translated by Alan Sheridan. New York: Vintage, 1995.

_____. *The History of Sexuality, Vol. 1: An Introduction.* Translated by Robert Hurley. New York: Vintage, 1990.

_____. *Madness and Civilization: A History of Insanity in the Age of Reason.* Translated by Richard Howard. New York: Vintage, 1999.

Freud, Sigmund. *Civilization and Its Discontents.* Edited and Translated by James Strachey. New York: W.W. Norton, 1961.

Greene, Doyle. *Lips Hips Tits Power: The Films of Russ Meyer.* London: Creation Books, 2004.

_____. *Mexploitation Cinema: A Critical History of Mexican Vampire, Wrestler, Ape-man and Similar Films, 1957–1977.* Jefferson, NC: McFarland, 2005.

Greene, Naomi. *Pier Paolo Pasolini: Cinema as Heresy.* Princeton: Princeton University Press, 1990.

Hegel, G.W.F. *Phenomenology of Spirit.* Translated by A.V. Miller. New York: Oxford University Press, 1977.

Hoberman, J., and Jonathan Rosenbaum. *Midnight Movies.* New York: Da Capo, 1991.

Horkheimer, Max, and Theodor W. Adorno. *Dialectic of Enlightenment.* Translated by John Cumming. New York: Continuum, 1998.

Jameson, Frederic. *Late Marxism: Adorno, or, the Persistence of the Dialectic.* New York: Verso, 1996.

_____. *Postmodernism, or, the Cultural Logic of Late Capitalism.* Durham: Duke University Press, 1990.

_____. "Third World Literature in the Era if Multinational Capitalism." *Social Text* 5: 3 (1986).

Jodorowsky, Alejandro. *El Topo—A Book of the Film.* New York: Douglas, 1971.

_____. Interview. *Penthouse*, June 1973.

_____. Interview with Jarrod LaBine. *Fad* no. 36 (1996). Archived at "The Symbol Grows: Alejandro Jodorowsky" website: *www.hotweird.com/fadinterview.html.*

_____. "The Movie You'll Never See." Archived at "The Symbol Grows: Alejandro Jodorowsky" website: *www.hotweird.com/jodorowsky/dunestory.html.*

_____. "Wrapped in Salamander Cloth, He Played House" [interview]. *Forced Exposure* 17. Archived at "The Symbol Grows: Alejandro Jodorowsky" website: *www.hotweird.com/jodorowsky/forced.html.*

Jones, Jim. "The Last Testament of Rev. Jim Jones: Jonestown, Guyana, 18 November 1978." In *Secret and Suppressed: Banned Ideas and Hidden History*, 121–126. Edited by Jim Keith. Portland: Feral House, 1993.

Judge, John. "The Black Hole of Guyana: The Untold Story of the Guyana Massacre." In *Secret and Suppressed: Banned Ideas and Hidden History*, 127–165.

Lacan, Jacques. *Écrits.* Translated by Alan Sheridan. New York: W.W. Norton, 1977.

Landis, Bill, and Michelle Clifford. *Sleazoid Express: A Mind-Twisting Tour Through the Grindhouse Cinema of Times Square!* New York: Fireside, 2002.

López Moctezuma, Juan. Interview with J.P. Bouyxou and Gilbert Verschooten published in *Cine*

Girl (1977). Text available on the Mondo Macabro DVD reissues of *Alucarda* and *Mansion of Madness*.

Loud. L. "The Virgin Mary Is a Chicken." *American Film*, March 1990: 80. Also archived at "The Symbol Grows: Alejandro Jodorowsky" website: *www.hotweird.com/jodorowsky/chicken.html*.

Lowe, Donald M. *History of Bourgeois Perception*. Chicago: University of Chicago Press, 1983.

Marcuse, Herbert. *Eros and Civilization: A Philosophical Inquiry Into Freud*. Boston: Beacon Press, 1966.

———. "A Note on Dialectic," in *The Essential Frankfurt School Reader*, 444–451. Edited by Andrew Arato and Eike Gebhardt. New York: Continuum, 1994.

Marin, Louis. "Disneyland: A Degenerate Utopia." *Glyph* 1 (1977): 50–67.

McNeil, Legs, and Gillian McCain. *Please Kill Me: The Uncensored Oral History of Punk*. New York: Penguin, 1996.

Mitchell, Lee Clark. *Westerns: Making the Man in Fiction and Film*. Chicago: University of Chicago Press, 1996.

Mulvey, Laura. "Visual Pleasure and Narrative Cinema." In *Film Theory and Criticism: Introductory Readings*, 4th ed., 746–757. Edited by Gerald Mast, Marshall Cohen, and Leo Braudy. New York: Oxford University Press, 1992.

Nichols, Bill. *Ideology and the Image*. Bloomington: Indiana University Press, 1981.

Nietzsche, Friedrich. *The Antichrist*. In *The Portable Nietzsche*, 565–656.

———. *Beyond Good and Evil*. Translated by Walter Kaufman. New York: Vintage, 1989.

———. *The Portable Nietzsche*. Edited and translated by Walter Kaufman. New York: The Viking Press, 1954.

———. *Thus Spoke Zarathustra*. In *The Portable Nietzsche*, 103–442.

———. *Untimely Meditations*. Edited by Daniel Breazeale. Translated by R. J. Hollingdale. Cambridge, UK: Cambridge University Press, 1997.

O'Neill, William L. *Coming Apart: An Informal History of the 1960s*. New York: Times Books, 1971.

Pasolini, Pier Paolo. "The Cinema of Poetry." In *Movies and Methods, Vol. I*, 542–58. Edited by Bill Nichols. Berkeley: University of California Press, 1976.

Peck, Abe. *Uncovering the Sixties: The Life and Times of the Underground Press*. New York: Pantheon, 1985.

Poe, Edgar Allan. *Complete Tales and Poems*. Edison, NJ: Castle Books, 2002.

Rashkin, Elissa J. *Women Filmmakers in Mexico: The Country of Which We Dream*. Austin: University of Texas Press, 2001.

Reich, Wilhelm. *The Mass Psychology of Fascism*. Edited by Mary Higgens and Chester M. Rafael, MD. Translated by Vincent R. Carfagno. New York: The Noonday Press, 1970.

Reis, George R. "Guyana, Crime of the Century (Cult of the Damned)." Archived at: *www.drive-in.com/reviews/e-h/guyanacrimeofthecentury7980.htm*.

Rubenstein, Anne. "Bodies, Cities, Cinema: Pedro Infante's Death as Political Spectacle." In *Fragments of a Golden Age: The Politics of Culture in Mexico Since 1940*, 199–233. Edited by Gilbert Joseph, Anne Rubenstein, and Eric Zolov. Durham: Duke University Press, 2001.

Sibley, Mulford Q. *Political Ideas and Ideologies: A History of Political Thought*. New York: Harper and Row, 1970.

Studlar, Gaylyn. "Masochism and the Perverse Pleasures of Cinema." In *Film Theory and Criticism*, 4th ed., 773–790. Edited by Gerald Mast, Marshall Cohen, and Leo Braudy. New York: Oxford University Press, 1992.

Todorov, Tzvetan. *The Poetics of Prose*. Translated by Richard Howard. Ithaca: Cornell University Press, 1977.

Waters, John. *Crackpot: The Obsessions of John Waters*. New York: Vintage, 1986.

Wilt, David E. "Films of El Santo" website: *www.wam.umd.edu/~dwilt/santo.html*

———. "Juan López Moctezuma" website: *www.wam.umd.edu/~dwilt/lopezmoc.htm*.

———. *The Mexican Filmography, 1916–2001*. Jefferson, NC: McFarland, 2003.

Žežik, Slavoj. *The Sublime Object of Ideology*. New York: Verso, 1989.

Zolov, Eric. *Refried Elvis: The Rise of the Mexican Counterculture*. Berkeley: University of California Press, 1999.

Index

Numbers in ***bold italics*** indicate pages with illustrations.

Adam and Eve 19–20, 29–30, 41, 77, 158
Aesop 25
Agamben, Giorgio 105–106
Age of Enlightenment 56, 66
Aguilar Camín, Héctor, and Lorenzo Meyer 3, 143
Alexander the Great 7
Alice in Wonderland (Carroll) 26
Alien 138, 192c6n9
El alimento del miedo (*The Food of Fear*) 184–185c2n4
Alive 94
All the President's Men 108
Althusser, Louis 149, 186c2n33, 194con.n1
Alucarda, la hija de las tinieblas (*Alucarda, Daughter of Darkness*) 1, 4, 17, 31, 47, 52, 66, 68–69, ***70***, 71–75, ***76***, 77–79, ***80***, 81–91, 99–100, 103, 115, 168, 173
Amos, Sharon 96, 190c4n42
Angel del fuego (*Angel of Fire*; Rothberg) 192c6n20
Anger, Kenneth 190c5n5
Antiquity 22, 50, 54, 56
Antonioni, Michelangelo 71, 116
Apocalypse: theme of in films 37–40, 90–91, 115, 132–133
Arau, Alfonso 179c1n12, 181c1n44
L'Architecte et l'empereur d'Assyrie (*The Architect and the Emperor of Assyria*) 8
Argento, Claudio 139
Argento, Dario 68, 139
Arrabal, Fernando 8–10, 180c1n17, 191c5n13
Artaud, Antonin 1, 8–13, 42, 77, 137, 180c1n28, 184c1n95, 187c3n19
Ashley, Jennifer 97
Atacan las brujas (*The Witches Attack*) 91
Ataque de los pájaros see *Birds of Prey*
Atkins, Christopher 117–119, 122, 126
Authoritarianism 4, 17, 34, 40, 44–45, 65, 101, 106; see also Fascism; Nazism
Aztec civilization 26, 62
Aztec Mummy trilogy (Portillo) 84

Bakhtin, Mikhail 192c6n20
Barenholtz, Ben 10
El barón del terror (*The Baron of Terror*) 84, 86, 90–91, 185c2n11
Barry, Gene 96
Barthes, Roland 157
Bataille, Georges 69
Baudrillard, Jean 191–192c6n5
Bava, Mario 1, 47, 68, 165
Bazin, André 13
Beaks: The Movie see *Birds of Prey*
Beckett, Samuel 8, 10
Bedlam 63, 186c2n31
Bellour, Raymond 192c6n19, 194c6n53
Benjamin, Walter 48
Bergman, Ingmar 10
Berkin, Jorge 52
Besson, Luc 192c6n13
La Bête humaine (*The Human Beast*; Zola novel) 191c5n19
Bible 11, 17–18, 20, 29, 32, 41, 133, 169
Bienvenido Maria (*Welcome Maria*) 184–185c2n4
The Birds 5, 116–117, 120, 123, 125–126, 128, 130
Birds of Prey 1–2, 5, 94, 103, 116–133, 173
Birth of a Nation 113
The Birth of Venus (Botticelli) 156
Blake, William 53
Blame It on Rio 119
Blanchot, Maurice 115, 189c4n33
Blood symbolism 31, 34, 44, 69, 77, 79–83, 87, 143–144, 146, 159, 166
The Blue Lagoon 119
Blue Velvet 192c6n21
Bogart, Humphrey 109
Bonnie and Clyde 14, 180c1n25
Bosch, Hieronymus 56
The Brainiac see *El barón del terror*
Brave New World 59, 172–173, 186c2n29
Brecht, Bertolt 24, 118
Breton, André 184c1n95, 185c2n7

Index

Bride of Frankenstein 158
Bring Me the Head of Alfredo Garcia 187c3n28
Brook, Claudio 53, *58*, 63, *64,* 75, 7*6, 80,* 84–85, 93, 185c2n18
Browning, Tod 35, 38, 149
Buddha/Buddhism 11, 21, 24, 35–36, 39–40, 44, 134
Buñuel, Luis 1, 10, 12–13, 16–17, 47, 49, 53, 57, 70–71, 88, 122, 137, 158, 180c1n28, 180–181c1n33, 181c1n42, 185c2n19

The Cabinet of Dr. Caligari 54, 60, 77, 165
The Caine Mutiny 109
Calinescu, Matei 55–56
"Callabro negro" (song) 140, 155
Canby, Vincent 11, 179–180c1n14, 180c1n21
Candide 11
Cardinas, Gojo 139
Cardona, René 84, 92–94, 191c5n13
Cardona, René, Jr. 1–2, 4–5, 92–94, 96, 103, 105, 108, 113, 116, 120, 123–124, 126, 132–133, 139, 152, 172–173, 186c3n6, 188c4n3
Cardona, René, III 191c5n20
Carradine, John 68, 186c3n1
Carter, Rosalynn 95
Cartoons (animation) 18, 51–52, 62
Cartwright, Veronica 117
Castration 11, 15–16, 18–19, 21, 24, 34, 78, 145, 150–152, 160, 169, 194c6n53
Catholicism 37, 52, 62, 88, 143–145, 155, 162, 169; sexuality and 70–71, 74, 78, 82–83, 85–87
The Centerfold Girls 97
Charro ("Cowboy") 14, 28, 141, 146
Chevalier, Maurice 8
Un Chien andalou 12
Christianity 35–37, 40, 43, 52, 73, 86, 137, 162, 170
Chrome and Hot Leather 97
Church 41, 61, 88, 169–171
Ciclón (*Cyclone*) 116
Cleopatra 164
Clover, Carol J. 124, 186c3n2, 194c6n51
I Clowns 149
Cocteau, Jean 8, 10, 12, 180c1n28
Colonialism 50, 135, 138, 141, 146–147, 152; U.S.-Mexico relationship as 4, 37, 139, 141, 146–147, 149–150, 155, 159–162, 165–166, 169
Color symbolism 42, 81, 143–144, 150, 193c6n30; black and/or white 14, 57, 60–62, 64–65, 78, 82, 144, 146–17, 158; national 140–144, 150–151, 153–155, 157, 160, 169–170, 192c6n22, 193c6n35
Colors 192c6n21
Communism 143
Como agua para chocolate (*Like Water for Chocolate*) 179c1n12
Confucius 134
Contreras, Gloria 157
Corman, Roger 1, 47–48, 51, 53, 65, 93
Corona Blake, Alfonso 53, 91
Cotten, Joseph 96
Counterculture 2, 4, 9–12, 14, 17–18, 21, 23–24, 26–29, 35–36, 38–39, 41, 43–45, 56, 58–59, 66, 95–96, 136–137, 139, 143, 182c1n64, 183–184c1n94, 184c1n102
Cowboy: as symbol of U.S.A. 36, 40, 141, 164
Craven, Wes 118
Crevenna, Alfredo B. 127
Cronos see *La invención del Cronos*
Crowley, Alistair 57
Crucifixion/crucifixion symbolism 18, 28, 32, *33*, 35, 57, 72, 86, 89, 91, 101, 144, 151, 166
Crusades 44
Cunning 22–23, 25–27, 29, 41

Dalí, Salvador 9, 12, 42, 138, 152
Dante's Inferno 57
Darkness/Light: symbolism of 42, 54, 56, 60–61, 67, 77, 86, 114–115
Death Instinct (Freud) 104–105, 114, 189c4n27
Debord, Guy 189c4n30
De Carlo, Yvonne 96
De Gaulle, Charles 3
De Laurentiis, Dino 138
Deleuze, Gilles 77, 136, 161, 180–181c1n33, 187c3n19, 189c4n25, 193c6n42, 193c6n42–47
Deleuze, Gilles, and Félix Guattari 2, 106–107, 128–129, 131–132, 134, 136, 170, 186c2n32, 189c4n27, 189c4n29, 189c4n31, 191c5n22–24, 193c6n43, 194c6n54
Delgado, Miguel M. 49
Del Toro, Guillermo 46–47, 185c2n18
De Meriche, Julián 181c1n44
De Mille, Cecil B. 10, 134
Descartes, René 42; duality of mind and body, 26–27, 166
Il deserto rosso (*Red Desert*) 71–72
Les Deux Bourreaux (*The Two Executioners*) 8
The Devils 70–71, 86, 187c3n26
The Devils of Loudun 187c3n26
Díaz Morales, José 91
Díaz Ordaz, Alfredo 188c4n14
Díaz Ordaz, Gustavo 188c4n14
Dillman, Bradford 96
Doctor of Doom see *Las luchadoras contra el médico asesino*
Dr. Tarr's Torture Dungeon see *La mansión de la locura*
Don Quixote 54, 56
The Doors of Perception 186c2n29
Dracula (character) 69
Dragnet 97
Drum 103
Dune 137–138
Dworkin, Andrea 192–193c6n25
Dwyer, Richard 108, 189–190c4n34
Dystopia *see* Utopia

Eagle: as symbol of U.S.A. 140–141, 145, 147, *148*, 149–150, 168, 192c6n18
Eastern philosophy/religion 21–22, 137
Eastwood, Clint 13
Easy Rider 14, 181c1n35
Ebert, Roger 96, 106, 188c4n15, 194c6n51
Eisenstein, Sergei 38, 185c2n10, 187c3n12

Index

Elgin (movie theater) 10, 12, 180c1n27
Emasculation 17–19, 36, 147, 151, 159–160, 163, 168–169
Enlightenment 7, 12, 21–23, 34–38, 40–45, 55, 59, 84, 136, 169
Entr'acte (*Intermission*, Clair) 193c6n27
Epic (Homeric) 10, 13, 21, 40, 44–45, 136
Eros (Freudian life instinct) 104–105, 114
Europe 50, 52, 185c2n14
Eurotrash cinema 1, 47, 69–70, 85, 93, 133
Evil Birds see *Birds of Prey*
The Exorcist 71, 86
Expressionism 1, 13, 53–54, 77, 155

Fábulas Pánicas (Panic Fables) 9
"The Fall of the House of Usher" (Poe) 193–194c6n50
Family 4, 139; as "holy family" 14, 19, 38, 40, 74, 146, 149, 160–161, 170; *see also* Oedipal relationships
Fando y Lis (*Fando and Lis*) 7, 9–10, 46, 179–180c1n14
Fanon, Frantz 181c1n46, 193c6n32
Fascism 18–19, 40, 43, 45, 56, 65, 95, 102, 106, 109, 181c1n43, 183c1n70, 183c1n89, 184c1n112, 189c4n27, 193c6n47
Faster, Pussycat! Kill! Kill! 31
The Father *see* Patriarchy
Fellini, Federico 1, 4, 10, 13, 47, 64, 71, 141, 149, 159, 179–180c1n14, 194c6n52
Feminism 11, 21, 28–29, 31, 182c1n64
Ferrare, Cristina 68
Ferrari, Marco 137
The Fifth Element 192c6n13
Final Destination 118
Fistful of Dollars 13
For a Few Dollars More 13
Ford, John 13, 16, 23, 113
Foucault, Michel 2, 42, 51, 53–54, 57, 70, 75, 77, 81, 104, 107, 136, 186c2n28, 187c3n21, 187c3n25, 189c4n30
Foss, Christopher 138
Franco, Francisco 65
Franco, Jess 1, 47, 85–86, 93
Frankenstein 158
Freaks 35, 38, 149
Free indirect subjective (free indirect discourse) 71–73, 75, 83, 88, 153, 158, 162, 168, 187c3n10, 187c3n12, 192c6n22
French, Tina 71
French Revolution 56, 66
Frenzy 125
Freud, Sigmund 15–16, 104, 20, 57, 62, 75–76, 83, 140, 170, 189c4n26–27, 189c4n31, 191c5n15, 193c6n42
Freund, Karl 158
Friedman, David F. 12
Frogs (McGowan) 117, 190c5n1
Fulci, Lucio 90, 165
Futurism 55

Gandhi, Mahatma 14, 181c1n46
Garden of Eden 19, 62, 156

Garry, Charles 96
Garza, Lily 89
Gender: politics and 12, 17–22, 24–26, 28–32, 35, 37, 41, 135, 150, 157, 163–164; vilification of women in films 21–23, 32, 34, 41, 135, 158, 163; *see also* Feminism; Patriarchy; Phallus/phallic power; Sexism
Genesis (Book of) 18–19, 31, 34, 156
Genet, Jean 49, 53
Gentlemen Prefer Blondes 157
Giallo (Italian horror genre) 4, 68, 139, 149, 156, 164–166, 180–181c1n33
Giger, H. R. 138
Giraud, Jean ("Moebius") 138, 192c6n13
Godard, Jean-Luc 10, 66, 120, 137, 181c1n49, 190c5n4
The Good, the Bad, and the Ugly 13
Grand Guignol 164
La Grande Bouffe (*The Great Feast*) 137
Great Society 95, 109, 113
Griffith, D.W. 113, 129
Guerra, Blanca 142, *151*, 159, *167*
Guevara, Ché 14
Guyana, Cult of the Damned see *Guyana, el crimen del siglo*
Guyana, el crimen del siglo (*Guyana, Crime of the Century*) 1, 5, 92–96, *97*, 98–101, *102*, 103–112, *113*, 114–115, 117, 130, 173
Guyana Tragedy: The Story of Jim Jones 95–96, 99–100, 108–109, 188c4n11, 189c4n28, 190c4n38

Halloween (Carpenter) 194c6n51
Hammer Studios (horror films) 47, 49, 90
Hansel, Arthur 49, *58*
Happenings 11, 58
Harris, Don 94, 97
Haskell, Jimmie 188c4n14
Hatchet for a Honeymoon see *Il rosso segno della follia*
He Who Gets Slapped (Sjöström) 194c6n52
Heatherly, May 117
Heavy Metal (magazine) 192c6n13
Hedren, Tippi 117, 190c5n5
Hegel, G.W.F. 30
Herbert, Frank 137
High Noon 181c1n39, 182c1n61
Las hijas de Elena (*The Daughters of Elena*) 93
History 59, 121, 129, 172–173, 186c2n28; as consolidated events 49, 53, 56, 64, 90; as cyclical events 40, 59; as frozen events 91, 115; as repetition of events 98, 105–106, 114–115, 173; unhistorical versus 188c4n13; *see also* Macrohistory/microhistory
Hitchcock, Alfred 4–5, 103, 116–117, 123–126, 140, 156
Hitler, Adolf 65, 72, 99, 106, 184c1n112
Hobbes, Thomas 105, 189c4n26
Hoberman, J., and Jonathan Rosenbaum 9, 12, 31, 36, 43, 46
Holocaust 53, 55–56, 64–65, 101, 110–111, 115
The Holy Mountain 7, 59, 134–137, 155, 191c6n3, 192c6n31
Holy Roman Empire 64
Homer 10, 22, 40–41, 44

Index

Homosexuality: equation with authoritarianism in films 17, 36–37, 51, 103–104, 135, 183c1n84
Hopper, Dennis 181c1n35, 192c6n21
Horkheimer, Max, and Theodor W. Adorno 2, 22, 40–41, 44–45, 101–102, 181c1n43, 193c6n33
El horripilante bestia humana (*The Horrible Human Beast*) 84, 92–93, 127, 191c5n10
Horror y sexo (*Horror and Sex*) 92
Huxley, Aldous 59, 172–173, 186c2n29, 187c3n26

The Incal (graphic novel series) 192c6n13, 194con.n3
Incan civilization 121
Incest 106, 141, 156, 159, 162
Industrial Revolution 53, 56
Infante, Pedro 14, 191c5n13
Infante, Sonia 117, 191c5n13
The Inquisition 44, 56, 87
Insanity *see* Madness
Intolerance 129, 132–133, 194c6n52
La invención del Cronos (*The Invention of Cronos*) 46, 185c2n18
The Invisible Man 158, 160, 162–163
Ionesco, Eugène 8, 192c6n38
Ireland, John 96
Isunza, Augustín 181c1n44

Jameson, Fredric 182c1n55, 191–192c6n5, 192c6n17
Jaws (Spielberg) 116
Jefferson, Thomas 13
Jesus Christ 18, 27–28, 32–33, 35, 40, 43–44, 73, 86, 89, 91, 101, 129, 134, 162
Jodorowsky, Adan 141, **148**
Jodorowsky, Alejandro 1, 4–5, 7–16, 18, 20, 24, 28–29, 32, **33**, 34, 36, 38, **39**, 40–47, 59, 83, 134–135, 137–139, 141, 146, 150–151, 156, 158–159, 172–173
Jodorowsky, Axel 139, 159, **167**
Jodorowsky, Brontis 14
Jodorowsky, Teo 152
John, Robert 37
Johnson, Michelle 117–120, 126, 187c3n14
Jones, Jim 92, 95–96, 98–100, 102, 109–110, 112, 188c4n5–6, 188c4n17, 189c4n32, 190c4n42
Jonestown 94–96, 98, 100, 102, 108–109, 115, 190c4n35
Juárez, Jesús 141
Judge, John 95–96
Jung, Carl 20, 23–4, 27, 37, 39, 52, 183c1n80, 183c1n92
The Jungle Book 138
Justine 74, 181c1n43

Kael, Pauline 11–12, 37, 44, 180c1n25
Kamini, Susana 58, 71, **76**, 187c3n12
Kant, Immanuel 9
Katsaris, Maria 97, 190c4n42
Keaton, Buster 180c1n19
Kent State University (May 4, 1970) 39
Kerlow, Max 64
Keystone Cops 62
King Lear 54, 56
Klein, Allen 10, 134, 137, 180c1n17

Kobayasy, Kunio 126
Kramer, Wayne 28
Kurosawa, Akira 182c1n52

Lacan, Jacques 30, 78, 147, 191c5n15
Landis, Bill, and Michelle Clifford 188c4n9, 188c4n18
Lane, Mark 96
LaSalle, Martin 49
The Last Movie 181c1n35
Laurel and Hardy 62
Law 15, 57, 65, 78, 101, 103–104, 108, 161, 170
Layton, Larry 111, 190c4n38
Leary, Timothy 59, 136, 186c2n29
Lennon, John 10, 180c1n17
Leone, Sergio 13, 15, 44, 181c1n45
Leppert, Richard 45, 181c1n43
Leviathan (Hobbes) 105–107, 189c4n26
Liberation theology 143–144, 155, 157, 169–170
Lifeboat 116, 190c5n6
Little Caesar 66
Looking Backward (Bellamy) 172
López Moctezuma, Juan 1, 4–5, 17, 31, 42, 46–49, 53, 68–69, 71–74, 82, 84, 87, 91, 93, 99, 168, 172–173, 185c2n18
Lorenzio, Mara 14–15
Lorre, Peter 48
Loud, L. 138
Lowe, Donald M. 12
Lucha libre films 3–4, 14, 49, 93, 164
Las luchadoras contra el médico asesino (*Wrestling Women vs. the Killer Doctor*) 93
Las luchadoras contra el robot asesino (*Wrestling Women vs. the Killer Robot*) 92
Luchadoras films (series) 92, 191c5n13
Luis, Jacqueline 15
Lynch, David 138, 192c6n21

Macrohistory/microhiostory 128–133
Mad Love 158–159, 162
Madness 4; asylums and 50–51, 54, 56–57, 70; binary of reason versus 42, 51, 54, 60–62, 64–67; collective 4, 42, 70–71, 87, 91; dazzlement and 42–43, 54, 56, 64, 67, 114; discourse and 53–54, 75, 79; dream and 76–78, 88; eroticism and 69, 87; historicism and 54; the individual and 4, 54, 57; nature and 81–82; *see also* Reason
Magritte, René 13
The Man from Laramie 13, 15–16
Man Ray 156
Mandingo 103
Mann, Anthony 13, 15
Mann, Thomas 8
La mansión de la locura (*The Mansion of Madness*) 1, 4, 17, 42, 46–57, **58**, 59–60, **61**, 62, **63**, **64**, 65–70, 73, 75, 81–82, 86, 89, 100, 106, 114, 173, 187c3n12
Manson, Charles 43, 95, 184c1n102
Mao Zedong 116
Maoism 26, 184c1n102
Marceau, Marcel 8, 193c6n37
Marcuse, Herbert 2, 43, 56, 104–105, 114, 170, 189c4n27

202

Index

Marin, Louis 172, 194con.n1
Marinetti, F. T. 55
Marquis de Sade *see* Sade
Martial arts films 164, 182c1n52
Martínez Solares, Gilberto 186c3n6
Marxism 95, 143, 170, 184n1c95, 189c4n29, 194c6n54
Mary Mary Bloody Mary 68–69, 82, 184–185c2n4, 186c3n1
Masochism 141, 161–162, 166, 189c4n25, 193c6n42–43, 193c6n46–47
The Masque of the Red Death 47
Master-Slave dialectic (Hegel) 30, 38, 160–161, 163
Master-Slave morality (Nietzsche) 31, 44, 183c1n70
Matar a un extraño (*To Kill a Stranger*) 184–185c2n4
Matriarchy *see* the Mother
Maximilian 65
Maya (Buddhist concept) 21, 135, 137
MC5 28
El médico loco y el sexo (*The Mad Doctor and Sex*) 92
Metropolis 77, 194con.n3
Mexploitation era/films 3–4, 14, 47, 49–50, 69, 74, 76, 84–85, 88–89, 91–93, 127
Meyer, Russ 1, 12, 31, 180–181c1n33, 182c1n68
Michelangelo 77
Middle Ages 54
Milland, Ray 117
Mirror-stage (Lacan) 30, 147, 149, 163
Mr. Blood and Miss Bones 137, 192c6n6
Mitchell, Lee Clark 13
Modernity/modern world 1–5, 9, 14, 17, 23, 41, 45, 47, 51, 53–57, 59–61, 64–67, 72–73, 81, 84–85, 87–94, 96, 104–106, 115, 118, 127, 130–131, 134, 136, 172–173, 191c5n19
Moebius *see* Giraud, Jean
Mohammed 134
Mongolian Cluster Fuck 28
Monroe, Marilyn 157
La montaña sagrada (*The Holy Mountain*) *see The Holy Mountain*
Monty Python's Flying Circus 52, 65
Morality 4–5, 12–14, 32, 36–37, 40–41, 43–44, 54, 57, 81–82, 92, 94, 131, 156–157, 159, 170, 180–181c1n33, 181c1n46
Morgan, Robin 29, 182c1n66
Morrison, Jim 14
Moscone, George 95
The Mother 14, 23–5, 30, 133, 140, 154, 159, 161–164, 166, 168, 193c6n45–47, 194c6n52
Mulvey, Laura 32
Mussolini, Benito 18, 65, 184c1n112
Myth 40–41, 43–45, 55, 172–173

Nadiuska 107
Napoleon 50, 56, 65
Napoleonic Wars 50–51
National allegory 4, 139–140, 144, 146, 150, 160–161, 164, 166, 169–170, 192c6n17
Native Americans 23, 182c1n56
Native societies 23
Nature 50, 55, 62, 67, 75, 81–82, 84, 116–118, 120–122, 127–128, 130–133
Nazism 43–45, 50, 106, 110–111, 184c1n112

Neo-Conservatism 2, 172
Nichols, Bill 113
Nietzsche, Friedrich 9, 11, 13, 31, 34–36, 40–41, 43–45, 170, 181c1n46, 183c1n70, 183c1n89, 188c4n13
Night of the Bloody Apes see *El horripilante bestia humana*
Night of the Living Dead 112, 165
1984 172–173
La noche de los mil gatos (*Night of a Thousand Cats*) 93, 126
North by Northwest 103–104
Nosferatu 46, 77
Nunsploitation films 47, 70, 86, 186c3n6, 186c3n8

O'Bannion, Dan 138
O'Brien, Glenn 44–45
Odysseus 7, 22–23, 37, 41, 44–45, 139, 193c6n33
The Odyssey 7, 11, 22, 41, 183c1n85
Oedipal order/relationships 4, 14, 139–140, 145–146, 149, 152, 154, 158–162, 164–166, 170–171, 181c1n39, 189c4n29, 194c6n54
The Old Dark House 165
The Omen 118
One Flew Over the Cuckoo's Nest 49–50
1, 2, 3, 4, 5 a Go-Go! 9, 179c1n12
O'Neill, William L. 14, 186c2n29
Operación 67 (*Operation 67*) 93
Orwell, George 102, 172–173

Paganism 52, 81–83, 86
Pan (ancient mythology) 19, 181c1n47
Panic Movement 8, 10, 180c1n27, 181c1n47
Paradise Lost (Milton) 52, 57
Pasolini, Pier Paolo 1, 17, 23, 36, 47, 56–57, 64, 71–75, 79, 105, 181c1n43, 186–187c3n9–10, 187c3n23, 193c6n47
Patriarchy 4, 14–15, 19, 34, 38, 40, 59–60, 78, 85, 93, 100–101, 103, 105, 110, 117, 139, 147, 149–150, 159, 161, 170–171; 192–193c6n25, 193c6n45; *see also* Family; Oedipal order/relationships; Phallus/Phallic power
Peck, Abe 11, 19
Peckinpah, Sam 13, 15, 44, 66, 90, 126, 164, 180–181c1n33, 187c3n28
Peeping Tom (Powell) 191c5n9
People's Temple 94–98, 102, 109
Phallus/Phallic power 15–21, 23, 25, 28–32, 34–35, 59–60, 103, 110, 145–147, 150–151, 160, 193c6n47
Phallic symbolism 19–21, 59–60, 68–69, 78, 103, 125–126, 163–164, 182c1n60; 191c5n9; guns as, 15, 18–19, 23, 28–32, 35; knives, 76, 141–142, 145, 147, 149, 151, 155–6, 158
Philosophie dans le boudoir (*Philosophy in the Bedroom*) 58
Phoenix (mythological bird) 40, 140, 168, 194c6n53
Pineda, Salvador 117
Pink Floyd 138
Los placeres ocultos (*Hidden Pleasures*) 126, 191c5n13
Playback see *Los placeres ocultos*
Poe, Edgar Allan 47–49, 51, 53, 57, 63–64, 66, 73, 185c2n7

203

Poetics 48, 73–75, 83, 168, 180c1n28, 185c2n8
Pom Pom Girls 97
Pontius Pilate 18
Pop Art 135, 137
Pope Benedict XVI (Cardinal Ratzinger) 192c6n24
Pope John Paul II 143–144
Porcile (*Pigpen*) 72, 75
Postmodernism 1, 4, 9, 11, 41, 45, 116, 118, 135–138, 191–192c6n5
Potemkin 38
Prado, Pérez 140, 153, 155–156
Price, Vincent 51
Profundo rosso (*Deep Red*) 139
Prokes, Michael 97
Prostitution 36, 141, 152–155, 193c6n46
Psycho 124–125, 140, 156, 159, 161, 165–166, 168, 191c5n9, 193c6n53

Rains, Claude 163
The Rake's Progress (Hogarth) 186c2n31
Rashkin, Elissa J. 192c6n20
The Raven 48
Reagan, Ronald 127
Rear Window 124
Reason 41, 45, 183c1n92; light of 42–43, 54; unreason and 42–43, 54, 56, 60–62, 64–67, 82, 87–89, 91, 114, 173
Reich, Wilhelm 34, 71, 183c1n74
Religion 4, 12, 44, 55, 71, 74, 91, 95, 100, 134–135
Renaissance 54
Revolutionary *machismo* 14, 17, 19, 29, 45, 181c1n38
Riddle, Nelson 188c4n14
Riefenstahl, Leni 99, 184c1n112
Rimbaud, Arthur 8
"Rime of the Ancient Mariner" (Coleridge) 59
Robinson, Edward G. 66
Robinson Crusoe (Cardona film) 152
Robinson Crusoe (Dafoe novel) 119, 152, 193c6n33
Robinson Crusoe and the Tiger see *Robinson Crusoe* (Cardona film)
Robson, Mark 63, 130
The Rocky Horror Picture Show 4
Rollin, Jean 1, 47, 185c2n13
Roman mythology 135
Romero, George 90, 165
Romero, Tina **70**, 71, 73, **76**, 77, **80**, 187c3n14
Romo, Paula 15, 181c1n44
Il Rosso segno della follia (*The Red Mark of Madness*) 165
The Roszakodore 41–42
Rubenstein, Anne 14
Russell, Ken 53, 70, 86, 137, 187c3n26
Ryan, Leo 94–96, 102, 108

Sacramental Melodrama 8–9
Sade 8, 31, 56, 58, 68–69, 74, 80, 87, 161, 180c1n22, 181c1n43, 193c6n43
Sadism 11, 86–87, 101, 122, 141, 161–162, 189c4n25, 193c6n42–43, 193c6n45, 193c6n47
Salò o La 120 giornate di Sodoma (*Salò, or the Days of Sodom*) 17, 36, 56–57, 64, 72, 75, 105, 183c1n84, 189c4n25, 193c6n47

Sambrell, Aldo 117, 190c5n2
Samson (Bible) 18, 35, 150
Samson in the Wax Museum see *Santo en el museo de cera*
Samson vs. the Vampire Women see *Santo contra las mujeres vampiro*
Sanders, Ed 28, 184c1n102
Le Sang d'un poète (*Blood of a Poet*) 12, 180c1n27–28
Santa sangre (*Holy Blood*) 1, 4, 7, 14, 30, 36–37, 40, 83, 139–147, **148**, 149–150, **151**, 152, **153**, 154–166, **167**, 168–171, 173, 183c1n83
Satanico pandemonium (*Satanic Pandemonium*) 186c3n6
Santayana, George 98
Santo/*Santo* films 14, 53, 91–93, 158, 163–164
Santo contra las mujeres vampiro (*Santo vs. the Vampire Women*) 91, 185c2n11
Santo, el Enmascarado de Plata contra la invasión de los marcianos (*Santo the Silver-Masked Man versus the Invasion of the Martians*) 127
Santo en el museo de cera (*Santo in the Wax Museum*) 53, 84
Santo en el tesoro de Drácula (*Santo in the Treasure of Dracula*) 84, 92
Santo y Blue Demon contra Drácula y el Hombre Lobo (*Santo and Blue Demon vs. Dracula and the Wolf Man*) 49
Satyricon 64, 179–180c1n14
"Scent of Irises" (D.H. Lawrence) 59
Schacht, Larry 96
Science 7, 41, 55, 91, 93, 127, 133; supernatural versus 84–85, 87–89
Science fiction (genre) 194con.n3
Scream 118
Scream 2 118
Serna, Mónica 49
Serpent (Bible) 29–31, 156, 158
Sex/Sexuality 4, 12, 16–17, 20–21, 26, 29–30, 37, 41, 68–71, 103–105, 110, 114, 123–126, 132, 139, 141–142, 144–145, 156–157, 192–192c6n25; *see also* Catholicism; Gender; Phallus/phallic power
Sexism 11, 14, 20, 24, 28–29, 32, 139, 182c1n64, 183c1n70
The Shape of Things to Come (Wells) 172–173
Sherman, Ellen 57, **61**
Sibley, Mulford Q. 173
Silva, David 17, 52, **63**, 71, 86, 90, 93, 181c1n44
Simón del desierto (*Simon of the Desert*) 53, 185c2n19
Sirens 21–22
Slasher films 68, 117–118, 186c3n2, 194c6n51
Sodom 36, 99
Soviet Union 3, 102
Spaghetti Westerns 11, 13, 21
Speiers, Jackie 107, 190c4n39
Spirituality 12, 21, 25, 32, 34, 41, 44, 136, 140, 142, 152, 168–169
Stagecoach 13, 113
Stalinism 3, 102, 143
Star Wars 138
the State 41, 59, 61, 106, 131–132, 143–144, 154, 169–171, 191c5n22, 191c5n24
Stewart, James 15

Index

Stockwell, Guy 141, *148*, *153*, 183c1n83
Stoker, Bram 69
Stone, Oliver 108
The Story of O 137
La strada 149
Strindberg, Joseph 8
Studlar, Gaylyn 193c6n43
Sufism 24
Sunset Boulevard 160, 168
Superchick 97
Los supervivientes de los Andes (*Survivors of the Andes*) 94
Surrealism 1, 9–13, 46, 48–50, 53, 133, 168, 180c1n28
Survive! see *Los supervivientes de los Andes*
Suspiria 139
Swanson, Gloria 138, 160, 168
"The System of Doctor Tarr and Professor Fether" (Poe) 47–49, 51, 57, 63–64, 66

Tapia, Faviola Elenka 142
Tarot 11, 23, 137
Taylor, Elizabeth 164
Taylor, Rod 123, 190c5n2
The Ten Commandments 137
Tenebre (*Darkness*) 139
Teorema (*Theorem*) 187c3n23
El tesoro de Moctezuma (*The Treasure of Moctezuma*) 93
The Theater and Its Double 8
Theater of Cruelty 1, 8, 11, 13
Theater of the Absurd 1, 8, 49, 51, 53, 116
Third Reich see Nazism
The Three Musketeers 62
Three Stooges 62
Thus Spoke Zarathustra 34
The Tibetan Book of the Dead 136
Tinti, Gabriele 190c5n2
Tintorera! (*Tiger Shark!*) 116
The Tixoulma 141
Tlatelolco (October 2, 1968) 1, 3–5, 10, 15–17, 19, 36, 38, 89–91, 93, 115, 164, 172, 188c4n14
Todorov, Tzvetan 185c2n8
El Topo (*The Mole*) 1–2, 4, 7–23, *24*, 25–32, *33*, 34–38, *39*, 40–45, 46–47, 54, 65–66, 80, 133–134, 136–137, 139, 141, 146–147, 150–152, 158, 160, 163, 169–170, 173, 180–181c1n33
Toppor, Roland 8
Traficantes de pánico (*Traffickers in Panic*) 188c4n4
The Transposed Heads 8, 179c1n5
Trashman (underground comic) 181c1n46
El triángulo diabólico de las Berumdas (*The Diabolical Bermuda Triangle*) 190c5n6
Triumph of the Will 43, 99, 184c1n112
Tusk 138, 141, 146–147, 159–160
Twilight Zone (TV series) 118

Übermensch 18, 35, 41, 43
Ulysses see Odysseus
Underground comics 11, 19, 28, 182c1n64
The Unknown 149
Urueta, Chano 84
Utopia (More) 172–173
Utopia 40, 43, 55–56, 64, 96, 106, 113, 129, 170; "Degenerate utopia" 172–173, 194con.n3; dystopia versus 172–173

Vampirism 68–69, 71, 77–78, 81, 84, 145
El vampiro y el sexo (*The Vampire and Sex*) 92
Venus di Milo (sculpture) 144, 154, 160
Venus in Furs (Masoch) 161
Viaje fantástico en globo (*Fantastic Trip in a Balloon*) 152
Vietnam 3, 26, 40, 55, 62
Villa, Pancho 14
Violence 4, 10, 13, 16, 19, 27–28, 39, 43–44, 68–69, 123–126, 132, 139, 143, 156, 165–166
Vitti, Monica 72
Viva la Muerte (*Long Live Death*) 180c1n17
Voice: as transmission of power 24, 28, 78, 81, 96, 99, 101–102, 110–111, 155, 169; writing versus 101, 110
Von Ryan's Express 130

Waiting for Godot 10
Walden (Thoreau) 50
War machine (Deleuze and Guattari) 131–133, 191c5n22–24
Warner Bros. cartoons see Cartoons (animation)
Watergate 108–109
Waters, John 94
Wayne, John 14, 181c1n34, 182c1n53
Weathermen/Weather Underground 44, 184c1n102
Welles, Orson 138
West Side Story 153
Westerns 13–16, 18, 25, 40, 42, 44, 52, 103, 111–113, 139, 181c1n39
Whale, James 158, 160, 163, 165
"White Rabbit" (Jefferson Airplane song) 26
Whitman, Stuart 96, 107, 109, 112, ***113***
The Wild Bunch 13
Wilson, S. Clay 11, 180c1n22
Wilt, David 49, 184–185c2n4, 187c3n16
Winchester '73 15
Wong, James 118
Woodstock 43
World War II 53, 56, 101

Young, Tony 97

Zappa, Frank 137
Zarathustra 34, 44–45
Zen Flesh, Zen Bones 38
Žežik, Slavoj 128, 191c5n15
Zolov, Eric 9
Zona Rosa (*Pink Zone*) 9, 179c1n12

www.ingramcontent.com/pod-product-compliance
Ingram Content Group UK Ltd.
Pitfield, Milton Keynes, MK11 3LW, UK
UKHW050527150426
5217IPUK00026B/1828